HOOKED

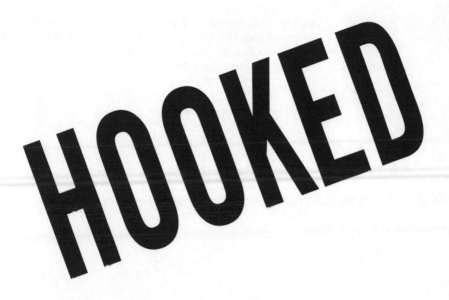

HOOKED

MATT RICHTEL
A THRILLER ABOUT LOVE AND OTHER ADDICTIONS

TWELVE

NEW YORK   BOSTON

Twelve

Hachette Book Group USA

237 Park Avenue

New York, NY 10169

Visit our Web site at www.HachetteBookGroupUSA.com.

Twelve is an imprint of Warner Books. The Twelve name and logo are trademarks of Hachette Book Group USA.

Printed in the United States of America

First Edition: June 2007

10 9 8 7 6 5 4 3 2 1

Library of Congress Cataloging-in-Publication Data

Richtel, Matt.

Hooked : a thriller about love and other addictions / Matt Richtel. — 1st ed.

p. cm.

Summary: "The protagonist, Nat Idle, narrowly survives an explosion in an Internet café after receiving a note warning him to leave immediately. The handwriting on the note belongs to his deceased girlfriend, a Silicon Valley venture capitalist, whom he has obsessively been mourning"—Provided by the publisher.

ISBN-13: 978-0-446-58008-3 (alk. paper)

ISBN-10: 0-446-58008-2 (alk. paper)

1. Journalists—Fiction. 2. Bereavement—Psychological aspects—Fiction. 3. Computer industry—Fiction. 4. Venture capital—Fiction. 5. California—Fiction. I. Title.

PS3618.I36H66 2007

813'.6—dc22   2006019620

For My Parents

HOOKED

1

I'm guessing that the moment that your life begins to unravel is often unceremonious—heralded by a whimper. The bang should have told me something.

I remember mostly details.

The extra foam sliding down the side of the mocha. A couple arguing over whether to put the "Mighty OJ" juicer on their bridal registry. The rottweiler tied outside the café, standing on hind legs, paws pressed urgently against the window.

When she walked by, I was reading a languid description of a Boston river, somewhat guiltily speeding through the imagery to get back to the book's action. I wouldn't have noticed her at all had she not put a small, folded square of paper on the corner of my table. I registered graceful hands, and a ring on the index finger. Then I focused on the piece of paper. Was I being picked up?

When I looked up again, she was nearly out the screen door, purposeful, and not stopping to look back. I dog-eared a page in my book, picked up the folded note, and followed her.

I scanned the street. The young transplants who call San Francisco's Marina District home meandered with designer sunglasses and designer baby strollers, enjoying a fogless July afternoon. Through the crowd, I could see she was halfway into a red Saab parked in front of the Pita Parlor.

Something kept me from calling out. I figured I'd wave her down, but she was in the car and pulling away before I could get close enough to yell without making a scene. I looked at the textured beige stationery in my palm. I unfolded the corners, and saw words like a bullhorn:

"Get out of the café—NOW!"

The café exploded.

Smoke. Car alarms. Glass, ashes, a cloud of dust. A sound inside my head like a hangover delivered via freight train. I don't think I ever lost consciousness. The blast took me three feet through the air, dropped me on the pavement, but seemed to leave me intact.

I've seen footage of war zones, where the world seems to be coming undone. This was nothing like that—just a single moment of extraordinary violence, followed by haze. Like a bloody version of the time my father slammed a stainless steel pot on the kitchen floor to get my brother's attention.

The front window of the café was blown out, and a side wall was ripped, though not torn down, exposing metal and concrete innards. A couple wandered out from the screen door; he held an arm limply at his side, her bloody legs churned between step and stumble. The owner of the rottweiler checked his pet for wounds.

These days, you imagine the first thought at such a moment would be of terrorism.

My first thought was of Annie.

She was rarely far from my mind, even four years after the accident that took her life at the age of twenty-eight. Mostly, I'd thought of her at moments of transition—when I got up, climbed into bed, or on a long drive between interviews. It said as much about me as us; it was in those moments, the quiet instances when life lacked structure, that I most needed a place to focus.

I wouldn't defend my relationship with Annie as perfect, but it defined love for me, and endured. She was always chewing strong breath mints, causing our kisses to taste spicy, and I got sad when I smelled cinnamon. Sometimes at night, I told an imaginary Annie stories aloud and tried to guess at which point she would have sleepily asked me to wrap it up.

But it was more than longing that made me think of her as a thin layer of dust settled over me. It was the note I'd been handed. I'd know Annie's handwriting anywhere.

"Can you move your legs?"

The words came through my fog from a police officer, kneeling beside me. I waved my hand to say, "I'm fine." I started to stand, and he helped guide me up by the elbow.

"We need to get you out of this area."

As my awareness returned, so did the sounds and colors, and the chaos. Police and firefighters, the sound of radio chatter, helicopters. I was embedded in the evening news.

The officer led me toward an area apparently being set up for the wounded. Was I hurt worse than I thought?

"*Mystic River*," the police officer said.

I looked at him with confusion.

"Good book," he added. "But you really should invest in the hardback. It's a sign of a fully committed person."

I looked down and saw I still had the novel I'd been reading in the café. My white knuckles told me I'd been clutching it like a life preserver. The note. Where was it? I fished in my pockets, but came up empty. I turned around and headed back to where I'd been lifted off the ground.

"Hold on, pardner. We can't have you going back there. Too dangerous."

"I lost someone," I said.

"You lost someone?"

"Something. I lost *something*. Please."

"Well, you're not going back to get it now."

With a powerful hand on my shoulder, he turned me around, walked me down the block to a concrete patch cordoned off by yellow tape, and set me on the ground with the others.

* * *

The cop's name was Danny Weller, and he was a chatterer. He told me about growing up in Oakland, and learning to fish in waders in the Sacramento River with his father. His dad, he said, was a fierce wordsmith, the outer casing of a union man covering a dictionary. Danny stayed nearby—my personal caseworker.

He kept my state of mind numb, but his friendly rambling didn't slow the background din of questions. Who would do such a thing? Did someone try to save my life? Was that person connected to Annie?

And what happened to everyone else in the café? How many hurt? How many dead? Those questions I asked aloud.

"We have three fatalities and a couple people in critical," Danny said. "Not as miraculous as it first appeared."

"What do you mean?" I looked at a half dozen people sitting on the street around me, nursing various wounds. Each was attended by police and emergency medical personnel. The idea that anyone survived seemed miraculous.

"The explosion was confined to one area of the café—it's not as bad as we first thought," Danny said. "At this point, we don't know if it was intentional or an industrial accident."

"You mean it might not have been a bomb?"

"What makes you think it was a bomb?" Danny looked at me intently, with curiosity but not accusation.

I took him in for the first time. I noticed hair and gut; he had a lot of both. I figured him at around forty-five years old. Worn, blue-collar hands, no wedding ring, but that didn't mean anything anymore. He had soft, droopy eyes that reminded me somehow of the black and chocolate-brown-colored glass polar bear eyes from the taxidermist's office where I interned the summer before my senior year in college.

Before I could get out an answer to Danny's question, a paramedic knelt beside me.

"He seems okay," Danny said. "He was outside when it happened."

"Let's have a look," the paramedic said, tilting my chin

up so I could look him in the eye. "I'm going to ask you some basic questions. Indulge me. What's your name?"

"Nathaniel. Nathaniel Idle."

"Nat Idle," Danny the cop said. I'd told him my first name earlier, but not my last.

The paramedic and I turned our heads to look. Danny turned his eyes to the side, the way a bad poker player fails to mask emotion, and I can't say I was surprised.

A year earlier, when I was researching an article about the HIV epidemic faced by the city's immigrant prostitution rings, I'd come across a disturbing tip. Several officers assigned to crack down on the residential brothels were sampling the fare rather than bringing the violators to justice. One of the cops, upon learning he might have contracted HIV himself, beat a twenty-year-old Malaysian prostitute with the battle end of a flashlight. The cop—Timothy Aravelo—and two colleagues were convicted.

Publicly, a number of police officers lauded my efforts. It was politically correct to do so. Privately, they said I had exaggerated the problems of one bad cop and his own domestic dispute and turned it into a crusade. I was viewed as a member of the corner-cutting sensationalist media.

"No obvious broken bones, a laceration on the forehead, scrapes to knees, elbows, and hands. Consistent with a forceful fall," the paramedic said.

"You did the right thing," Danny said.

The paramedic thought Danny was talking to him. I knew what he really meant.

"Thanks," I said. "Danny, look, something's not right. Something is very strange, and—"

Danny cut me off. "We're doing preliminary interviews with everyone who was in the area. We like to get impressions while they're fresh. You're our next contestant."

He pulled me up by the hand and bent in close. "Ordinarily, Lieutenant Aravelo would ask you a few gentle questions and then give you a pat on the back. But you might get slightly rougher treatment."

2

The cops had constructed a makeshift command center under a temporary open-air tent in front of the Kuma Sushi.

Law enforcement, especially the branches of the military, get a reputation for the ability to destroy—houses, front doors, villages. I'm equally impressed by their ability to construct things. Give a galvanized troop of men in uniform shovels, poles, and canvas for roofing and flaps, and within an hour you'll have a tent city complete with his and hers field toilets and showers.

Danny had walked me over to the command center. "Perch," he said. He left me outside the yellow police tape that surrounded the tent and wandered in, presumably to let them know their next interview candidate had arrived. I flashed on a memory of my barber analyzing the 1996 presidential election based entirely on Dole's and Clinton's respective haircuts. We can't help but see the world through the eyes of our daily pursuits, and sitting there, even having been nearly blown up and saved, I couldn't help but see the scene as a journalist. Stories everywhere, blossoming narratives, a boy wearing a too-long tattered shirt, with an image on the back of a frog playing drums, comforting his mother while *she* cried.

"Let's go," Danny said, guiding me through an opening in the police tape. "The lieutenant's ready."

Under the tent, a half dozen cops whirred with various tasks. Several barked commands into walkie-talkies, one typed into a laptop, another set up what looked like an industrial-strength radio, but they all shared an intensity. This was the moment these men and women had trained for and they met it with a palpable feeling of authority and purpose.

Danny steered me by the elbow to the corner of the tent and whispered, "I told him who you are, and that you're pretty shaken. I tried to warm him up, but he can be a bit unforgiving."

And, as it turned out, a lot large.

The Aravelos seemed to have been conceived after their mother mated with the side of a mountain. Big bones holding big chests, and the strong, meaty hands that make politicians. Maybe that's why I fixated on the one small thing—the lieutenant's disproportionately small Adam's apple. It looked like a genetic hiccup.

"Dodo," he said. I found him staring intently at me.

I turned to Danny.

"The lieutenant's a habitual nicknamer," Danny said. "It suggests intimacy but he's really letting you know who's in control."

"That'll be all, Danny boy. Beat it," the lieutenant said without a hint of self-awareness. "We can do without the surveillance."

Danny's jaw tightened. He turned around and walked away, and Aravelo pulled his chair nearer.

"The dodo bird—extinct. Like print journalists. You'll be killed off by the Internet and its much more efficient means of distribution."

In San Francisco, even the cops were fixated on business models, to say nothing of the double meaning of "dodo."

"The first thing is this: I'm not going to get screwed on this investigation," the lieutenant continued. "Within hours we'll have feds, and state investigators, and probably the goddamn Marines turning this place upside down. But I'm the point guy on this for the SFPD, and I do not intend to lose this assignment, however small our role may wind up being."

I must have squinted, indicating my confusion.

"I'm going to treat you like any other person in that café—not like the guy whose fancy prose took down my brother. As far as I'm concerned, that's in the past—or the future. Not now."

He figured if he had some conflict of interest, he'd be tossed off potentially the biggest case of his career. "You're the one who brought up my job," I said quietly.

Aravelo ignored me and turned to his underling note taker. "Start scribbling," he said, then turned to me. "What were you doing in the café today?"

The question was innocuous enough, but it had an unpleasant whiff.

"I was hanging out and reading a book."

"So that's why you came into the café?"

"Yep, like I just said."

Aravelo studied me. "No, you said that's what you were *doing*. You didn't say *why* you came into the café in the first place."

"Yes, I came in to read, drink coffee, and hang around other people doing the same thing."

"Do you often read in public?" The way he said it made me feel like I was an exhibitionist.

I shrugged.

Aravelo glanced at the note taker, then locked into my gaze. "Look, I've got more than fifteen people injured by a totally bizarre incident. This type of thing doesn't happen. So there are no dumb questions. Now, where were you when the explosion happened?"

I sighed. Much as I didn't like his style, he was right. "I was actually at the front door. I was . . . heading outside for a minute."

"You were leaving the café just when it exploded," he said, pausing momentarily. "Any reason you decided to leave just then?"

I'd known this was coming, but I wasn't sure what I'd say. If I didn't come clean, I could hurt the investigation. But I'd be implicated if I told everything precisely as it happened. I split the difference.

"I saw a woman," I said. "She walked by my table. She struck me as . . . "

I searched for the word. All that surfaced was an emotion, a worthless one, the simultaneous feeling of hope and intense loneliness.

"As what?" the lieutenant said. "Describe her."

"Graceful."

"So you followed this random stranger out into the street?"

Maybe it sounded a little odd, but not really. Every guy has been struck by a woman, then followed her for a block, or sat beside her at a bar, hoping for an opening. I explained what happened—mostly. I told the lieutenant that I never got to talk to the woman, or even close to it, because she walked out, seemingly in a hurry, and jumped into a late-model red Saab.

Aravelo jumped on it. "All points search for a red late-model Saab driven by an attractive . . ."

He looked at me for help finishing his sentence. Without being sure of it, I said, "She had light brown hair."

"Brunette," Aravelo parroted forcefully to his note taker. "Now, go!" He looked at me. "One more question. What stories are you blowing out of proportion these days?"

I shrugged. Aravelo dismissed me and told me he'd be in touch.

I assessed my surroundings: countless emergency vehicles; high-tech law enforcement equipment; onlookers and media held back by blue barricades at the far end of the block; nearby, several lightly injured café patrons waiting for Aravelo's inquiries; and, across the street from the police tent, a blonde woman. She was pointing a telephoto lens at my head. Was she taking my picture?

I walked hurriedly in her direction. She stood behind yellow police tape, still shooting the scene. A scar that looked faintly like the coastline of California marked the tip of her chin. When I got close, I was struck by her camera. It was old, not digital, held in a leather case with a soft maroon lining, and, while it had a telephoto lens, not particularly sophisticated by professional journalist standards. I asked the woman if she was taking my picture, and why.

"Freelancer," she said. "Just doing my job."

She turned her camera on me. I waved my hands in front of my face, and, surprising myself, I blurted, "Do you know Annie Kindle?"

Just then, a boy and his father walked beside us on the sidewalk, holding hands. "Daddy, what happened to that man?" the boy said.

I looked down my torso to what had caught the boy's attention. My shorts and shirt were torn, my knees scraped, hands pink with dried blood, and my right elbow bandaged. Pebbles were embedded in my shins. A plausible target for a photographer.

I took a deep breath. I closed my eyes and returned to a lost time, to Annie's laugh. I may have been the first person to ever fall in love at first sound.

3

It danced across Jeremy's Bar and Grill. It floated above the din of romancing couples. It froze me over my Guinness. Her laugh was pure, confident, free.

I didn't usually drink alone. But I didn't usually come to small mountain towns to make major life decisions either.

Kings Beach is three hours northeast of San Francisco. It calls itself a beach. I always thought "beach" implied "ocean." But it's really lakeside, on the north side of Lake Tahoe.

The town is a stretch of modest motels and eateries, and places that rent out kayaks in the summer and skis when the sun gives way to snow. It's a fun family spot, or, in my case, a temporary resting place for mixed-up graduate students.

The laugh belonged to a slender brunette with shoulder-length hair and a dark hue to her skin, as if one of her grandparents had been Asian. It might not have been beauty to everyone, but it was my definition. She looked soft, passionate, and kind, or maybe eager to please.

Her friend was another matter.

As they approached, I realized that the only open bar seats were right beside me. That gave me only seconds to act, and I did. I quickly turned away from them, raised my beer to my lips, and began staring intently at a baseball game on the TV. Had I reacted a moment later, they would have seen me staring at them. I'd have been locked up for leering, and, worse, I'd have lost the advantage of feigned indifference. A finger tapped my shoulder. The friend. "Are these seats taken?" she asked. Her tone discouraged anything more than a "yes" or "no."

"They're all yours," I said, turning to face them fully. "Welcome to the neighborhood."

The woman of my dreams smiled and said, "Thanks." Her friend sensed my interest and leveled a preemptive strike. "It's girls' night out, so we're not doing the flirting thing," she said, adding with at least a touch of softness, "Now return to your beer."

I hadn't planned on drinking more. Now I had no choice. I ordered another beer. I made small talk with the bartender and watched the game. I talked to a couple sitting to my right who, after spending six hours together on a mountain bike ride, were plenty happy for a third-wheel diversion.

I glanced at myself in the bar mirror—hoping for something less than haggard. In terms of pure physical attractiveness, I'm in the 80th percentile, but with wide fluctuations. I'm five feet eleven inches, fit, stocky, with more torso than leg. I'm an ethnic mutt—dark brown hair and a strong nose. I sometimes invited comparisons to the ethnic character actor of the moment. The observer would always seem to add, "in a good way," in a tone that made me wonder. The X factor in my looks is my haircut. With a good one, I creep up to the 90th percentile. With a bad one, I've seen the low 70s.

When I looked away from the mirror, I noticed I had at last caught a break. My beauty's friend stood and headed to the bathroom. I waited the customary ten seconds and pretended to discover the friend's absence.

"Are we allowed to talk now?" I said. "I want to respect the Geneva Convention and all other applicable rules."

"Only if we're very quiet," she whispered. "I can't spend another afternoon in detention."

I had read an article by some dating guru who advised you should wait for the woman to introduce herself. That way she's the one expressing interest. But this woman deserved better than parlor games, and I didn't have much time. "Nat," I said.

"I'm Annie."

I said, "I have an escape plan. Do you think it would be hard to tunnel through the bar?"

Annie picked up her drink—something red in a short glass. "Don't mind Sarah. She's just trying to protect me—from jerks, and men who don't know a real lady only escapes using duplicity and lies."

She smiled.

"Break it up, you two," came an approaching voice. Sarah was back, and she wasn't interested in our relationship going any further. "You were warned, young man. No conversation of any kind."

Annie shrugged. Was it indifference or resignation? She picked up her jacket too. "See ya," she said.

"You'll thank me later," said Sarah, and they started walking away.

I couldn't think of any way to stop them that wouldn't have made me seem like a desperate, obsessive loon. Then, just before they hit the door, Annie stopped awkwardly—if I had to guess, caught by thought or indecision—spun back, took two steps toward me, and just on the edge of earshot said, "Pink salamander," or at least that's the way it sounded. And she was gone.

If it was a salutation, it was lost on me, ditto if it was a coded message. I spent half a day looking in phone books, around town, and down alleys for a hotel, bar, restaurant, or anything else named the Pink Salamander, or any conceivable derivation of the name. The closest I came was a tattoo and nail salon called the Chameleon, whose frumpy, heavily pierced proprietor said she appreciated my "Don Quixote" quest but said I'd keep searching in vain until I found a relationship with God.

I spent another day driving around town, hoping to "run into" Annie. I spent an inordinate amount of mealtime at Jeremy's Bar and Grill. I asked around. No Sarah, no Annie, no luck.

I'd already extended my stay by one day. I had to give up. I packed up the 4Runner and began the rationalizations. She wasn't that pretty, she was a passive follower of her friend, or she didn't find me attractive enough. So what was the point?

In at least one respect, the trip had been a success. I'd decided to undertake a major career change—and to abandon my pursuit of becoming a doctor. I'd finished medical school two months earlier. I had to admit to myself that I hated the training.

The question I had spent the better part of a week in the mountains contemplating was whether to go ahead with a residency. Instead, I was thinking about becoming a medical journalist. Writing about public health issues, and trading pragmatism and respectability for the idea of helping to change things, and gaining relative control over my time—at least compared to playing doctor. The fact that I faced $100,000 in debt and was still considering journalism suggested to me I had just the kind of idealism necessary to make such a career blunder.

At town's edge, heading home, I drove by the entrance to the marina and was struck by a last-ditch thought to check the boat slips—salamanders living on the cusp of both land and water.

The slip rental office was at Ernie's Tackle and Dive Shop. The seemingly very stoned employee said he couldn't give me information on boats and their slip homes without the approval of a manager who was due in shortly. The idea of going slip to slip seemed one step too many, particularly given the numerous launch points around the lake.

I waited for the manager and tried on dive masks.

A voice said, "At last, my knight in shining scuba gear."

The *Salamander*, slipped nearby, was the boat on which Annie and Sarah had been bunking.

"I was really hoping we'd meet again," I said.

"Me too," said Annie.

4

For our first date, I had suggested a funky Mexican bar in the Mission District. The food was authentic. So was the mariachi band, which could cover the silence should wit evade us.

I am not generally superstitious, but when I was walking to the bar to meet her, I found a nickel with a jagged edge on the sidewalk, picked it up, and, figuring it five times more powerful than a penny, made a wish and threw it over my left shoulder. I'm pretty sure I was mixing rituals. I was clearer about the wish. There had to be someone who would let me lose myself so completely in a moment that I was no longer watching from the outside. Hopefully, that person liked margaritas.

Annie wore a snug, sleeveless T-shirt, looking confident enough to err on the side of casual.

"I'm so sorry I'm late," she said. "The traffic on 101 was murder."

Annie commuted to Palo Alto, the suburbs of San Francisco. The rest of the world knows it as Silicon Valley.

I set a drink in front of her. "Let us toast to a world where children don't go hungry, the homeless live at the Four Seasons, and the freeways have no stop-and-go traffic," I said.

She told me the basics. She was twenty-six. She grew up in

San Francisco. She graduated from a fancy northeastern college. She wasn't big into dating because people took her laughter to indicate passion and she wound up with suitors whom she preferred as friends. She said she might try to steer future dates onto dire topics to forestall joviality.

"Like phobias."

She laughed. "I actually have one: Q-tips in the ear," she said.

"Fear of indented brain?"

"Not so much that. The inside of my head is the only private place left on earth."

"How about something that makes you sad?"

She had one of those too: the last thirty seconds of *Saturday Night Live*, when the credits roll and the cast is waving. She said it meant the host's dream week has come to an end and the workweek was coming.

Annie said she worked at her dad's investment firm, Kindle Investment Partners, to test the idea that she had a knack for putting money in small companies and turning them into big ones. It wasn't something she felt particularly suited to. She said her father felt otherwise. He was, she said without bragging, one of the Valley's most potent venture capitalists. When she talked about work, she sounded tired.

"So what would you be doing if you weren't getting rich and creating technology to change the world?" I said.

She chewed on it.

"Well, I majored in computer science."

"And your enthusiasm for it runneth over."

"I don't know, maybe I'd be a shrink. I got a minor in psychology," she said, then her eyes turned more whimsical, like she was discovering an idea. "I'd be a veterinarian."

"Or a combination—pet psychiatrist," I said. "I had a dog once who could have used a few hours on the couch."

"You always know where you stand with animals. Feed me, love me. Feed me. Feed me," she said. "They're easier to trust than people."

"People need to eat too."

"It would be amazing to be with someone incorruptible."

I told Annie my basics. I had grown up in Denver, the son of generous but middle-class government employees. I spent every possible weekend in the mountains—backpacking, climbing, fishing. Partly, I loved the outdoors. Partly, I needed escape. "My brother was all-everything."

"I've got one of those," she said.

"Brother?"

"Shadow. My father. He's got big plans for me. He calls me his 'Smiling Assassin.' Do I look like I'm smiling?"

"More like grinning."

"He thinks I'm like him. He says I'm made of steel," she said, then lowered her voice an octave. "'Annie, the Kindles are conquerors!'"

"You dress beautifully for a Hun."

"I've got you right where I want you," she said.

Annie was a great listener. Her eyes rose and fell with each revelation.

I told her about the incident that helped undo my medical career. During my third year of medical school, I'd been on a rotation in the pediatric oncology ward, and I'd grown close to a nine-year-old boy suffering from leukemia. On Wednesday afternoons, I found an extra hour to hang out with Jacob, usually spent playing Chutes and Ladders.

Then he contracted pneumonia, which in his weakened state would have killed him within two weeks. The attending doc thought we should let nature take its course, but I argued we should use antibiotics to kill the lung infection and then hope for remission of the cancer. It wasn't unreasonable, but I'd learned of the pneumonia one day after I'd missed my regular Wednesday board-game ritual with Jacob, and, guilt-ridden,

I disagreed vigorously with the doctor in front of the parents. He asked me to step into the hallway and told me I was too attached—medicine's code word for "unprofessional."

Annie's eyes were wide. "What'd you say?"

"Well, I kind of compared him to Dr. Kevorkian."

Annie started laughing.

"You called your boss a murderer." She sounded impressed. "That's either really courageous or really stupid."

"The parents agreed with me. They gave the antibiotics. The boy lived two more months."

I got a hefty reprimand, not for Jacob's death, of course, but for protesting too much.

The more I told Annie my story, the less I focused on her, and the more on the remains of a plate of petrifying nachos. But I was hyper-aware of her reactions. It felt like she was embracing my worldview, endorsing it. It was a change from the majority of people, including friends, who saw my decision to quit medicine as failure. Sometimes I had to fight off sharing their perceptions. I looked up. Annie held my gaze. "I'm glad you came to find me in Tahoe." She looked down. "I've been looking for you too." She leaned over and kissed my cheek, and I melted into the linoleum.

We strolled past the taquerias and the five-and-dime stores. "Few places are as romantic as a darkened alley," I said, taking Annie's hand as we stepped into a small separation between two buildings. We launched into a kiss. She took my hand and wrapped it around her back, and I pulled her into me.

"You're not okay to drive," I said when we came up for air.

She pulled out her cell phone, excused herself, and dialed a number. When she returned, we resumed kissing, until a horn honked. Outside of the alley, a dark BMW sedan had pulled up.

"My ride," she said.

She held my hand as she opened the door, then she climbed into the dark car and it pulled away.

5

I was still dazed from the explosion when I headed home to my apartment on Potrero Hill, a neighborhood whose industrial roots had become overgrown by residents. During the Internet boom, there hadn't been enough housing to accommodate the gold-rushing twenty-somethings and so they bled into Potrero.

Across the street from my apartment was Meatless Ray's, an organic grocer featuring tofu-based homeopathic remedies and meat substitutes. Next door, tucked into a veritable shoebox of a retail space, was a Laundromat whose owner sold computer tech support services on the side. This was post-boom San Francisco, a city fighting to return to greatness, jacked up on wheatgrass and e-mail attachments.

But the establishment I loved most was the Past Time bar; three blocks from my apartment, and open until 4 a.m., the bar itself was unremarkable, but the clientele left an impression, particularly Dennis "Bullseye" Leary, and his wife, Samantha.

There is every reason to believe, as some suggest, that the Learys cross over the fine line into certifiable. I preferred to think of them as colorful. They are, at least, savants. You've got to give credit to anyone who can name the lifetime batting average of every starting player to ever spend more than two seasons with the San Francisco Giants.

That was Bullseye. His strength was math—doing it and

memorizing it. His weakness was just about everything else. He wasn't much at the big things, like holding down a job or practicing regimented hygiene. The small things challenged him too. Once, during a game of darts, he misfired so badly that he hit a waitress standing at about forty-five degrees to the dartboard. Bullseye.

The unconfirmed understanding at the bar was that Bullseye once owned a Chevron gas station, made a decent chunk of money, and went into retirement after a series of loud disagreements with the corporate office.

Samantha had her own specialty. She is, in New Age parlance, a spiritual healer. Samantha has a knack for laying hands on someone to cure headaches, sports injuries, and work-related aches. Some people call it acupressure. We just called her the Witch.

Samantha could tell someone's mood—where it had been, and where it was headed. She also professed to be able to rid houses of ghosts and specters, though since their actual presence is tough to prove in the first place, this remained a subject of intense and ongoing bar speculation. You could always recognize Samantha from blocks away, thanks to the loud homemade knit hats she wore that she claimed regulated her temperature.

Samantha and Bullseye argued too, once viciously for days over whether he was obligated to her in the afterlife, should it exist. Sometimes it seemed they didn't like each other at all, they just loved each other. It was a relationship that regularly tested their self- and mutual acceptance; after all, Samantha gave massages, platonically but vigorously rubbing people's bodies and spirits, and if I had been Bullseye, I'd have thrown a lot more tantrums than he did.

On their worst days, the Learys provided comic relief. On their best, they were real friends. After Annie died, I pulled back from a lot of my old buddies—a mutually agreeable separation. I needed a hiatus from my life, and from what became persistent and well-meaning efforts to set me up with new women. My old friends needed a break from the heaviness that enveloped me. Many were in their medical residencies anyway, and their lives revolved around work and sleep. Samantha and Bullseye filled the void. Often, they just listened. Tonight, they were in for an earful.

"Bonds went two for four," Bullseye said when he saw me. "That's not the interesting part."

Bullseye doubtless had heard what happened at the café. But he couldn't have known I was there. So the fact that he ignored my torn shirt and shorts was just par for the course for his social skills, not an extraordinary example of the theme. "Division of labor," I said. "I'll get the beers and you tell me the interesting part."

"He walked in the tenth," Bullseye explained. "Therefore, his on-base percentage is the highest not just for any player this late in the season, but for any player at any time after the first month of a regular season."

I set down a round of beers. "I was at the Sunshine Café."

Bullseye didn't say anything, but I could feel him shrink his head back into his neck the way it did when his left brain was poked with a stick. Samantha put her hands on my knees, studied my face, and then dove into a full-fledged bear hug.

"I survive the explosion only to be asphyxiated in my local bar."

"Breathe through your mouth. It will release the toxins." She finally released her hug.

I told them about the explosion and its aftermath.

"You're *sure* it was Annie's handwriting?" Samantha asked.

All I could do was shrug. I could have sworn the looping script was hers, but how could that be possible?

"Isn't that place in Annie's old neighborhood?"

I nodded. "I had a basketball game and an errand in the Marina. I rarely go to that café anymore. We used to have Sunday brunch there." It came out slightly defensive.

Samantha knelt in front of me.

"So maybe Annie was in the back of your mind, sweetie. You were shaken by the explosion and it opened a portal in your memory. It was another level of consciousness."

"Mumbo-jumbo," said Bullseye gruffly.

I thought I caught a whiff of judgment in Bullseye's eyes. He had met Annie only once, but professed a dislike of her immediately. I heard from someone else at the bar that he had described her as a "Peace Sign," seductive, but bigger on symbolism than substance. There was a class distinction Bullseye just couldn't abide, or maybe he thought my love was a little too intense for his mathematical view of the world.

The further I got into the story, the less it made sense. If I believed that the explosion was an accident, then I couldn't possibly explain the warning I'd been given.

But the idea of someone blowing up a neighborhood café seemed nothing short of insane. What could it possibly have to do with Annie?

We had two more rounds in virtual silence. At some point, Samantha sat on Bullseye's lap and fed him peanuts while he watched the game. I finally slinked out. Was someone trying to blow me up? Or was someone trying to save me?

Or both.

6

I got back to my loft sometime after midnight. I toted the laptop to the couch and tried to check e-mail, but somehow I'd left the computer on all day and was without power. I plugged it back in at the desk, and that's where exhaustion overtook me. Head bobbing at chin, I fell into a deep sleep, and dreamed of Annie, evaporating into millions of tiny computer pixels.

I awoke with a start to two sounds: a meow and ringing. The meow was a cat. The ringing was a magazine editor calling. Both were hungry.

Samantha Leary had given me Hippocrates, the black cat sitting on my chest bleating for breakfast. The critter, Samantha said, was designed to teach me to be less of a "dog" and to develop my inner feline. I looked at the cat and barked, causing it to flee toward the kitchen. The phone call was from Kevin. He said, "Got a sec to chat?"

Somebody should study how editors and writers communicate. A remarkably high number of conversations begin with an editor saying, "Got a sec to chat?" But this doesn't refer to a short exchange of ideas. It means: Do you have half an hour? I need to tell you precisely how to write your story.

Writers respond, "Absolutely." By which they mean: You talk. I'll ignore you. I'll write the story the way I want to.

My dynamic with Kevin—and with other editors—demanded

subtler strategies. As a freelance journalist, I needed to be particularly sensitive to editorial demands. If I ticked them off,
they wouldn't hire me and I, by extension, wouldn't eat, or
pay rent.

Kevin worked for *American Health Journal*, for which I
wrote three or four times a year. The stories weren't of particular interest to me, but the magazine paid well—on time.
"We've got an idea about the cell phone story," he said. "We
want to do an informational graphic mapping the path of the
radio wave as it passes through the brain."

Editors say "we" when they mean "I."

Kevin went on to explain an idea for an elaborate but simplistic illustration. It would show the radio wave taking a path from
a phone tower through the major regions of the brain and to its
ultimate destination—the phone being held at someone's ear.

He stopped talking abruptly and changed directions.

"We need the story by Friday. You still on track?"

I looked at the half-foot-high stack of research I'd amassed
on the kitchen table. I hadn't begun to look through it, but
I'd told Kevin I'd done the interviews and read the literature.
I spent a few minutes trying to manage his expectations. The
generally accepted theory is that the effect of radio waves on
the brain is small, if not nonexistent, and I told Kevin not to
expect any revelations. Still, the paranoia about cell phones is
understandable, and not just because the idea of having radio
waves crashing against the frontal lobe is disquieting. We har-
bor a general distrust of machines. Just look at the number of
movies that make technology the enemy; wayward computers
have replaced Commies, aliens, and Nazis.

Maybe our fear was a reflection of our growing dependence on gadgets. In every ear, an earpiece. On every belt, a
pager—millions of devices connecting us to millions of other
devices with streams of data. We've come to rely wholly on a
bunch of things that most of us couldn't build or fix.

"Emphasize the fact that we just don't know how bad the

medical impact could be," Kevin said. "I'm thinking about two thousand words."

Maybe I should have played the sympathy card—and tried to buy some more time to finish the story. The café that had exploded was all over the news. I could have told Kevin I'd come within a double cappuccino of being blown up with it. But he would have just said, "Oh my God. Are you okay?" He would have meant: Get me the story by Friday.

I tried to focus on the pile of research, but the papers were highly scientific, boring by most standards, and not particularly informative. On any day it would have been tough; on this day, doubly so.

And, besides, the laptop was beckoning again.

Home office workers know it is taboo to spend a couple of hours watching TV, but they have no reservations about surfing the Web. TV is deemed sheer entertainment and a waste of time, while monitoring Yahoo! News, catching up on stocks, and checking e-mail every two minutes is barely a misdemeanor. Procrastination under the guise of productivity.

I called up the *San Francisco Chronicle* home page, which had three stories related to the café explosion. The main headline read, "San Francisco Eatery Torn by Blast." The story said that police were frantically hunting down leads, but had no suspects or motives. There was no credible evidence of terrorism. There were five fatalities.

According to the *Chronicle*, the blast would have killed more people if the weather hadn't been so good. A half dozen patrons who might have been inside were sitting at the thick oak tables outside of the café. Those who were inside weren't so lucky. I read their obituaries.

Simon Anderson was a thirty-five-year-old aspiring novelist. He left behind a wife and two kids, one adopted and with autism. Andrea Knudson, twenty-five, had just finished law school and was preparing to take the bar exam. Darby Station was a single, thirty-something regional marketing manager for a company based in Texas. And Eileen and Terry Dujobe were retirees, evidently spending an afternoon sipping their unexpectedly last latte. They were all residents of San Francisco.

The stories said several people inside the café survived the blast unscathed. At least one was mentioned by name. Police said that a waitress named Erin Coultran had walked into a small employee bathroom milliseconds before the blast. Concrete reinforcements had kept the restroom, and the waitress, virtually intact.

There was a picture of Erin. She appeared, not surprisingly, frazzled. She was thirty-three and pretty, maybe beautiful. Even in two dimensions, she had eyes that conveyed kindness and depth.

I felt a surge of adrenaline return. My legs twitched and I bit the inside of my cheek so hard that I winced. With an unsteady index finger, I drew an imaginary circle around Erin.

I looked at her eyes. Had she seen the woman who handed me the note in the café?

7

Highly skilled journalists learn techniques for finding people. Like using the phone book and the Internet. That's why we're so handsomely paid.

It turned out that Erin Coultran belonged to a performance art troupe in the Mission District, the Heavenly Booties. The troupe's Web site described the group as committed to socially conscious women's free-form improv dance style. It left a lot up to the imagination, though I could at least surmise that if I ever had a chance to dance with Erin, I wouldn't be the one leading.

I doubted anyone would be staffing the headquarters of a performance art troupe. If they were, some other entrepreneurial journalist had probably gotten there first, but the key to unraveling a story was to muster the energy to start somewhere.

When I got there, a handful of journalists were indeed out front on the sidewalk, lingering or, rather, fidgeting. That's what reporters do. It's a product of the attention deficit disorder that is a prerequisite in the profession. A journalist not involved in a moment of intensity is seeking one out.

I walked to the dance troupe's modest storefront. A crème-colored blind hung halfway down the window. I knelt and peeked through the bottom, but could see only two wooden tables on a linoleum floor.

I turned around and found myself looking into the sun. And felt a dull ache where the adrenaline had worn off.

*   *   *

Two months earlier, I'd written a story about how the vending machines in San Francisco's schools were stocked with high-calorie crap sold by the same companies sponsoring extracurricular sports programs. To call it investigative journalism would have been an impossible stretch. It, like most of what I did, just involved noticing connections. Nothing cloak-and-dagger about my trade. I was a guy with a pen, curiosity, and deep thanks for the First Amendment. This quest was already demanding a different kind of grit.

I stopped at a Mexican grocery store two doors down from the dance center. Varieties of jalapeños, plantains, and tomatillos on the outside produce stand catered to the neighborhood's concentration of Spanish-speakers, but inside the place smelled thinly of the barbecued duck I could see behind the deli glass. Many of the local stores had been purchased of late by Chinese, a demographic shared by the young man who sat behind a counter watching *Wheel of Fortune*.

"I've got a strange question."

"Condoms are over there, bro," he responded, pointing to aisle three.

"Good. Now where are your inflatable dolls?" I said.

I pulled out a newspaper clipping of Erin's picture. "I'm trying to find someone."

"Are you a pig?"

"Reporter. She survived an explosion the other day. I want to ask her how she's feeling."

Suddenly, that seemed like enough information. He picked up the photo and whistled. "Legs"—he held his hand three feet in the air—"up to here, bro."

"So you've seen her. Today?"

No, but he'd seen her. She came in all the time, shepherding hungry kids from a tutoring center that was a block away. He pointed me in its direction.

*   *   *

A block away, I stood outside a storefront with its window covered with colorful and haphazard crayon drawings. A sign read, "Guerrero child-care and tutoring."

I made my way through the sea of rug rats. I found her sitting in the back, huddled over a cup of coffee. I got ten feet away and stopped, just as she looked up.

Erin's eyes widened. I saw her look to the left. I followed her gaze—to the back door. Over its top was a banner drawn in thick purple, green, and yellow markers with the words "Adios Amigos." By the time I turned back toward her, Erin was already standing and heading full stride toward the exit, dangling a pair of keys from her left hand.

"Erin!"

She wasn't stopping to look back.

8

My view of Erin was a ponytail poking through a baseball cap, heading purposefully in the other direction. I flashed for a moment on whether I might tear my hamstring again, then gave chase into the alley where she was putting a key into the lock of an aging green Honda with a ski rack.

Even without having time to think, I knew on some level I didn't like what I was about to do. I stepped forward, put out my hand, and pushed her driver's side door shut so she couldn't open it.

"Leave me the fuck alone," she said, with a mix of terror and anger, and a touch of resignation. I played on it.

"I was at the café. Please, I need your help."

She wore a sweatshirt with a Tsingtao logo. She was tall and thin, with smooth, pale skin. Her face was mildly round, suggesting cheeriness in some circumstances, but at that moment just as if it had been slightly overinflated with air.

When she spoke again, it was less with venom and fear and with more than a little confidence. "Are you going to let me go? Or am I going to start screaming and kicking?"

I pulled my hand away from the door.

"I don't know who you think I am," I said. "But I just need your help. I mean you no harm."

Even as I said it, I had to wonder whether I meant it entirely. After all, she was aggressively fleeing the scene.

"You've got the wrong person."

I shook my head. Wrong person? She wasn't Erin, the café waitress? Then I realized that wasn't what she meant. What exactly she did mean wasn't clear. I didn't figure I'd get a chance to ask, not without a subpoena. But instead of closing the door, she put her hand over its top, curling her fingers down over the window. For the first time, she seemed to study me.

"There are reporters everywhere," she said. "I came here to think, and to . . . clear my head."

It struck me she could be suffering from a muted version of post-traumatic stress disorder. She was highly alert and sensitive, her responses exaggerated.

"Give me five minutes of your time." I tried to affect my least threatening tone. "I saw your picture in the paper. I needed to talk to a fellow café survivor. I . . . I lost someone . . ."

I launched into a concise version of what had happened to me at the café.

"This woman saved my life. I thought maybe you'd seen her too." I didn't bother to mention Annie. I did say, "I know it sounds insane."

She listened. She closed her eyes, seemingly concentrating, but part of me wondered if her pause was affect. "I didn't see a woman leave the café. I didn't see anyone hand you a note, but I do remember you," she finally said. "You ordered at the counter then sat by the rack where we keep the magazines. I was trying to figure out if and when you'd need a refill or something to eat. Maybe the person you're talking about never sat down. I tend not to notice people unless they're sitting at a table."

I clenched my teeth and spoke with an edge. "She had long hair. You're sure you didn't see her?"

"I was on my break in the back, checking e-mail. I went to the bathroom just before the explosion. Maybe that's when she showed up."

I couldn't repress the confrontational question bubbling from my gut. "Why did you pick just that moment to go to the bathroom—right before the explosion?"

"This conversation is over."

"Erin . . ."

She opened her car door. She looked at me intently.

"What's *your* sin?"

"What does that mean?"

"Please, I need to go. Let's continue this later," she said.

She scribbled her cell phone number on a piece of paper and handed it to me. As she pulled off, I realized she'd written down only six digits. Just then, my own phone rang. I answered, and heard an unfamiliar voice.

"Nathaniel, it's Danny Weller." The policeman from the café.

"Sergeant," I said.

I could hear traffic in the background. "Listen, I'm wondering if you have a few minutes to get together," he said. "I thought you should know about some interesting developments."

9

When I got to the Bus Stop Bar, Sergeant Danny Weller was already there. He was seated in a booth near the back, wearing a button-down shirt, and looking more like a dentist than a cop. He was nose deep in a newspaper. Beside him sat a dark-skinned cop in uniform who was at least a head taller and thick, scrawling on some paperwork.

I neared the pair. "I need a three-letter word for 'organism,'" Danny said without looking up from a folded-in-half *Chronicle*. "Zoa," he added, mostly to himself.

Danny introduced the other cop as the Big Samoan, Officer Edward Velarde. He had a vise-grip handshake and he looked vaguely familiar. Near his left ear, by his hairline, was a red rash, the flaky scales indicative of psoriasis. As a medical student, you learn to identify people by their pathologies. I couldn't place where I'd seen him before—maybe after the explosion. He asked for Sergeant Weller's signatures on the paperwork he'd been working on, stuffed them in a briefcase. "See you back at the fruit farm, sweetie," he said to Weller with a pronounced mock lisp, and excused himself.

"What's going on, Sergeant?" I said pointedly.

"When I was a kid, my dad and I drove up Highway 80 almost every weekend. We'd fish in Sacto, or hike in Tahoe. The traffic was always terrible. So Dad would have me read him the crossword while he drove. He loved puzzles," he said. "The art of the crossword is memorization, really, not analysis. I've been stocking away clues since I was twelve. Back then, if I used a word incorrectly in conversation, Dad would make me carry a dictionary around all day."

He was going to do this on his terms. I fought the impulse to demand answers.

"Do you and your dad still fish?"

"He's living in Fremont, in a group home. Sick as a dog, the kind of dog that needs a new liver," Danny said. "Hell, I shouldn't be talking about tragedy to you, considering what happened yesterday. How're you feeling?"

Actually, I still wasn't sure. I'd been experiencing such an adrenaline rush that I hadn't paused to put it in any perspective. "Tired."

And mystified and frustrated. I wanted to know about the new developments the sergeant had alluded to on the phone, but I had learned over the years as a reporter that one of the most effective ways of eliciting information is to not let on about your desperation. Sources usually want to divulge something, tell the story, take the spotlight.

One strategy to get people talking is to do the talking first, so I decided to tell Danny what I knew. It was a gamble, of course. Just because he had allowed me to call him by his first name didn't change the fact that he was a cop, with his own allegiances and priorities.

I told him the little bit I knew. About the note, and a bit about Annie—and her handwriting—about going to see Erin, her hostility, the brief story she told me.

"She ducked into the bathroom—nice time for nature to call," he said.

"In a suspicious way?"

He shrugged.

"Nathaniel, do you believe that the woman who handed you the note was your ex-girlfriend?"

It was the one question I hadn't permitted myself to fully consider.

"I don't think so, Sergeant—how could it possibly have been?"

I didn't say aloud the rest of my thought: No way Annie was alive, or she would have contacted me long before.

He studied me. The more he did so, the more resolute I felt. Annie was gone, end of story. But someone had singled me out, was messing with me on a grand scale, and it was time to try to get what I came for.

"I need to know what's going on, Sergeant."

He lifted his glass, dropped his neck, and finished off the last of his Coke. "The district attorney has reopened the investigation into the charges against Lieutenant Aravelo's brother."

"What?" I said, quickly, sharply. "Why?"

Timothy Aravelo was a first-class thug. He'd nearly killed a twenty-year-old woman, then conspired with a couple of other cops to cover it up. I'd come to suspect the corruption went high into the police department. That I could never prove. But I was damn sure the younger Aravelo was one badge away from being a gang member.

"High-priced attorneys. They convinced an appellate judge to reexamine some of the sworn testimony."

I clenched my teeth.

"It's probably not a big deal," Danny continued. "But I wanted to let you know things could get a little dicey. You'll probably have to talk to investigators again."

We were interrupted by a buzzing sound coming from the sergeant's pants. He pulled out a pager. "Damn," he said.

He rose from the seat.

"I'm not in charge of the café investigation. It's Lieutenant Aravelo's baby. But I'm tracking it."

He explained that San Francisco's homicide rate had spiked in the past couple of years. Lots of the murders were unsolved, especially in the poor black corners of the city where gangs roamed. He reminded me that the mayor had made a big deal out of addressing unsolved murders, earning himself enemies on the police force by publicly questioning their capabilities, and then issuing a directive that high-profile murder cases would have two teams of investigators—one official team, and then one or two shadow investigators who investigated independently, found their own leads, and were supposed to feed information to the main group. Sometimes they preferred to take credit for a collar.

It created competition, but also distrust.

"What you told me—about the note—needs to be in the right hands. I am tight with a couple of the lead investigators on the café case. I'll have them get in touch, if you don't mind," he said. "Or you can contact Aravelo directly—if you feel comfortable going that direction."

I couldn't let him go. There was so much I wanted to know.

"Sergeant Weller. I was hoping you'd be able to tell me more about what happened at the café. Who did this? Why would I be warned? Is this a random act of violence or some insane attack that I've wound up in the middle of?"

He studied me, then shrugged. "I think you put it correctly yesterday. Something very strange went down."

He turned, then looked back over his shoulder. "Call me anytime you want to talk."

I needed another beer—or several—so I drove across town to my local joint. Samantha and Bullseye were parked at their usual spot, watching the Giants game. I barely said hello before launching in with my story.

"Your chi is way out of balance," Samantha said, grabbing my hand and vigorously rubbing my palm. "I can do some healing with massage. But you really need to come down to the studio for acupuncture—and energy work."

"What my chi needs is a pizza and some sleep," I said.

She was right. In the preceding couple of years, despite sometimes protesting otherwise, I'd come increasingly to appreciate Samantha's witchcraft. I made an appointment for the next day.

I walked outside of the bar and studied the piece of paper on which Erin had written her six-digit number. Maybe she'd left one out by accident. I tried a couple of combinations, adding a different last digit each time. Three weren't real phone numbers, and a fourth was answered by an old lady with a slur in her voice who seemed like she wanted to talk anyway.

When I got home, I was beyond exhausted, but I saw my laptop sitting there and I couldn't help myself. I sent an e-mail to my attorney, telling him about Sergeant Weller's revelation that the Aravelo case had been reopened, and seeking his advice.

Then I started looking for news of the day's events. There wasn't much I hadn't learned earlier from the *Chronicle*, and from Danny. I saw a picture of the eviscerated café and felt a wave of nausea.

I read about the café's owner, Idelwild Corporation, a holding company with some powerful corporate owners. They wanted a piece of the Starbucks café phenomenon and what it represented: the confluence of technological and interpersonal communications. Cafés were like campfires but with wireless access and better pastries.

I followed link after random link for four hours. Even as my body yearned for bed and sleep, I couldn't pull myself away, the mystery and memory stoking my quest. Finally, I drifted off, and woke up in the morning to a decision. It was time to visit the dead.

10

The paper said Simon Anderson's funeral and memorial service would be held graveside in Colma. The City of Souls. More than one million people are buried in cemeteries on a lush hillside setting just south of San Francisco. The only thing more crowded than life in the Bay Area is the afterlife.

The obituary said the deceased was a former investment banker focusing on technology who had done well enough to take on his dream of becoming a writer. He'd published a children's book through a vanity press.

A crowd was gathering. A woman next to me pulled out a bottled water and a pouch of raw mixed nuts. She told her friend she'd brought her own snacks in case the funeral food wasn't organic.

A tent had been set up over the gravesite and a woman I took to be Anderson's wife sat underneath, with her daughter and autistic son, who bounced excitedly, seemingly oblivious to the solemnity. Surrounding us were tombstones big and small, death's haves and have-nots. The Silver family mausoleum was big enough to fetch $3,000 a month without renovations if rented as a one-bedroom apartment in Noe Valley.

I had come to the funeral looking for a place to start, maybe someone who had been at the café to whom I could show the picture in my breast pocket. I pulled it out and looked at Annie.

Our second date took place two weeks after our first. We'd

had little contact because she'd been on a work trip to New York and relatively unresponsive to e-mail. But when I got to her apartment to pick her up, we immediately launched into a kiss, which threatened to get heavy, until a little girl from across the hallway opened the door.

She told Annie that her cat had again crawled behind the stove and had been there for hours. Annie promised to help, went inside her own apartment for a second, slyly showed me a bag of catnip, and then we went over to retrieve Edmund. Annie knelt beside the stove and made a show for the girl of coaxing out the cat with a fantastical plea about how everyone involved would be better off by its appearance.

When Edmund emerged it set off genuine joy from the girl, and also Annie, who wiped cobwebs from the cat's face and scratched the base of its ear. Annie, the cat whisperer. I'd always been a sucker for a woman who could nurture a pet, figuring if she could love something that habitually puked on the carpet she could cope with whatever hair balls I brought up. Annie startled me by reading my thoughts.

"If you run behind the stove, you're on your own." She smiled.

"I'm not easy. I've had sex with only three people," Annie said.

"You mean at once?"

"Pig." She paused. "This is going to be something special."

She pulled me into her apartment. At a glance, not much registered. I could tell one thing, though: The place was neat. Hospital corners all around.

"Nat, this whole thing is freaking me out," Annie said. She lowered her voice, like she was too embarrassed to finish her thought. "Is this real?"

I laughed. "I was wondering the same thing."

She led me to the bedroom. I noticed that tacked neatly around the edges of the ceiling were Christmas lights—blue, red, yellow, and green—but unlit.

"I should have removed them six months ago," Annie said. "I'm better at putting things up than taking them down."

"Sure, putting things up is exciting—it means holidays and vacation and presents are coming. Taking things down means it's over. Hibernation."

"Very deep," she said. "I don't know where their box is."

She giggled and her eyes shone joy, and desire. I dove into them.

Afterward, I looked at her bedside table. It was bare, except for a tick-tock clock with metallic black hands, and two hardbacks: *Heart of Darkness* and *Horton Hears a Who*.

"Nat, have you ever saved a life?" Annie asked. "You know, in the line of duty."

I told her the story from two years before when I'd seen an SUV back over a pregnant woman outside a mall. I administered CPR, as anybody with basic training would have done. The woman died, the baby survived. The woman's husband sued me for failing to stabilize his wife's cervical spine. His case was tossed out, but not before it made the experience even more painful.

"I would have wanted that man's head on a platter," Annie said, then added after a pause, "Why are you smiling?"

It was true. She was right. In a millisecond, my mood had shifted.

"I haven't felt angry about that for a long time," I said. "The thing is, I haven't felt much of anything for a long time."

From the bedside table, I picked up *Horton Hears a Who*. It was autographed, inscribed to "Annie, A Wondriferous Girl, Who Someday Could Rule The World."

"Why did you ask me if I'd ever saved a life?"

"Why, Doctor," Annie responded playfully, "you never know when a girl will need saving."

We spent the next two days prone. Not necessarily in the throes of passion—we talked constantly—but there were a lot of throes. It was a bit surprising, given the relative lack of contact between our dates. She dismissed my questions about her inattentiveness on her work trip by noting that she had been overwhelmed. Her father had sent her to size up a small technology company in upstate New York. The work was all-consuming. She told me that she'd thought about me all the time.

All in all, it was two days of great conversation, take-out food, and Strawberry Too, her Labrador retriever, named after her first childhood dog. We took a crash course in each other. Annie got nervous when people touched her neck; she preferred watching television with the light on because it reminded her that what was happening on the screen wasn't real; she once had a "little brother" from East Palo Alto from whom she learned Spanish to better communicate with; she had a high tolerance for liquor but not beer; she monthly wrote handwritten letters to her mother, who had divorced her father several years ago and moved to Washington State. She liked writing letters, and theorized that her handwriting changed slightly depending on who they were written to; with her mom the script was a little rounder, bespeaking sympathy.

It wasn't one single thing that inspired me about Annie, one accomplishment or trait I could point to that summed up her allure. It was how she made me feel—that she was clearheaded and passionate but waiting, like me, and I could be the thing she was waiting for. When I woke up Monday morning, I was truly hooked—until we had our first fight.

I was sitting in an antique chair in her living room a few weeks later. I leaned my head back over the back of the chair, reveling in the greatness of the moment. I over-reveled. The chair fell over backward and a leg snapped. Annie rushed over. To the chair.

"Can I get you a sledgehammer?"

"Don't worry about me," I said, holding up my bleeding hand.

I walked into the kitchen, turned on the faucet, and ran warm water over the cut that ran inside the webbing of my thumb. I'd need a butterfly bandage. Behind me, I could hear Annie trying to put the wood pieces back into place. Finally, she walked over and inspected the wound, but she remained cold.

"That's the first thing I ever bought myself," she said.

I held my tongue. I left in a dark silence and spent the night replaying the event. Maybe it was just a function of upbringing; Annie was Prada, I was Levi's. Then with the light of day came a delivery on my doorstep. It was a baby snapping turtle in a terrarium. There was a note. It read, "I am so horribly sorry for snapping. Please forgive me. A."

In the coming months, when one of us lost track of our priorities or blew things out of proportion, that person was deemed "turtle." Our first pet name. As time passed, it became our singular term of endearment.

But I didn't give in immediately. Following our fight, I slowed the engine. I started peeking around corners. One night, we were about to climb into my car after going to a movie. Annie asked for the keys and told me she was driving. I sat in the passenger seat, she put a finger to my lips, encouraging silence. Then she pulled out a black scarf, wrapped it across my eyes, and tied it behind my head. I laughed as we drove in circles around town for half an hour. She was trying to confuse me as to our destination. I was imagining we would wind up in a hotel bed, with me wearing only the blindfold.

We finally parked. She led me into a building and up a set of stairs. It felt familiar. I remember the smell of cinnamon cookies coming from somewhere nearby. She leaned in close and whispered, "Please trust me . . . again."

I heard her put a key in a lock and open the door. She undid the blindfold and held my gaze.

"I'm getting there," I said.

I realized we were standing in the doorway of my apartment.

"Surprise," Annie said, pointing me to a pile of gifts: a quill pen, a stack of crepe stationery with my initials, and a new Mac with a big, dazzling screen, all of it sitting on an antique mahogany desk. Annie said she wanted to share the wealth of a deal that had yielded her father's firm tens of millions of dollars. I ran my hands over the carved side of the desk.

"I can definitely be bought," I added, mostly joking.

"No you can't," she said, taking my face.

"They're a writer's rocks and sticks—his tools. *Your* tools," she whispered into my ear. "Keep creating. Keep building."

From then on, I wrote Annie poems, and left goofy messages on her answering machine, and put notes on her car, and I never doubted her again.

Back at Cypress Lawn, I was shaken from my memory by the voice of a minister delivering a by-the-book eulogy. Simon Anderson, loving father and husband, charitable man, passionate in his pursuits, taken from us too soon. Anderson's brother spoke next. He was strikingly attractive, as were many of those in attendance. The kind of gene pool drawn to San Francisco, but even more so. Many men wore ties, a fashion relegated to weddings and funerals. Anderson's brother described his sibling as a wicked-quick study, who would have struck it rich even without help from the dot-com boom; a pilot and adventurer with an effortless charisma, and a husband and father who cherished his family.

"I know things got a little rough at the end," he said, looking at the widow. "He wouldn't have wanted pity from anybody. You know Simon. He would've wanted a proper wake. So let's drain one more keg."

The crowd began to disperse, and I noticed a hundred hands reach into pockets to extract cell phones. It was like the airplane had just landed. I looked for an in-person conversation. I saw one mourner in a dark suit hobbled by a leg cast. His face was scabbed. I started walking toward him just as he was approached by two serious-looking gents, one bearing a notepad. Cops. I turned in the other direction and took a stroll on the giant lawn, which reminded me of the setting of Annie's memorial service, with hundreds mourning a tragic death at sea. By then, there was little hope her father's no-holds-barred search effort would yield a miracle, or even a body.

A line of Anderson's mourners began an orderly exit. In one of the nearby cul-de-sacs of the massive cemetery I noticed one car staying put, and out of the way—a beat-up green Honda with a ski rack and its driver slunk behind the wheel.

Erin Coultran was lurking.

11

I expected Erin to hit the throttle when she saw me, but she didn't. She did start rolling up her window. Then she paused and stared at me through dark glasses with purple frames, seemingly lost in analysis.

"Get in," she said, with a sudden sense of purpose.

We drove in silence away from the procession. She didn't like a crowd—certainly not this one. We parked by a tombstone proclaiming "Frisky" to be a "cat above."

"When you mourn, you really like your privacy," I said.

"So how did you first learn that the cop had nearly killed the Malaysian girl?"

I'd done it enough times myself to know when I'd been Googled.

I reached into my breast pocket. I felt the small square picture. Maybe it would jog Erin's memory. Then again, maybe Annie was all in my imagination and there was no jogging to be done.

I kept the picture tucked. And, seeing no harm in it, I told Erin the Aravelo story from the beginning. I had friends from medical school who worked at San Francisco General, a take-all-comers urban triage center. They often gave me tips about interesting health issues that they felt (1) wouldn't be of interest to the mainstream press, or (2) wouldn't be fully understood and explained by someone without a medical background.

Erin said, "So are you a doctor?"

"I'm a nonpracticing, ill-qualified, not-up-to-date, medical school graduate."

"So you are a doctor."

Signs of life. She seemed to smile without moving her lips. She'd removed her glasses, revealing eyes deep brown and magnetic.

I explained that my doctor friends started seeing a spate of young Asian women with HIV. It was clear they were prostitutes. The trick was finding where they worked. It turned out that the brothels were actually advertised under various euphemisms in the neighborhood papers. I called for an escort, and was given an address in the Sunset District. From there, I did the basic grunt work of journalism. I met several prostitutes, including Azlina Hathimar, also known as Daisy. They'd been shipped over from Malaysia and Vietnam and were essentially buying freedom through the sex trade.

"So why didn't they go to the police?" Erin asked.

"Some of their johns were cops and they didn't know who to trust."

"Fucking police," she said, looking away.

I had planned to go to the cops myself, but events overtook us. I'd gone back to the brothel to do more reporting, arriving not long after Patrolman Aravelo had dealt out his beating. I'm not sure Azlina would have survived if I hadn't gotten there and begun treating her; her pimps might not have bothered to call for an ambulance.

"So now you're investigating the café explosion? You're looking for another project?"

She started the car.

"Where are we headed, Erin?"

"Cole Valley. I'll take you back to your car later."

It was a different Erin than the one who'd fled at the tutoring center. This one was driving, literally and figuratively. This one seemed highly capable.

Erin held out a ballpoint pen. It looked like it had been chewed in half.

"What do you make of this?"

"I diagnose you with raccoons."

"Andy did that. With his teeth."

I had no idea who Andy was, or why Erin was telling me about him.

"Andy killed himself two weeks ago," she said. "They say he walked off the bridge. He's the last person on earth I would ever have expected to do that."

"Who's 'they,' Erin?"

She just shook her head.

"Andy was your boyfriend?"

"Not exactly. He was so kind, and funny. He . . . Two months ago, he . . . started getting these terrible headaches."

I had seen water bottles on the backseat. I twisted my body around to grab a couple. On the seat and spilling onto the floor were a jumble of clothes, discarded food wrappers and balled-up paper, and a worn Bible. Unlike Annie, Erin apparently didn't gravitate to order.

"Back up," I said. "Can you give me some basics?"

I wasn't asking because I particularly cared, but I realized the best thing I could do was to keep Erin talking. Maybe she'd say something that would help me get closer to understanding the café's connection to Annie—if there was one.

Maybe I could just get a better handle on Erin.

She said she'd been working at the café for two years when she met Andy Goldstein, tall and lanky with a glob of sandy blond curly hair that some days looked like an overfertilized plant. He taught fifth grade at a private school. During the school year, Andy would occasionally stop by after the final bell to put the day—and the brats—behind him. He joked that he believed in the healing power of root beer.

Erin and Andy grew extremely close. They used to go to

the skateboard park and talk above the background noise of boarders testing their courage against the pavement, though sometimes Andy earnestly told the kids he was a scout for MTV to see which ones got more courageous and focused and which were more mistake prone. Andy had theories about everything; he swore to Erin that you could tell the quality of a Chinese restaurant by its rice. He also insisted that the world could be broken down into two groups of people based on their elevator-riding habits—there are those who press the button of the floor they want only once, and those who press it again each time the elevator makes a stop. Andy was strong, and centered, and made her laugh and feel calm. "When I was with him, it always felt like it was Sunday afternoon," Erin said.

"Meaning?"

"Safe enough to nap."

Andy had planned to spend summer break from school traveling in Vietnam and Thailand, but decided instead to finish up a master's thesis. Waitress and patron grew very close, until Andy started acting strange.

"Andy became . . . excitable for a few weeks, and then tired. He turned irritable, and mean," she said. "He freaked at me for screwing up his latte."

He knew something wasn't right. He said he was having restless sleep and strange, vivid dreams. "He was almost relieved when the headaches came," she said. "It gave him something more concrete to talk to the doctors about."

The initial tests didn't show cancer, but they were inconclusive. Then he went to see a neurologist who'd used some sophisticated tests that found something weird. Erin never got a full explanation, but there was at least reason for hope.

Two days later, he jumped from the Golden Gate Bridge.

I tried to recall my basic training in psychology and neurology. Andy was irritable. He had vivid dreams. Suicidal ideation. Evidence of a psychotic or schizophrenic break? I remembered that it did typically happen to people in their thirties. But it didn't seem to fit with the rest of the story.

What didn't seem unusual was that his death took place at the bridge. The spot has one of the highest concentrations of suicides in the world, a fact that has inspired intense debate over whether San Francisco should erect a guardrail that would make leaping more difficult. Critics said it would be a costly eyesore, which made me wonder whether my fellow San Franciscans had any right to claim, as they often did for sport, that they were less superficial than the fine people of Los Angeles.

I asked Erin if she'd told the police about Andy.

"I talked to them just after the explosion."

"Lieutenant Aravelo?" I asked.

"You too?"

"Yeah." I grimaced. "It's tragic, Erin, and I'm sorry. But I don't see what this has to do with the explosion, or anything else."

She shook her head. "It's a strange coincidence." Her voice was distant, but resolute. "Something went wrong at that place—I mean, at the café."

I let the proposition run over me. Her tone implied a certainty lacking from her substance.

"Erin, when I first ran into you—ran after you—back at the tutoring center, you said, 'You've got the wrong person.' Then you asked me what my sin was. Why would you say those things?"

Erin shrugged. "I guess I felt guilty."

"Guilty?"

"That I survived," she said softly.

Then she said, "There's something I want to show you."

12

Cole Valley is situated just above Haight-Ashbury, famed home of the 1960s love-in turned semicommercial zone for hawkers of tie-dyed T-shirts. Cole Valley, by contrast, owns up to its yuppiedom. There are more than a few Audi A4s owned by holders of Pottery Barn credit cards.

It was also home to Andy's apartment, a mélange of milk crates used as bookshelves, mismatched and multicolored furniture, and a hammock. On the wall above a television from 1970 was a poster of Einstein. Garage-sale chic. Fashion du Math Professor. Erin served us tea in plastic drinking glasses with logos from the annual Bay to Breakers 10K run.

Erin explained that she had a key to Andy's place and that she was getting the time and courage to clean it out.

She held out a photograph. He sat at a campsite. The sun seemed brilliant overhead, but it was almost outshone by Andy's goofy grin. He had scruffy blond hair, and his clothes looked like quick pickups from the Salvation Army. Andy was easygoing.

"I'm not a doctor," I said, repeating my earlier admonitions.

"You finished medical school. And you're obviously smart. I just want to understand what happened. Listen to my story."

I suddenly didn't have the heart, or the patience.

I fumbled in my breast pocket. I felt the picture. I put it on the table. It was 3-by-5, the way they used to make them, with a white border. Annie was standing on a rock, with Lake Tahoe behind her.

"She's beautiful," Erin said. "Is that the woman who handed you the note?"

I told her I didn't know. She picked up the photo.

"I've never seen her."

"You're absolutely sure?"

"Sorry."

Our eyes briefly met but Erin looked quickly away. I picked up Annie's picture and slipped it into my pocket. I felt the need to escape the memory. I turned my gaze to the Bic pen.

"It's not that tough to chew through a pen."

I regretted it the moment I said it. I sounded sarcastic. What did I mean? It wasn't tough to chew through a pen, but why would anyone do so—stress or an aggressive oral fixation?

"Andy rarely had a bad mood. He was the kind of guy who could fall asleep on the floor watching TV and not get up until morning. But about two months ago, he came into the café saying he'd had a sleepless night. He talked about watching infomercials. He was hyper. He did a pretty funny impression of a guy selling mood-improvement tapes for dogs."

Then it stopped being funny. He didn't sleep the next few nights.

"Was he doing anything differently? Was he drinking more caffeine? Was he stressed out about something? Did he change his exercise regimen?" I asked.

"No. He got pretty scientific about it too. We were reading the nutrition labels on everything he ate."

"What about his daily routine?"

"He did seem more intense."

"Intense? Like agitated—from lack of sleep?"

Erin took a sip of her tea. "I guess he was really focused on his research."

I noticed Erin had a way of not answering some of my questions directly.

Andy was finishing a master's project about the habits of kids who are in joint custody of divorced or separated parents. He was looking at the impact on kids of moving between homes each week. He wound up amassing a decent group of students he corresponded with over the Internet.

"You're telling me that a grown man was corresponding via e-mail with kids? Did Andy tick some parent off? Could he have been threatened?"

Nope, Erin said. She said Andy had asked for and received permission from every family he worked with, under the auspices of the university.

Besides, she asked, how could that possibly explain the headaches?

I considered her question. Why Andy had been sleepless was not clear. The fact that he was agitated and had headaches was easier to understand. It was simple physiology. When a body doesn't get enough rest, its systems don't regenerate. To function, it relies increasingly on adrenaline. A kind of fight-or-flight mechanism kicks in. The body loses rhythm, and the mental functions follow.

When I looked up again, Erin had put a laptop on the table. She turned the screen in my direction. On it was a single word, "ping," typed thousands of times.

"One night when he was feeling sick, I came over to watch a movie, and wound up spending the night on the couch. I found Andy on the front stairs, typing away. He was typing the word 'ping' over and over. He said he'd been at it for hours, just passing time."

I noticed that the laptop's space bar was indented and cracked.

"I asked Andy about that, and he said that he must have been pressing too hard on it," she said.

I wondered if Andy had written any diary entries that might explain his frame of mind.

"That's what I want to know," Erin said, suddenly animated. "There's a diary file, but I don't know the password to get in."

That's what Erin really wanted from me—to get some help

looking at Andy's private thoughts. I was always struck by people's carelessness around technology. We e-mail off-color jokes and naked political views across a medium that records every conversation forever. Even when we try to erase what we've done, we leave traces and footprints. Or, in public settings, we talk on our cell phones about the most intimate matters. Maybe we really don't care. Or maybe we all secretly just want to get caught—at being ourselves.

I fiddled around with the computer for a moment, trying to open the file. The guy was dead, so I wasn't infringing upon his privacy. As it turned out, I couldn't have infringed upon it if I'd wanted to; I lacked the expertise to open the file.

I couldn't really imagine what Andy, or his laptop for that matter, had to do with the explosion at the café, but I also could understand Erin's desperate curiosity—and I wasn't much above grasping at straws myself.

"Mind if I borrow it for a day or two?" I said. "I have someone I can show it to. A wiz at technology."

I told her about the story I was working on—about the impact of cell phone radiation and the brain. I'd been consulting Mike Thompson at Stanford Technology Research Center. He could speak to that topic and just about any other thing having to do with technology.

"Is there anything else you think I should know?" I asked.

Erin seemed so sure something had gone wrong. Was there something else driving her instincts? Something she was purposefully holding back?

Erin had a faraway look. She shook her head no.

"My husband was an alcoholic."

"Your husband?" I asked, trying to make sense of her apparent non sequitur.

"Ex," she said. "When he was on the bottle, he became a different person. Like night and day. It was the same thing with Andy."

"Like he was drunk?"

"No. That's not what I mean. I just mean that Andy turned

into a different person over the last six weeks of his life. I knew him. Even if he was getting sick, he wasn't the same person. He was . . . hijacked."

"I don't mean to dismiss your instincts, Erin, but I do know that tumors can really impact mood. So can changes in brain chemistry. That's the essence of depression."

I asked her for the name of Andy's neurologist. She handed me a business card for Murray Bard, MD, and said he'd been recommended to Andy by Simon Anderson. Andy had become good friends with Simon at the café, and sometimes would babysit Simon's kids over in West Portal.

"Simon could get anyone to do whatever he wanted," Erin said. There was a quickening in her voice, like the way I'd sound when making an excuse to an editor.

"And Simon was friends with a neurologist?"

"Simon knew everyone."

I offered to take a cab back to my car, but Erin insisted on driving me back to the cemetery. I grabbed the Dell laptop, and we headed out the door. Just two paces out, I nearly tripped on my face. A workman was fixing the lights in the apartment hallway, and I was so distracted and tired I hadn't noticed his wires. I shouldn't have overlooked him. He was a burly man with an overgrowth of curly hair for a beard. He grunted dissatisfaction at me.

"Walking is not for the meek of heart," Erin said.

Suddenly she let out a big laugh, and the mood brightened. I hadn't heard a laugh that pure in a long time.

But laughs like that can be deceiving. Recovering my balance, I was struck by an idea—after dropping off the laptop, I could take a detour that might bring Erin and the café into better focus.

13

Erin decided to join me on a drive to Stanford Technology Research Center to drop off the laptop. I needed to go there anyway to pick up some papers for my dreaded cell phone/brain story. The deadline taunted me.

I'd gotten used to being on time for everything—Silicon Valley had a way of doing that to you. There were timepieces everywhere. Not watches or clocks necessarily, but cell phones, PDAs, pagers—every one of them gave you an up-to-the-minute digital readout. One friend of mine claimed he didn't wear a watch, as if to suggest he was too mellow to be constrained by time. The real reason was he had seventeen other gadgets to keep him honest.

Erin and I faced a forty-minute drive directly south to Palo Alto, the heart of the Valley. It's made up of people with a wicked combination of two seemingly disparate skills: math and marketing. They've managed to get their inventions into every home, car, pocket, and company in every industrialized nation.

Compared to Valley people, the robber barons were suckers. Sure, they were financial titans. But every time they built a new car or railroad, it cost them money. They spent money to make it.

This is Silicon Valley's genius. The most successful companies have almost zero manufacturing costs. Once they create a computer program, they can re-create it with the press of a button, just like printing greenbacks.

As we entered the highway, I was plugged into my mobile phone. I'd put in a call to Leslie Fernandez, a friend of mine from medical school who had since become a neurologist. I figured she could put me in touch with Murray Bard, the doctor who had treated Andy. The best way to get to a doctor was through another doctor.

As luck would have it, Leslie immediately took my call. It probably didn't hurt that we'd spent a few nights during medical school playing doctor.

"Nat. Long time," she said. "My first question is: Is everything okay? My second question is: Can I buy you dinner?"

I'd forgotten how direct she could be.

"I'm good. Are you still hooking electrodes up to people's brains just to make their limbs flop about?"

"Ooh, Nat. I love when you talk dirty."

Even from her side of the car, Erin could sense Leslie's voice thick with flirtation.

Leslie and I spent a moment catching up. Then I got to the point and asked if she knew Dr. Bard and could give me an introduction. I told her I'd heard he was doing some interesting work with electrical signals of the brain. Leslie knew I was doing medical journalism; she'd draw her own conclusions about my request.

"Just your luck. I know Murray quite well."

"Well, like . . . well?"

"Gross. I'll put in a call to him. Try his office this afternoon," Leslie said. "So, I'm guessing we're not going to get drunk this weekend and take the sleeping bag back to Golden Gate Park."

"Rain check."

She laughed. "Okay, gotta go."

I smiled sheepishly at Erin. "Old flame."

"How long ago did you two date?"

Her question sounded rhetorical. The next one didn't.

"So, tell me about the person you lost."

* * *

We were passing the exit to Atherton, the chichi community Annie's parents called home. Unlike the surrounding municipalities, Atherton referred to itself not as a city, but a township.

On the frequent occasions when Annie's dad and stepmom were out of town, we got the run of the Atherton mansion. We always gave the night off to the staff—the cook, a maid, and the guy whose sole purpose seemed to be to watch the cars sit in the garage. Then Annie and I would see how many rooms we could kiss in for at least ten minutes, removing only one piece of clothing after completing a room. One night, I showed up wearing six layers of ski gear as a joke, and Annie permanently amended the rules by undressing me in the entryway, where we wound up spending the night.

One time when we had the mansion for a week, Annie and I vowed we'd try to keep our entertainment novel by trying a new activity every night. We managed drunk bowling, followed by a Lenny Kravitz concert, but gave up when, on Wednesday, with nothing to do, we somehow wound up at a Palo Alto city council meeting. Midway through a presentation to the redevelopment board, we were giggling in the last row when a city staff member asked us our business. I earnestly declared, "I demand a national holiday in this woman's name."

The staff member asked us to leave.

Outside, a local chess club was holding a nighttime tournament under lights in the city green. Contestants eliminated from the tournament played one another or deigned to accept challenges from the stragglers looking on. Annie and I challenged a toothy fourteen-year-old. He pasted us in about ten minutes—twice in a row.

"No chess for our son. Too dangerous," Annie announced as we walked off. "Just football, and heli-skiing."

"Sons—plural."

"Really?" she asked.

"Really."

"And daughters."

"Two of each, and one hybrid. Half man, half woman, half turtle."

"You're not saying anything?"

The voice was coming from Erin.

"You're thinking about her."

For the second time, I almost jumped into the conversation, but again was interrupted. Again by my phone. It was Sergeant Danny Weller.

"How are you doing, Nat?" he asked. I'm not sure he was too interested in the answer, given how quickly he spoke again. "Can you spare a moment?"

"Sure."

"I wanted to let you know that they found a red Saab."

"Where?" It came out sharp.

"They pulled it out of an isolated inlet near Half Moon Bay," he said. It is a small coastal town. "A fisherman hooked the bumper."

I was speechless. Danny laughed.

"Dad and I never caught anything that big."

"Danny. Did they find a body—in the car?"

"Nope."

Silence again. This time I filled it in. "I didn't read about the car in the morning paper."

Earlier, I had glanced at the *Chronicle*. It didn't have much new about the investigation. Lots of speculation and "no comment" from the cops. At this point, the reporters either knew far less than I did, or they were reporting less than they knew.

"You're not going to," Danny explained, referring to what I would continue not to see in the newspaper. "We never tell the good stuff to the press."

Why was he telling me this?

"Have you heard from the investigators?" he asked.

"Nope."

He coughed, then cleared his throat.

"How about you? Have you learned anything else—have you talked to your waitress friend?"

I glanced at Erin.

"Want to get together later?" I responded. "I liked that bar—it was dingy, dark, and the glasses seemed particularly dirty."

"See you at six," he said. "I'll bring the soap."

When we got to Stanford Technology Research Center, Mike wasn't around, so I dropped off the laptop with a note asking him to check under the hood. Nothing specific, and nothing urgent.

On the way back, I suggested we take a detour to Simon Anderson's house. Maybe mourners would still be there and we could talk to his wife. Erin didn't seem interested but I pressed her into duty. She knew the location. We drove in silence until we were almost there.

"You didn't like Simon much," I said.

"He was a player, or so he thought. He figured there wasn't anyone he couldn't seduce."

"Despite his marriage?"

I remembered something from the funeral. Simon's brother had mentioned that things had been rough toward the end of his life. I asked Erin what he might have meant.

She shrugged. "I don't really know. Things might have been tense with his wife, or he was sick or something. You hear rumors. Trust me, this is not worth dwelling on," she said, then changed tone, and topic.

"His true passion was wizards."

"Well, really—whose isn't?"

"He was writing a fantasy book for teenagers."

"Like Harry Potter?"

"He went *crazy* when people said that," Erin said. "It became a running joke at the café. We would sometimes bring up Harry Potter just to watch his face contort."

"They got pretty close," she said.

It sounded distant, and very much like a non sequitur.

"Who did?"

"Andy and Simon. Andy watched Simon's kids. It was a big responsibility, since his youngest son is pretty sick," Erin said, sounding focused again. "The Andersons have an exquisite place."

Had an exquisite place.

As we turned the corner, we saw the home of the deceased aspiring novelist Simon Anderson on fire.

14

Notwithstanding the wild coincidence that another structure was ablaze, it seemed momentarily innocuous, like watching it unfold on CNN. Whatever had happened had just started. A wisp of flame jutted out from a front window. The house was three-story beige stucco, with black trim and a bright red front door. It looked to be intact and sturdy.

Then I heard a throaty boom. A surge of heat coursed across the yard. Fire burst out windows on the first floor. A man in athletic gear stood on the sidewalk holding a tennis bag and a cell phone. I scrambled over to him. He was on the phone with the fire department. "Thank God they're all at the memorial service," he mumbled.

Small miracles, but just small ones. No sooner had we concluded that the family wasn't home than the man pointed to a window on the second story. A heavyset woman opened the window and waved her arms. She had a look of sheer panic.

"Back door," he yelled.

"I'm gonna die up here."

"The fire department's on its way," he chimed back, "Stay calm."

"You stay fucking calm!"

Two boys on bikes jutted around the front and screeched, "The back porch is on fire!" Then I noticed the woman again. She gulped big fast breaths, hyperventilating. Not from fire, but fear.

Like a lot of San Francisco homes, the garage level was partially belowground. The effective second floor wasn't more than twenty feet above terra firma.

"Just open the window all the way and slide your butt onto the ledge. Then let yourself down and we can grab your feet. You can hold on to the drainage pipe," I found myself saying. "I promise you this will be very simple and easy and safe."

The pace of her breathing increased. She was lost in her fear, and not hearing me. Panic attack. From what I could see, the worry here was less that she'd be engulfed by flames and more that she'd pass out and be helpless. I could see the physiology unfold; eventually the airways would clog with dark soot, constricting oxygen to the blood, heart, and brain.

The decision to quit medical school still haunted me. Partly because I sometimes found myself defensive when challenged by people with a résumé-centric view of existence. More so because of the periodic weight of a responsibility I couldn't really bear. I could see a medical problem, or evidence of one, but not have the expertise to fully grasp or do anything about it. It turns out doctors aren't generally lifesaving heroes, but I couldn't even muster the illusion anymore.

What could I do here? It didn't take a neurosurgeon to see she needed to stay calm.

"Put your head out the window," I said. "Slow, deep breaths."

She remained paralyzed.

"Hey!"

Nothing.

I took a step toward the house.

"Boost me."

Instinctively, the man standing next to me grabbed my arm. Don't be an idiot, he was thinking.

But then, he didn't understand it was not nearly as idiotic as I was capable of being. That was spending my twenty-first birthday climbing Mount Aconcagua in Argentina, a 23,000-foot, highly challenging high-altitude ascent amid wicked winds.

I looked at the water drainage pipe running up the side of the house next to the window. This didn't qualify as a particularly treacherous climb. And the woman was now slumped. If someone didn't get up there to calm her down, she was going to suffocate at the summit and get cremated.

I looked around at the gathering of neighbors. No one seemed to know what to do. The first-floor doors and windows weren't options.

I moved under the window.

I grabbed the pipe, and tested a foot against the stucco. It slipped off. I looked at my feet. Not an ideal time for the slippery black leather shoes I'd worn to the funeral. I pulled myself onto the pipe again. The man I'd been talking to, and one other, perched underneath me, and the pair hoisted my feet. With their help, standing on their hands, I'd have to pull myself only a yard on my own to reach the window's ledge.

My feet balancing me on the house, I clung to a metal strap holding the drainage pipe to the building. I reached for a similar strap a foot above, and felt my grip loosen. I started sliding down the pole. I landed on my feet, then my butt.

I yanked myself up again and got a boost from the men. And I hung there, three feet below the ledge, looking less and less like Spider-Man every second.

Who was I kidding? I wrote medical stories for a dollar a word, played recreational hoops two days a week, and faced such hero-inspired challenges as eating tuna sandwiches with mayonnaise that was nearing the end of its freshness date. I didn't even play a doctor on TV.

But I felt a surge of adrenaline, an almost foreign urge to act. Maybe it was Annie inside my head. I pulled myself within two feet of the window's ledge and realized I wasn't going to get closer. I could hear nearing sirens. I looked up to see the woman's head against the window frame. Her lumpy chin rested on the sill, still rapidly gasping for air.

"Hey!" I shouted to her. "You ever see a guy fall and break his neck?"

"What?"

"What's your name?"

"Agnes."

"You're going to be fine, Agnes."

She turned her head to the side and threw up. Her head rolled back. She was so panicked that, given her weight, I was afraid she might arrest. Her blood pressure had to be skyrocketing. Her eyes were open. "I don't want to die."

Suddenly, an explosion rocked us. I barely was able to hold on to the pipe, my feet were blown away from the house, my legs waving out like a tattered flag. I pulled desperately to keep from falling. A howl of heat blew out the window, the flames near.

She started breathing quickly again. She was tremulous and crying. I had to get her talking. I had to get her to focus on me.

"What happened, Agnes?"

No answer.

"Agnes! I need you to tell me what happened here."

Something in her eyes snapped open. "I'm just the housekeeper. It's not even my regular day," she said, pausing. "I was . . . I was cleaning. It got hot. Then everything . . . so goddamned fast."

"Did you smell gas. Was there . . . anything strange?"

I heard the thump on the windowsill. I had been so entranced, I hadn't noticed the arrival of the firefighters.

"Gas, maybe. I don't know. There was an electrician when I got here. The house was empty because of the funeral. The electrician said she was doing some wiring in the basement . . ."

She was cut off by another explosion, just as the firefighters made their ascent. One wrapped his arms around her. I felt a hand on my shoulder, guiding me down a second ladder.

On the ground, I swam through a growing crowd in search of Erin. She was still sitting in the car, looking stunned.

"Oh."

That was all she said, as if the ability to express more complex emotions had left the building.

"Bad news, worse news," I said.

"What?"

"All of this—the explosion. Andy, Simon. The fire. It's all somehow connected to Sunshine Café," I said. "The café is . . . at the center of all this violence."

That was a revelation, at least to me. Up until then, I had no pattern I could discern.

She touched her palm to the side of my face. "What happened?" she finally said.

I told her what the woman said. Maybe someone had sabotaged the Andersons' electrical system.

The electrical system.

I jerked forward.

"Andy's place," I said.

Erin sniffled. "What about Andy?"

"Outside his apartment. Someone was working on the lights. A worker, or an electrician. They're going to try to burn it down."

I turned the keys in the ignition.

"We have to go," I said. "Now!"

15

Erin dialed 911 and I flew down Laguna Honda, a secret passage to Cole Valley—and Andy's apartment.

I pulled around a Windstar minivan, eliciting an orchestra of honks.

"I'd like to report a possible fire," Erin said.

I heard her end of the conversation.

"No. No flames. No smoke."

The operator slowed her down, and asked her a couple of questions. She gave Andy's address. I gave the accelerator a punch. The tires squealed. The odometer hit 50.

"Please, his place may be . . . a target."

Erin closed the phone and said they were sending an officer by.

I sped into the Haight-Ashbury, then screeched the brakes. Half a block ahead was a logjam. Or, rather, a peace jam—about a dozen twenty-somethings imitating peaceniks had gathered on the corner and were slapping tambourines and hoisting signs. They were for something. Or against something. You live in San Francisco long enough, you quit reading the placards. All I knew was they were standing between us and the next block.

I pressed palm onto horn. Big mistake. There's no better way to antagonize a group of informal protesters. They had the look of people who had gotten stoned, watched Fox News, become angry, made signs, and headed down for the corner between pizza slices. They needed a common enemy, and they'd found me.

A couple paused in crossing the street to approach my window. The woman wore a flowing white skirt from the 1960s and a trendy windbreaker from North Face. "You're polluting the earth with your death machine," she said.

I rolled down the window. "You know the trouble with these big SUVs," I said. "You barely feel it when you run over someone's foot."

I turned the wheel sharply and drove onto the sidewalk, narrowly missing the back of a Saturn and evading the protesters.

"What are you doing?" Erin cried.

In my new worldview, there were no longer stop signs, or anything close to speed limits.

"Nat! Look out!"

A teeny-bopper on a foot-fueled scooter appeared from outside my vision and laid rightful claim to the crosswalk. I slammed on the brakes. Erin and I lurched forward.

"Nat," Erin said, when she sat back up. "Look."

We were just around the corner from Andy's house. I didn't see anything unusual. I said so.

"That's what I mean," she said.

She was right. There was a complete absence of everything. No fire trucks, emergency vehicles, or smoke. No chaos.

We dropped into a moment of silence.

"What are we doing, Erin?"

She didn't immediately offer an answer. There probably wasn't one.

Or, rather, there were probably too many possible interpretations of the question. We had just flown across San

Francisco in six thousand pounds of seething gas guzzler. Why? Was I overreacting? Was there any real danger? What about our own safety?

"You're a little high-strung," Erin said.

Should we leave this all to the police?

Perhaps this last question was born of subliminal observation. Pulled up behind us was a member of the San Francisco Police Department.

This was not going to be a friendly law enforcement encounter.

16

"icense and registration please."

"Officer," Erin said. "We were the ones who called in a report about a possible fire."

I extricated my driver's license. I tried to remember where I had put my registration. Don't cops know that no one actually has any idea where they put their registration?

"You called in about a fire?" said the officer, whose name-tag read Sampson. "You called the San Francisco police?"

"Nine-one-one," Erin said.

I held my driver's license up to the open window. The patrolwoman took it and scrutinized my height, weight, and picture like it could tell her everything anyone could ever need to know about me.

"Mr. Idle, can you please step out of the car," she said.

I tried to remember if I'd done something wrong. The answer dawned on me just as Officer Sampson said it.

"You nearly killed a skateboarder," she said.

She got points for hyperbole.

"We got two calls about a Toyota sport utility vehicle tearing through Cole Valley," she said.

She seemed to take pains to enunciate when she said "sport utility vehicle," like my car of choice would cost me points when we came to the me-making-excuses portion of our program.

"I didn't see the incident," she continued. "But I could hear the screeching of brakes and tires from around the corner. I could have heard it in the Castro."

It was kind of funny. She didn't smile. Still, the way she said it, it sounded like good news. Like maybe she wasn't going to dig into my bank account for something she hadn't personally borne witness to. I decided to go for the jugular. I began begging.

"I'm sorry, Officer. I've had an unbelievably bad couple of days," I said.

She glanced at me without commitment. "Let's see what the box has to say."

She walked to the squad car. She sat. She started entering my information into her onboard computer.

"Underpants," Erin said.

She leaned closer.

"The one and only time I got in trouble with the law. The one and only thing I ever stole."

"Underpants?"

"A racy little pink number," Erin explained. "I was fourteen. I had some friends who were going through a theft phase. I wanted to prove myself, but I was terrified."

"By stealing big-girl undies."

She curled a strand of hair behind her right ear and trailed a graceful index finger along her jaw, letting it rest on her chin. I'd always found the great challenge of rock climbing to be deciding which jagged outcroppings were solid and secure enough to make reliable hand- or toeholds. I still couldn't decide whether to grasp on to Erin.

"Oh, no. My theory was much more flawed than that," she continued. "I figured that I would steal something that I could readily conceal. I would simply try on a pair of panties, then walk out of Kmart undetected. Not only did I get caught, I had to undress in front of the manager. She was a nice older woman. But still . . . I was stripped right down to my thong, which fortunately I was wearing over two pairs of my own regular underwear and a pair of shorts. My father nearly disowned me. He was strict, capital S. I think it was a year before he let me out of the house for a non-church function."

The cop exited her car and started heading in our direction.

"Anything short of a strip search, and I think you're having an all right kind of afternoon," Erin said.

"Mr. Idle," the officer said.

She was using honorifics. That didn't bode well.

"Are you familiar with the term 'reckless endangerment,'" she asked. "We got two calls from possible eyewitnesses, including the mother of a boy who claims you nicked the tail end of his scooter."

"What about the call to 911?"

It was Erin. She wasn't letting go. The officer took a deep breath. She seemed like someone to whom patience came naturally. The uniform had weaned it out of her.

"A call was placed," Officer Sampson said. "And responded to."

She explained that a patrolman had been in the vicinity. Officer Sampson looked at the notepad in her hand. "Officer Eldridge reported no smoke or fire."

She looked up.

"It's not all bad news, Mr. Idle," Officer Sampson said. She told me she was going to let me off in exchange for a favor.

"I'd like you to drive down to the station," Officer Sampson said. "Lieutenant Aravelo would like to have a word."

I said good-bye to Erin, and we headed downtown.

The only time I'd been in a police car prior to that was on career day in junior high. My friend and I pestered the stoic cop for exciting stories, but he wasn't biting. Finally, he drove us to a cemetery and said, "Make something of your lives. Make sure you get good grades." We laughed about it for years, but it was eerie and mysterious and we weren't sure if he was suggesting life was short, or that he might kill us if we didn't get straight A's.

Andy's death, his life, Erin's too, mine, all bubbling with uncertainty, and begging for interpretation. Maybe every life, and death, is its own unsolved mystery. Certainly, I was realizing, that was the case with Annie.

As we drove to the station, I found my thoughts turn distant—to another time when confusion and anger had visited in its purest form. Only to be followed by death.

17

Thightanic."

"Gross," Annie said.

I was trying to engage Annie in a word game we invented: making up stupid pornographic titles for popular mainstream movies.

"What about *Forrest Rump*?"

We were about to enter the Marin Boat Club. Annie put her head on my shoulder. It was a spectacular day—the late fall gala of the yacht club, and a turning point for me and Annie. After much cajoling, she'd agreed to let me meet her family. In their natural habitat.

Annie surveyed the scene. "The fancy cars and boats, the newspaper accolades, the self-congratulatory bullshit—it's infectious."

"We're not talking disease here."

"Make sure you hose down after shaking anyone's hand."

The joint was hopping. We were making a beeline for the bar when a joyful voice exclaimed over the din. "Princess." The people around us parted to reveal Annie's father. He looked younger than I expected; his hair was not yet gray, and he was dressed in khakis and a short-sleeved button-down shirt—the uniform of the high-tech titan.

"Daddy," she said warmly.

His arms were open. "May I have a quick word in private?"

"We'll be right back, Turtle," she whispered.

I watched her give him a hug, and the assembled parted back around them. I parked at the bar. I wasn't sure I saw the problem with the lifestyle. Alcohol and bite-sized snacks were free. I was one complimentary Swedish massage away from country club heaven.

"What's up, doc?"

I turned to face an alarmingly good-looking man. Or maybe I was just alarmed by the way he addressed me. It seemed strangely coincidental given my recent decision to abdicate a career in medicine. "So you came with Annie," he said.

"I'm the designated drinker."

"Nice work if you can get it," he said. "She's got an amazing ass."

When he saw me flinch, he started laughing. "Dave Elliott," he said, extending a hand. "Crass bastard."

Dave described himself as an old family friend of the Kindles. He had done a bunch of travel, most recently in Asia, and was finally settling down. He owned a house in Marin and worked as a lawyer in San Francisco, doing some work for Annie's father. He said they'd spent the previous weekend playing golf in Pebble Beach.

"Lucky man," I said.

"I'll give you a hundred bucks to burn my putter, then run your car over the ashes."

We bantered for a while in guy-speak, the fidgety concise language of two men feeling each other out and seeking common ground. We finally got a rhythm and wound up discussing skiing, which he'd done his share of too—albeit in Switzerland.

I took a big slug of my tonic.

"Is she down with you getting loaded?"

I shrugged.

"She calls the shots, doesn't she?" he said, like it was widely understood. "She picked out the last guy's clothes. Wouldn't let him wear plaid."

I saw Annie knifing through the crowd with a purposeful look. "Would you mind if we left a little early?" she said calmly.

Given the intensity of her look, I knew better than to ask questions. Dave took a different tack. "Relax, Annie. Have a drink," he said, then looked at me. "Solidarity, brother."

She responded, "Don't you have a trollop to be outwitted by?"

Outside, her face was flushed. She looked away from me, and started talking about problems the family was having with a start-up company in New York that they'd invested in. The problems stemmed from how to measure sales and projected revenue in an Internet start-up. She said she was trying to stay conservative but also move the company quickly to stay ahead of the market. He'd put her in charge, she said, but wouldn't let her do her job. She had a cold look.

"He can't treat me like this. He's obsessed with control."

I hadn't realized she was in charge of anything or that her father could provoke such mercurial moods. But the truth was, I had a larger concern. "What's the deal with Dave Elliott? Did you date him?"

Annie turned her head to me, then laughed. Like it was the funniest—and most stupid—thing I'd said in weeks. "God, no," she said. She shook her head. "He would have liked to."

We were in my car. From the passenger seat, Annie turned the key in the ignition, prompting a quick exit. "Dave and I used to be good friends. He was kind and a good listener. But he had designs on me the entire time. I trusted him. I confided in him. He felt sure we were developing a romantic relationship. The truth is, I never even considered it. He told me he loved me. He's never forgiven me."

* * *

Two days later, I was standing outside Sam's Deli, a couple of blocks from my apartment. I was a mouthful into a takeout turkey Reuben when a black BMW pulled up. I recognized it as the car that picked up Annie after our first date. The door opened.

"Annie?"

A male voice responded, "Hop in, Nathaniel. I'll give you a lift home."

The situation didn't particularly set off alarm bells. I couldn't imagine I'd be a kidnap victim. Particularly since (1) I was standing on a public corner on a bright San Francisco day, and (2) neither I, nor my family, could possibly have anything anyone could want. I peered in the car.

"Glenn Kindle," he said. "Annie's dad."

He sat in the back, separated by a dark glass window from whoever was driving. On his lap sat a magazine, the SkyMall catalog.

"The secrets to happiness herein." He held up the catalog. "You think this stuff is complete garbage, right? A vibrating putting green whose frequencies purportedly promote natural healing. I mean, give me a break. But see the bigger picture here. The SkyMall is the cutting edge of the capitalist dream. People love the hunt for something amazing. The sellers of this junk aren't cheating people, they are giving us a reason for hope. Consumers are knowingly swept up in the illusion. A transaction is its own mutual emotional success."

"Are you here to help me with personal philosophy or Christmas shopping?" I asked, smiling.

"I'd hoped to meet you last weekend—at the party." He set down the magazine. "I was in the neighborhood so I figured I'd make amends."

Amends for what? And how the hell did he know the location of my neighborhood?

I figured there was one decent way to get answers. I climbed in the car and we shook hands. I looked down at the half-eaten Reuben sandwich starting to sweat through the napkin.

"I didn't bring enough for everybody," I said.

He laughed and hit a button on his door. "Let's go," he said to the driver.

"I'm sorry we don't have more time to get to spend together. Those events are always more fun in theory than reality."

"Well, you're welcome to come upstairs. I've got a chilled six-pack of Anchor Steam. I might actually only have five left . . ." I said. I wasn't trying to be smart-ass. Not entirely.

"Listen, I'll speak frankly. Do I need to be worried?"

I considered his question as the car came to a halt. I looked out the darkened window. We were already at my apartment.

"I'm just wondering what you and Annie are up to."

"I honestly have no idea what you're talking about," I said. "Nothing. Really. No weird *X-Files* voodoo stuff. You know, if we become in-laws, we're going to look back at this and really laugh."

His smile was strained.

"Forgive me. I've grown careful, and maybe a little too protective."

"Nothing to forgive."

"You've got a lot of debt, you had a run-in with a superior when you were in medical school. Now you've given all your training up to make ends meet as a journalist. It doesn't quite add up."

"Well, we don't all need to make enough to spend the GNP of a small African nation on a car," I suddenly counterpunched.

He chuckled.

"She's right. You are funny. Forgive me. Let's just call this a mix-up. We can start over next time."

Just then, the car door popped open. It was being held by the driver. Glenn's last comment hadn't sounded much like a real apology. I lingered.

"Trust me, I know Annie is incredible."

He nodded blankly and then cruised way.

I immediately called Annie, told her what happened, and said I was going to Palo Alto to finish the conversation.

"Please. Please don't go see him," she pleaded. "It will just make things worse."

"Tell me right now. What is going on? Who does your father think he is? Who does he think *I* am?"

She said her father was just egomaniacal, overprotective, and feeling threatened by our relationship. He was also worried the dot-com boom might be petering out. They had to move fast.

Instead of confronting him, Annie suggested I join her on an upcoming business trip to New York. She promised that she would show me her world firsthand, tell me about her family, introduce me to Kindle Investment Partners.

I hoped the next few weeks would give me my desperately needed clarity.

They gave me the opposite.

18

Kiss me."

Annie and I stood on the observation deck of the Empire State Building, and I found myself thinking of the bird that my father claimed attacked him as a boy. The attack happened as my father walked across a span bridge, which, my father said, explained his fear of both birds and heights. Then, when I was a boy, my father passed down his acrophobia by pressing my brother and me tight against the chairlift whenever we went skiing.

Standing on the observation deck with Annie, I felt no fear. I think it was because I had my arms wrapped around her, imagining I was responsible for saving her from whatever tragedy might befall. Being with her had become such a rush it crowded out everything else.

It was two-thirds of a day I'd wish on anyone. We woke up in a midtown hotel, fed each other continental breakfast in bed, and then spent the morning at the Bronx Zoo. Annie looked at the monkeys, baby elephant, and tigers and seemed to feel unbridled joy, and I looked at Annie looking at the animals and felt the same thing.

My education began on the airplane, in the first-class cabin. En route, she showed me a bunch of documents relating to her work as an investor, which seemed as scintillating as organic chemistry.

"How the hell do you know what this means?" I said.

"I thought *you* might know," she said.

She explained that she and her father had reached a kind of a détente. He demanded she do things a certain way. She either obliged or did it her own way and risked his recriminations. But often, she would surmount his challenges and exceed his expectations. She earned respect—from herself.

The company we were going to visit was called Vestige Technologies. It made supply chain management software, which Annie translated as "automated inventory tracking."

She gave me her sales pitch and I understood why mom-and-pop investors were sinking their retirement funds into Internet companies, and why many of them were making a big mistake. Annie said that the companies that most investors understood, or could envision as breakthroughs, met consumer needs, like allowing people to go online to buy books or groceries. Some of these would succeed, most would implode.

The real money and market power, Annie said, was in infrastructure, and in serving corporate customers. To thrive, companies had to do things more cheaply. That meant cutting expenses, the biggest of which is often labor. Capitalism's next great leap forward was computer automation. Economic studies were showing it not only made companies more efficient overall, it made individual workers more productive. Long-accepted economic principles stood challenged. Profit per worker could soar.

One of the biggest drivers in reducing these costs would be supply chain management software. Corporations were just starting to use it to automate procurement of parts, relationships with manufacturers and customers, and internal management of employees.

Vestige wasn't sexy, but it was going to make billions. And the real financial winners would be the earliest investors—venture capitalists like Kindle Investment Partners and its limited partners. They were in a position to enjoy spectacular growth.

Annie said early-stage investment was not just something her father was very good at—he was one of the best.

"He wants you to follow in his footsteps," I said.

"I might have," she said playfully. "Until I met you."

The next day, after spending lunch in Central Park, we took a cab to the third tallest building in New York. We stood on top of the Empire State Building, about to lock lips.

"Why do you do it?" I said.

She kissed me. "Because you taste like pizza and bubble gum."

"This work," I said. "It always sounds like it makes you miserable. Then I see you making goofy faces at the zoo, and I think: Why not choose a life with more peace—whatever that might be?"

I felt a surge of wind and I pulled the collar of her jacket around her ears.

"Nat, make a funny monkey noise for me," she said playfully.

I eeped.

"I admire your decision to quit medical school, to take yourself off the beaten path. To take regular naps. I love it about you," she said, turning serious. "But just because my path isn't precisely serene the way you think of serenity doesn't make it wrong. I can thrive in this environment, build great companies, create a lot of opportunities for people, and make a fortune. Then I can come home and have plenty of time to spend at the petting zoo."

We never made it to dinner. I had showered and gotten dressed up. Annie was in the bathroom for an eternity. Finally, I knocked.

"Come in."

She was sitting on the toilet, fully dressed, in a short skirt and black stockings. She would have looked stunning, except there was a smudge of red lipstick that tapered off from the right corner of her lips. It looked clownlike and intentional, a defacing.

"Make another funny monkey noise," she said, trying to sound upbeat.

"What's the matter?"

"You don't really love me," she said.

"What?"

"This isn't real."

I snagged a tissue. "That's the smeared lipstick talking." I wiped off her lips and chin. "I love you completely," I said. "I have never felt anything like this for anybody."

Annie closed her eyes, lost in thought, opened them, then told me a story. When she was sixteen, her father arranged for her to spend a summer working for a local Republican congressional candidate. She volunteered instead to work for the Democrat. Her father walked into the Democrat's campaign headquarters and started yelling at her, humiliating her. Later, he showed her a newspaper clipping in which the Democrat had been discovered to have had an affair years earlier with the family's illegal-immigrant nanny. Annie said she suspected her father had leaked the affair to the paper himself.

"He's a maniac," I said.

Annie let the words sink in. "We did a thousand things together when I was little. We went to the zoo, we traveled. But my absolute favorite was when we went skiing. Not the skiing part, but the chairlift. It was just me and Dad suspended in the air and he would ask me question after question, what I thought about this, and what I thought about that. I hated when the ride was over and I skied as fast as I could down the mountain so we could do it again. Then I got older and independent."

She wiped the makeup off her chin.

"He feels like he's losing you?"

"Maybe. My father is a pragmatist. Relationships to him are important, but they are things to be temporarily sought, like consumables, then attained, checked off, and rejected if they get too unstable. He has his own definition of . . . love. To him, emotional pursuits have the same essence as materialism, entertaining and fun to a point but then a distraction if they get out of control."

The softness had drained from her.

I told her what he'd said about the SkyMall catalog, eliciting a thin smile. She said the basement was filled with gimmicky catalog items, like a dish that provided cats with fresh, aerated water, suitcases with ergonomically correct handles, and a remote-controlled shark. Her father was fascinated by capitalist seduction.

I started laughing. "If he ever figures out the channel for the Home Shopping Network we're all doomed."

"It's why my mom left him. He thinks of love the way he thinks of the solar-powered cooling safari hat. It's an illusion, and something to desire and sacrifice for, so long as it isn't too much trouble."

She turned away from me, to the mirror, and looked at me in the reflection. I waited for her to continue, but she didn't, and she didn't respond to gentle follow-up questions.

I surmised that she wanted to be alone, so I left her and sat on the bed and waited. Finally, the bathroom door opened. Annie had removed her clothes. What followed was ferocious lovemaking, which was nearly derailed when Annie, for the first time, started to talk dirty, uttering explicit instructions. I was getting into it, but something snapped in the mood, and Annie giggled, and then we both started laughing.

The next day was her big meeting. Annie's job was to convince some investment bankers to take the company public, which meant huge returns for Kindle Investment Partners. The meeting was down in a conference room in the hotel where we were staying. Moments after Annie rushed out the door, I noticed she'd left a manila folder with her presentation. I found the glass-walled conference room easily. Inside, I could see Annie holding court. Five men in suits listened rapt—one of them was Dave Elliott, the lawyer for Annie's father.

I rapped on the window, and Annie beckoned me inside. I handed her the envelope. "Nathaniel Idle, everybody," she said, eliciting bored nods. She took the manila envelope and looked inside it. She continued to exude professionalism. "Thanks," she said. "This looks to be in order."

I tried to catch her eye, but she looked back to the group and I unceremoniously departed.

Two months later, I got a ringside seat to the dynamic between Annie and her father.

We were at the Atherton house. Her father and his third wife—a thirty-something who was wiser and gentler than the clichés about rich guys and their blonde mates would have you believe—were supposed to be away. Annie and I were in the kitchen, blackening fish. We heard the garage door open.

Glenn Kindle was in an ebullient mood. He promptly took us to the garage and showed us why. Rather than go away for the weekend, he had had a change of heart and gone to the car dealership and bought a Mercedes convertible. He handed Annie the keys.

"NotesMail goes public next week, and thanks in no small part to our new junior partner," he said. He grinned.

The keys sat in Annie's open palm. She didn't say a word. She looked bewildered at first. Her father winked at me as he ran his hand along the beautiful metallic blue machine. Then he started walking toward a door leading back into the house.

"Shotgun!" I said.

I looked up to see Annie following her father. He turned and smiled at her. Almost like an afterthought, he said, "Ted won't know what hit him."

"What did you do?" she asked.

"I cut him out," he responded matter-of-factly. "He deserved it. We did the work. He was not, to say the least, pleased. He called me a ruthless cunt. No one's ever called me that before."

Annie seemed to smirk. "So unbelievably cold."

"Big fishes eating little fishies," he said. He held up his soda as if toasting, and walked out.

Annie turned back to me. She tossed the keys in my direction in a big arc. I dipped to my left to catch them before they hit the pavement.

"He's out of his mind," I said, recovering.

"It's a payoff."

"For keeping you quiet about Ted?"

"Junior partner is a euphemism. For lackey." Her lip seemed to quiver. "I put the deal together. I earned us millions by convincing NotesMail to let us be their lead investor."

"And Ted?"

"My father doesn't appreciate what I'm bringing to the table."

I took a step toward her. She continued her thought.

"There is so much competition to find viable companies and get them to agree to fair valuations. The other big firms would have killed for the position that I put us in. I put the projections together and I sold the founders on this and I shouldn't be treated like a second-class citizen."

I grabbed Annie by the shoulders as if to shake her and whispered, "Stop!"

She looked at me and took a step back.

"Annie Leigh Kindle. I love you. I'm going to marry you someday. I'm going to give you children, and dogs, and fish. *I'll* be the breadwinner. You can be the family vet. It doesn't matter, so long as we're together."

First Annie smiled, thinly. Then, for the first time I could remember in a long time, Annie cried. A single tear became a gathering. When she finally spoke again, it was in a whisper.

"I need out," she said.

"Sounds good. You'll quit. We'll go far away—to Italy or Brazil. Someplace like that. We'll move into a château."

Annie wiped her eyes. She pushed back from me and looked away.

"Out of us."

I was sure I'd misunderstood her. "What are you talking about?"

"Out," she whispered again, looking so distant.

"Where is this coming from?"

Annie turned her head and looked at me—square in the eyes. She tipped her face forward and pinched her nose with her thumb and forefinger. She held the pose for a long time. Then she put her hand to her forehead and laughed.

"Annie?"

The laughter continued.

"I'm kidding. Who am I kidding?" she said.

She took my hand.

"What am I talking about?"

She shook her head, like some spell had been broken.

"Annie, did you just try to break up with me?"

"Tell me about the château," she said. "Please."

"Why did you say that? What would cause you to say something like that?"

Annie took the keys out of my hand. She kissed my cheek.

"I know how you feel about me. You can't imagine how it makes me feel. It's so powerful. So incredible," she said, smiling. "I'm a woman. I'm temperamental. Can I fall back on that just once?"

I wasn't feeling playful. I wasn't smiling.

"I promise," Annie said.

"You promise?"

"I promise I will never ever break up with you as long as I live."

19

Annie was an experienced sailor—and she wasn't alone. Five of us had gone out on the boat. Friends of Annie's I'd come to like, including Sarah, from the night I fell in love at first sound.

It really wasn't raining that hard. It was a relatively warm day, but the deck was icicle slick. We were a little more than a mile off the coast of Santa Cruz, in Craft Kindle.

Annie went aft. She was tying down a rope when we got hit with a swell. I wasn't even watching, but I heard her call out my name. When I moved around to the front, we got hit with another wave. I caught her eye, just as she went overboard. At the exact moment, it didn't seem like a big deal. The waves weren't that high. It's not that we were calm, far from it; we just weren't completely panicked. I grabbed a life preserver and headed to the side, but when I looked over, there was no Annie. I called out. I saw nothing, heard nothing. I dove in.

The waves were ugly but manageable. Where could she have gone? Had she hit her head on the side and gone under? I did circles around the boat—as deep as I could swim. I held tight to a rope I'd been thrown, to keep me from drowning myself.

I almost lost my own life. I swam myself ragged. I had to be pulled from the water, anguished and inconsolable.

We'd dropped the anchor, of course, then an inflatable boat, and spent hours searching, the Coast Guard by our side. Her father hired a veritable army. They searched the water for days.

They found nothing.

20

I was still lost in the past when Officer Sampson delivered me to the San Francisco Police Department, filled out some paperwork, and set me down on a bench to wait for Lieutenant Aravelo. I tried to avoid eye contact with the passing cops, consumed with the idea that they knew what I'd done to Aravelo's brother and would relish an obnoxious comment or leer.

What could I hope to get out of this situation? Aravelo would doubtless be in full grill mode. He wasn't likely to tell *me* a damn thing. Not intentionally. Could he be convinced to trade information?

While waiting, I checked my voice-mail messages. There were two. My editor, Kevin, had called. "Wondering how the story is going," he said. "Call when you have a sec to chat." He hung up without saying good-bye. Typical. The other message was from Samantha, who wanted to remind me to visit her the following day for acupuncture. "I sense you need intensive work on your gallbladder meridian."

Anxious for distraction, I scrolled down the stored numbers file on my phone. I discovered one number I hadn't called in years. I wondered if it was even still valid. Louise Elpers, licensed marriage and family counselor. In my phone book, she showed up as "braindoc." I'd talked to her for a few sessions after Annie's death, and she helped me with the basic approach to processing grief. I remember her saying that I was glorifying Annie, that it was perfectly normal, and that, as she put it, knowing that didn't help a goddamn bit.

I did manage one reality check in the week just after Annie died. I'd gone to Costco, bought beef jerky in the industrial size, a four-pound bag of peanuts, and a case of Dr Pepper. I just didn't want to feel obliged to stop. I drove for nine hours due east, away from the ocean. I landed in Litham, somewhere in Nevada, population 814. There was a gas station beside a diner. They were connected, or co-owned, as denoted by the sign, "Gas-n-Steak."

Two teenagers, a boy and a girl, were flirting, wrestling in a light romantic way. The boy went to his waistband, pulled out a bright green water pistol, aimed, and fired. The girl covered her eyes and squealed with delight. She charged toward the boy and wrapped her arms around him. Started kissing his face. I began to sob, and I didn't stop even when the gas station attendant asked me to move the car away from the full-service island.

A cop approached me. "Lieutenant Aravelo is ready for you."

As a journalist, I'd always been in the power position when it came to interviews. I was the one asking the questions. I may not have been equal in wealth or power to the person I was interviewing, but the threat that I might write a story gave me a kind of clout in almost any interview situation. Not with Lieutenant Aravelo.

He was dressed in uniform with his crisp white shirt tucked in smartly. He was asking me to take a seat when a loud buzzing came from what looked to be an alarm clock on his desk. He shut it off, opened a desk drawer, and pulled out a bag of almonds and a banana.

"Small, regular meals," he declared.

He put a picture on the table. It was grainy, but in color, like it had been taken from a convenience store camera.

"Who is this?" Aravelo asked.

She was blonde, with angular cheekbones and a blouse that came high up onto her neck. I felt a spasm of adrenaline, but I wasn't sure why.

Lieutenant Aravelo seized instantly on my hesitation.

"What can you tell me about her?" he said. "I want to know everything you know, Dodo."

Even if I had seen the woman before, it would be tough to recognize from an image of such poor quality. The eyes seemed distant, foggy.

"How about cutting out the offensive and not very clever nickname."

"Tell me what you know, Mr. Idle."

"I can't help you. I have no idea who that is."

I must have sounded genuine enough. Aravelo paused. He took deliberate bites of his banana, chewing almost comically slowly, like it was part of a regimen.

"How about this one?" The lieutenant held out another photo.

This time my surge of adrenaline was justified. This time, I held it in check. On the table, he set down a photo that I guessed from the relatively smooth skin around the subject's eyes to be about a decade old.

"She's Erin Coultran," Aravelo explained. "Waitress at the Sunshine Café."

I held my breath.

"I recognize her."

He sat lightly on the edge of the table and waited. I paused, trying to make it look like I was searching. "The paper said she survived because she was in the bathroom?"

When I looked up, I found the lieutenant searching my face. If he knew that I knew Erin, he wasn't letting on. Had Weller not told him?

"Did you see her go into the bathroom?"

I shook my head.

"Did you order coffee from her?"

"I had water."

He wasn't amused.

"No."

"Did you remember her from the café?"

"Is she a suspect, Lieutenant?" I asked, trying to sound properly reverent.

Aravelo ignored me. "Tell me about the Saab."

I remembered what Sergeant Weller had told me earlier. The police had found a red Saab in the water near Half Moon Bay. Maybe this was why I had been on Lieutenant Aravelo's invite-only list to the police station. They'd found the Saab and wanted more details. After all, I was the one who had given them the tip in the first place. Could I recall anything else?

"Was the woman in the picture the driver of the red Saab?" I said.

"You remember any details?" The lieutenant dismissed my question. "The interior. Was it leather? What about the license plate? What about the frame around the license plate?"

Wouldn't they have known all this already? Maybe they wanted to verify they had the right car.

What was the harm in answering about the Saab? I mostly already had—the day the café exploded. I did it again. I told him what I'd told him before.

"I wasn't focused on the car," I said.

He seemed to consider this, and accept it.

"Why are you asking about the Saab?" I said.

No answer. I upped the ante. "Did you find it?"

Lieutenant Aravelo turned his lips upward into a tight, controlled grin. It could have meant anything. I interpreted it as: You're a better tactician than I thought.

"How did you know that?" he asked.

It was a fair inquiry. One I was totally unprepared to answer. It would have meant jeopardizing Sergeant Weller and my relationship with him. Maybe Weller and Aravelo were on the same team, maybe not.

Before I'd left Erin, she'd told me I would know what to say when I got into the interrogation room. The realization came upon me slowly, like a wave of nausea.

"The explosion is just the tip of this thing," I said. "Something went wrong at that café long before it turned into a fireball. You know it. *I* know it. Please stop treating me like a chump."

I steadied myself for whatever was coming and was still unprepared.

"From now on, I'm calling you Sleeve. Not Steve, Sleeve."

I squinted.

"Do you know why a woman hates when her man goes to a strip club?" He continued to not make sense. "It's not about the tits and ass and the lap dances that make weaker men cream their pants. It's because the men fall in love. For a few minutes, we soak in the belief that we are connecting. We *are* connecting. The best strippers are opening themselves up to us, and we, knowing it's a finite experience, open up right back. When it works, it's not about sex. It's about love."

He opened the top of a clear plastic container and took a swig of a thick, strawberry-colored juice drink.

"Being a great cop involves reading emotions and being honest about what motivates me and other people. I can see what's happening inside you right now; you wear your emotions on your sleeve. Your anxiety has a smell, and it's not just the kind that comes from sitting in the hot room. I can see where the edge is and I can see how close you are to it."

He clasped his hands.

"What did you have to do with the explosion?" he said.

"Give me a break."

Aravelo pulled a notebook from his back pocket and flipped it open. He glanced at it while he talked.

"You left the café just before it exploded," he said.

Then he listed the rest of the circumstantial evidence. I'd known about the red Saab. I knew it had been found, something that hadn't yet been made public. "Now you're telling me that there was a previous problem at the café. Would you care to elaborate?"

The way he asked it, I wasn't sure whether he knew about Andy or Simon Anderson.

"I want to talk to my lawyer."

When I said it, I was struck by a single thought: Why the hell didn't I insist on talking to my lawyer earlier? I guess it was because I never thought I was considered a suspect.

"You're not the only one trying to figure out what is going on here," I said, standing. "The difference is, maybe I'm doing a hell of a lot better job."

My frustration, confusion, adrenaline, and yearning boiled over. Aravelo slammed his fist into the table.

"You. Will. Stay. The. Fuck. Out. Of. My. Investigation!"

I walked out of the building in a rage. I pictured myself slamming a two-by-four into Aravelo, succumbing to a reckless adolescent fantasy.

I hadn't slept well in two days. My neck balled with tension—a clear demand of the brain by the muscles: Slow down or we will seize up or tear and enforce bed rest. I tapped my head against the side of the building and tried to calm myself by remembering the likely medical causes of my compounding stress. This was all just biochemical. I was experiencing acute stress disorder, the result of a highly traumatic event like confronting death or its prospect. The symptoms were potentially serious—anxiety, detachment, and even dissociative amnesia. Was I even accurately remembering what happened at the café?

I closed my eyes and inhaled deeply, just as the phone rang.

"We need to get out of here," Erin said.

21

Erin picked me up two blocks away. I noticed the smell. Groceries. The back was packed up with Safeway bags.

"Lieutenant Aravelo is a very dangerous man," I said.

"I got that feeling."

"He uses his brain the way his brother uses a flashlight."

"Which means?"

"As a blunt object."

"Elaborate, please." Erin was losing patience. "What did you learn?"

My head pulsed. I rubbed my temples.

"He asked me about you."

"What do you mean?" she asked. Alarm.

"He showed me your picture. He asked if I'd seen you at the café."

Erin took her hand off the wheel and put it to her mouth. She bit the tip of her thumb.

"Why would he do that?"

"I don't know."

"Did he tell you why he wanted to know?"

"I don't think it's anything to worry about," I responded. "He said he was interested in anyone who survived the explosion."

Even as I said it, I realized the comment would not mollify Erin, and it wasn't mollifying me. There were a handful of survivors. Why would the cops ask me about one of them?

I learned in medical school that when you perform surgery, you separate the patient's head from the body with a curtain. In theory, this is supposed to create privacy and protect the patient from seeing anything uncomfortable. The reality is that it protects a surgeon—from whatever case of the nerves might come from realizing that the meat puppet he or she is carving up is attached to a real human being. It lets the doctor be clinical. I felt a momentary urge to be able to look at Erin more clinically, protected by a curtain, and to make a cold assessment. Of her, Aravelo, Danny, the whole ensemble cast.

"I told them everything I knew," Erin said. "I didn't see anything."

"You went to the bathroom."

"I hate cops," she said.

The words hung in the air.

"What picture did they have of me?" she asked, sounding calmer.

"A head shot. You looked . . . well, a little younger. Maybe ten years. I think you wore a sweater."

Erin had a destination in mind. She asked me if I wanted to join her for a night in Santa Rosa. A friend of hers had a secluded house there and she said she needed to get away. She promised she would cook and that I could sleep. It was what the doctor ordered. En route, we stopped by my place so I could feed the cat, pick up a change of clothes, my laptop, and my work papers. I had what I knew would be a vain hope I'd get some work done on my soon-to-be-overdue article.

Erin told me how she'd spent the previous hours. She said she had checked out Andy's apartment and it was still intact, then called his landlord, who told her he hadn't ordered any electrical work. But he said the cable company had been doing some work in the building in recent weeks.

As we were crossing the Golden Gate Bridge, I realized I was supposed to meet Sergeant Weller in a few hours. More than that, I needed to meet him. He was a back channel for information and I was ready to demand answers. I started dialing.

"I have an idea," Erin said. "Why not turn that thing off for an hour."

I didn't precisely sleep, but I managed stupor. I tried a relaxation trick Samantha taught me that entailed slacking the jaw, softening the eyes, and focusing entirely on the image in front of you. Hocus-pocus, maybe, but it was the best I could do without Jose Cuervo and lime. I looked at the license plates of cars in front of me. I recited the digits, letting my jaw go slack. Still, I felt my eyelid twitch involuntarily, blepharospasm. My brain channeling its electrical activity. I blinked hard, but I couldn't zero out, couldn't rid it of Annie.

In the previous twenty-four hours, I'd learned about Andy and the Andersons, and some blonde in a yellow blouse in a grainy photo, and had been grilled at police headquarters. Underneath them all, there was Annie, her memory blurring with the scenery. Townships passed in a flash, then the hillsides farther north. Green bled into green.

You can have your Swiss Alps, your Italian coast, Aspen. Then bow to Northern California. Go a hundred miles any direction from San Francisco and you're in bliss. Santa Cruz. Lake Tahoe. Napa Valley. Mountains touching sky. Cliffs overlooking divinely created shores.

"Sarah."

I yanked out of my stupor.

We had pulled into the right lane. Preparing to exit the highway.

"Explain what that means," Erin said, "after you hand me a map."

I rummaged in the glove compartment for a Thomas Guide. Then I skipped ahead—in the story.

"Lieutenant Aravelo showed me a picture of a woman."

"Another picture?" Erin sounded surprised.

I hadn't recognized the woman, but I thought of someone who might—an old friend of Annie's. Her best friend—maybe Sarah could shed some light onto why I had been handed a note in Annie's script.

As uncomfortable as Sarah made me, I had a soft spot for her, particularly the eulogy she gave at Annie's funeral. Her opening anecdote revolved around a sizzling August day when Annie was eleven years old. There was a 10K run around the lake. Her father had set Annie up with a tub of strawberry ice cream in a cooler packed with ice, and a sign: "Ice cream scoops $1."

Annie didn't want to do it, but her dad insisted it would be a good learning experience. When he returned at midafternoon, the ice cream was all gone, but Annie only had one dollar in sales. He asked what happened. Annie said, "I started a foundation."

The church crowd had let go of their sadness with a huge laugh. But there was another punch line. Partway through the day, a benevolent passerby had seen her giving away strawberry scoops. He responded in kind. He had come to sell his blond Labrador puppies from a large wicker basket. He gave one of them to Annie.

"Permission to use my mobile phone again," I said to Erin.

She smiled and shook her head. It struck me as knowing, in a maternal way. "You've got a problem with that thing."

I dialed the number I had for Sarah and left a rambling message, concluding awkwardly that I had a question about our long-gone mutual friend.

Erin put her hand on my knee and smiled. "Put the phone down again—before you hurt someone."

* * *

"Shoes off," Erin said.

She was carrying a bag of groceries into the kitchen. The gentleman in me should have offered to help. But he was looking at the couch the way my cat, Hippocrates, looks at, well, the couch.

I plopped down. One last thing to do. I'd noticed when I called Sarah that I had two voice-mail messages on my mobile phone. One was from my attorney, Eric Rugger. Good man, smart as hell, huge fan of Bloody Marys. But, as far as I could tell, never during trial. Besides, he was what I could afford.

"Got your e-mail and your phone messages," he said. "I hadn't heard about the Aravelo case being reopened. I'll look into it. But, importantly: Don't panic. These things are not uncommon. Call me if you have questions, or I'll get back to you with details."

The second message was from Mike Thompson. It was classic geek brief. "It's Mike. Checked out your laptop. Give a call." Click.

I did, and when I got him on the line he made a techie joke I didn't understand, prompting him with silence to get to the point.

"I opened the diary, like you asked. Piece of cake. I wasn't sure what else you wanted me to do. I gave the computer a cursory look. I checked out the operating system and the applications. It seems to be in good working order."

I put my feet on the wood table.

"Thanks, Mike."

"I didn't mean to suggest there wasn't something unusual."

I sat up. "Can you say that part again—without the double negatives?"

His response came quickly.

"It's an encryption scheme."

"I thought you were able to get into the diary."

"Not that. Do you know what GNet is?"

I said no.

"It's an application I've never seen before. I found it attached to the operating system."

"What's it do?"

"Dunno," Mike said. "It's inactive."

"But it caught your attention."

"Not really."

"But you just said that—"

Mike cut me off. "It wasn't the program that interested me. It's the fact it's being guarded by the most sophisticated encryption scheme I've ever seen."

22

n English," I said.

"How's that?" said Mike.

"Explain in English what happened to the computer. Slowly. Like I'm the village idiot."

I was sitting straight up on the couch now, my posture mimicking my curiosity. Erin picked up the change in my mood and sat down next to me.

"There's a piece of software on your computer . . ."

"Actually, it's not my computer."

"Whoever's computer this is has a piece of software I haven't seen before," Mike ran over my interruption. "In the operating system, it has the name GNet."

"Like the letter 'G' then the word 'Net'?"

"Yep," he said. "It may not be a big deal. Can't really tell."

Erin put her ear next to mine. It wasn't speakerphone, but it would have to do.

I said, "If it's not a big deal, then how come you bothered to mention—"

He cut me off again. No one is more assertive than a geek who is in control of a technical situation.

"The program didn't catch my attention. It's the encryption scheme. *That's* what caught my eye. It's pretty sophisticated. Multiple layers and encryption keys. Seemingly unnecessary. Like locking your diary behind a vaulted door protected by armed guards."

I listened, tried to digest, then fell back on a classic journalism technique. I repeated what he said back to me—in my
words. This accomplished two goals: It helped me understand,
and it slowed him down.

"What you're saying is that there is some possibly unusual
program on the computer."

"Affirmative."

"And it is being protected by a definitely unusual, and very
impressive, different program that we'd need a supercomputer
to crack."

"You got it, dude," Mike said.

"What else can you tell me?"

Mike said he had a better idea.

"Why don't I show you?" he said.

I told Mike I'd come down to Palo Alto the next morning for
coffee.

He seemed mildly energized by the prospect of looking into
the matter further, but he didn't ask why I was inquiring, or
about anything else related to the computer. It surprised me
a little. Mike was different from a lot of geeks. He did care
about context, and he wasn't consumed exclusively with bits
and bytes. He wasn't at all a bad communicator. But he also
had no inkling about the potential significance of this computer. *Potential significance.* Maybe there wasn't any at all.

"So Andy's computer has an unusual program on it?" Erin
said.

"That's the way it sounds."

"So what does that mean?"

Maybe the program was innocuous. Maybe it was a video
game—that Andy had protected with a password. Who knew?
I gave the look that would embody such a response. Namely:
a blank stare. This had become utterly overwhelming, a buffet
of uncertainties. Erin laughed.

When she walked away, I gave a surreptitious look in her

direction. She wore jeans with a red flower embroidered on the right back pocket. I wanted to trust her. I felt like I was starting to, but I knew almost nothing about Erin Coultran. Nothing biographical, or geographical, or educational. We'd spent a day together in the foxhole. But, outside of knowing she was composed when it mattered most, I didn't have a clue.

I added it to the list. Of things I didn't know, but wanted to find out about.

I twirled my torso around to put up my feet. I then took the ultimate prerequisite step toward falling asleep in the modern age, and turned off my mobile phone. It didn't take; I turned the gadget back on again. Unfinished business tugged.

When I dialed, I tried to orient myself. Was Sergeant Weller one of the good guys? As he had done in the past, he put me immediately at ease.

"I need an eleven-letter word. The clue is 'lactose and wimpy.' "

"Aren't you on the taxpayer's dime?"

"That's why it's urgent I get the answer immediately. So I can get back to eating doughnuts. Hang on a sec," he continued. "Lemme get somewhere a little less within earshot of the chain of command."

It was more than a sec.

"Milquetoast," I said. I'd counted it on my fingers. Eleven letters.

"We are going to become good friends."

Danny asked me if we were going to get together at six, as planned, and I told him I needed to take a rain check. We agreed to meet in the morning. I told him where I was and with whom.

"The waitress?" he asked, sounding surprised.

I told him we needed to get somewhere quiet. He didn't say anything. It struck me that, looking at it from his perspective,

the idea of me and Erin hanging out might not just be confusing, it might be suspicious. After all, we were two survivors of
the explosion, who had discovered each other, and were holed
up in a remote location. To try to mollify Danny's concerns, I
told him that I had a lot to fill him in about, starting with my
dressing-down by Aravelo. Again, he seemed genuinely surprised. I was less surprised by what he said.

"He's not a good man," Danny said.

Danny said that the two men had long been rivals. Aravelo
had twice blocked Danny's promotion. Then Danny had been
put on one of the shadow homicide teams and the competition
between the men had intensified.

"He's got a little fiefdom. They're tough guys. Make their
own rules. Anti-intellectual," he said.

Their conflict, it struck me, was of minor importance to
me. I asked Danny what he'd learned about the café. He said
he had some things he'd prefer to tell me about when we got
together, then asked if there was anything from my end. I told
him about the laptop, and about Andy getting sick before the
café exploded. This too seemed to surprise him, and he di-
gested it slowly.

"Tomorrow," he said. "Something early—like breakfast."

We agreed.

"Nathaniel. Between now and then, I recommend that you
don't trust anybody."

23

You know what you need?" Erin asked.

"Human contact?"

"I was thinking tea."

She sat down beside me. She began kneading the webbing between my thumb and index finger. "It relaxes the shakras," she said.

Her hands were graceful. Her fingernails were grown out slightly and groomed. I realized how feminine she could be. Even soft?

It's the last thing I thought before I fell asleep and drifted away. On a tiny island of ice.

I sat cross-legged on my frigid block. Floating, in cloudy blue water. It would have been the Arctic, except for the black panthers, each sitting on an island of ice. Some glowered at me, others tended to themselves, licking paws and resting on their haunches. They were waiting for me to make a mistake. I was shivering, frigid. My arms felt like stalactites of blue ice.

A panther howled, then leapt. Standing on my chest, it said, "Bring me a chocolate milk shake, Turtle. I'm waiting."

Had I screamed aloud? It was dark. I was on the couch in the log cabin. I'd been out for two hours. It wasn't enough. I was still shaky after spending twenty minutes in the shower. The stress of the previous two days was catching up. The body can withstand much more than we give it credit for; witness the thirty-hour stints that doctors typically do in the first two years of residency. But the doctor knows the shift will end. A sustained period of stress without expectation of its conclusion adds an even higher dose of the fight-or-flight neurochemicals. A dangerous dose.

Erin had cooked a feast—a roast, mashed potatoes, string beans. She said it was the comfort food of her midwestern youth.

"It's even better if you're wearing pants," she said.

We sat down and had our first real chance to talk. Erin had grown up in East Lansing, Michigan, the daughter of a high school teacher and a church deacon. He was loving, but a disciplinarian and patriarch. He was outwardly nice to everyone but she knew how he felt about the people who lived in the black ghetto. "Yes, sirs" and "Thank you, ma'ams" were the family's vernacular. Her mother was a closet intellectual who didn't talk to her husband about the books she read. Several times when Erin was a girl, she discovered that her mother had put the cover of a romance novel around the subversive literature she was actually reading. When she was younger, Erin gravitated to the certainty of her father's path. But she said that, predictably, her own life's experience began to contradict her dad's rigidity.

To try to keep on the straight and narrow, she quit the University of Michigan after a year and married her high school sweetheart. He was in her father's mold—to a fault.

"My friends and I called him the Bible Belter."

"Religious guy?"

"Because he belted me," she said. She smiled when she said it, like she was remembering something she couldn't believe ever actually happened.

She blamed herself, lashed out at everyone else, then eventually had an awakening. To her mother's great sadness, she moved west. She tried to figure out if there had been some impulse or interest she'd been repressing. Like a lot of other people; Haight-Ashbury may have turned into a veritable outdoor trinket mall, but people still flocked to San Francisco to find themselves. There were far more southern and midwestern black sheep than you could squeeze into a VW microbus. They were part of the "to-do list" generation—people who got into new thing after new thing, from rock climbing to hot yoga to night golf. Sometimes in the same day. And sometimes it seemed they didn't really pause to enjoy the thing, they just liked marking it off the list.

For Erin's part, she experimented with the various Left Coast trends. She'd gotten political, attending various rallies and, in particular, women's rights functions. The women's socially conscious dance troupe in the Mission—where I'd first tried to find her—was the latest.

"Can socially conscious dance only be performed by vegans?" I asked.

She laughed. "It's centered around free-form, nonviolent movements. Although one month we practiced a routine where we attacked a domestic abuser—in rhythm. I developed a killer imaginary karate chop." She paused, turning contemplative. "I hate hypocrisy. I used to think it was Congress, or the church. But it's all over. Some of my friends are left-wing bigots. They hate any idea that challenges their way of thinking. They refuse to think. I wonder if I've strayed too far."

"From God?"

"Maybe. Maybe more generally. There are all these false idols. We think we'll be happy if we find the right cause or pursuit or hobby. Maybe it's more complicated than that. With religion, I—we—just wanted answers. But then I substituted answers with questions. One experiment after another. One serpent after another. Isn't it the opposite side of the same coin?"

She said she'd been trying to create a more tangible personal philosophy. Her current idea of courage was going to a horror movie by herself. She'd done it once, a Nicole Kidman ghost flick that terrified her so much that she spent part of the movie in the lobby. Going to a romantic comedy alone, she said, didn't qualify as love.

She said she'd had a few relationships, including a short but intense one with Andy that had wound up in a deep friendship. She joked she was taking her romantic cues from the cell phone industry. She'd started to measure a relationship's potential in terms of a phone's two LED indicators: strength of connection and battery life, and a good start would be if both were over 80 percent.

Then she asked about Annie. I told her about our relationship. When I described the boating accident, Erin briefly put her hand on my forearm. It wasn't exactly maternal, or romantic. Maybe she was just steadying herself. She asked if I was over Annie.

It was my own personal $64,000 question. Was I stuck in the past? The grief counselor I went to see after Annie died gave me a context for my relationship with Annie that I've alternatively embraced and rejected, depending on my mood, and how many beers I've had. Louise said Annie was my first experience with real intimacy. She was the mother duckling. I was the baby duck. She'd imprinted me. According to Louise, I overglorified Annie because I hadn't seen the extent of her flaws. It usually took two beers to deem the theory psychobabble.

I told Erin about my forays into dating since Annie. I'd had a bunch of short flings; the longest relationship had been six months with a woman I'd met at a cocktail party hosted by the Democratic Party. She was a lawyer, pretty, and devoid of humor.

"She used to say things like, 'This wine isn't as full-bodied as I'd expected.'"

"She'd better have been very full-bodied herself to get away with that," Erin said.

"I'm over Annie's death," I stated abruptly, feeling mostly sure of myself. I didn't add: I'm not over the loneliness that comes from her absence, but I have to believe someone else can make me feel that excited—that connected.

Erin seemed to have the ability not to overanalyze, but at the same time it struck me that she didn't believe the last thing I'd said. Then, quickly, I thought: Maybe I'm projecting. Maybe *I'm* still not sure I can feel true love with someone else.

"I've been wondering," Erin said. "Why did you happen to come into the café the day everything happened?"

I thought about it for a second, and found myself smiling.

"Would you believe: drapes."

A year earlier, my parents had visited. They'd been aggressively passive-aggressive in expressing horror over the state of my bachelor pad. They mentioned that adulthood required some basic amenities, like a real set of dishes and something other than a green flannel sheet tacked to the windowsill to keep out the morning sun. They'd given me a gift certificate to Pottery Barn. For some reason, the day the café exploded, I had played basketball, then gone to Pottery Barn near the café, having decided I was ready to embrace curtains.

"And whatever the heck they represent," Erin said.

It was funny, but I felt a wave of sadness. When a woman had put a note on my table at the café, I wondered if my future had finally arrived.

Erin and I had polished off a bottle of red wine. She put her head back on the couch and closed her eyes. In a moment, she was asleep. Her head lolled to the side, hitting my shoulder. Her hair smelled faintly of a purple flower I couldn't name. Even consumed with memories of Annie, it was impossible to deny Erin's allure. Objective beauty, heightened by effortless conversation. I closed my eyes too, hoping to join her in sleep. But I felt the familiar vibration in my pants. My phone was calling. I gently pulled my shoulder out from Erin. I extracted the albatross and looked at the number. I felt a bright burst of adrenaline. I thought: I wonder if I'll ever sleep again.

24

The caller ID read: Offices of Battat and Bard. The neurologist who treated Andy, and whom Leslie hooked me up with, getting back to me at 9 p.m., when doctors ended the workday. I let him off early and turned off my phone. I craved sleep. But the call had done its damage.

Suddenly, I was thinking about all the questions, the sudden urgency of my life. Notwithstanding Annie's death, I'd lived the comfortable, relatively slow and lazy American life. Being a journalist was like being a stem cell. I was an unformed, infant organism, waiting for some subject or article or two sides of a debate to define me. What was my purpose?

I sometimes thought about a quote from John Adams, the founding father. I could never remember his exact phrasing but it went something like: Be soldiers and politicians. So your children can be lawyers, doctors, and businessmen. So their children can be poets, musicians, and artists.

The first generations build infrastructure, the later ones, with bellies full, write rock and roll and look for truth. The inheritors of stability would go where their fathers hadn't gone. They'd write "Stairway to Heaven," or articles on medical journalism. Nothing earth-shattering and plenty of time for soul-searching naps.

Erin stirred. She mumbled something sleepily, put a kiss on the side of my cheek, and said good night. I felt the memory of adolescent angst, the disappointment when you realize the girl's going to get out of the car without you getting a kiss. It was pushed aside by another surge of adrenaline. The café explosion made everything fresh again. Restless, I pulled out my laptop and began to surf through memories, beginning with the Santa Cruz boardwalk. Or, at least, its Web site.

It was an April day on which Annie and I had gotten crepes. A beachside palm reader told Anne's future: She would come into money. What did you expect for $3.50?

I clicked off the boardwalk Web site and found the site for the San Francisco Opera. Annie and I had giggled so loudly during the first act that we had to excuse ourselves.

I began to slide and squirm my way across cyberspace, driven by spasms of nostalgia. Memory linked to memory, minutes into hours, our relationship evolving in bits and bytes. A site for every occasion—the Lake Tahoe Inn, where we spent a Saturday night by the fire playing Scrabble; the Berkeley Bowl, where we listened to Jimmy Buffett and ate pot brownies; Squid Row, a fresh-fish market where we bought swordfish and learned how to blacken it—something we were so proud to have figured out we made it at least once a month.

Squid Row. One of those rare dark memories. We'd gotten fish there the night Annie had threatened to break up with me, after her father told her about the NotesMail deal.

I found myself at the Web site for Kindle Investment Partners. Still posted there, at a link you had to know how to find, was Annie's obituary from the *Palo Alto Daily*. I read it for the umpteenth time. Glenn Kindle's creeping venom could be felt even on the company Web site—a grand tribute to the man's extraordinary public side.

There were links to recent news stories about his successes, and those of the companies he had backed. But since Annie's death, his fortunes had languished, at least in relative terms. He wasn't hitting the billion-dollar jackpots of the dot-com boom, and he wasn't getting the kind of attention he'd grown accustomed to. He was still funding high-tech start-ups and preparing IPOs, but he was no longer the hero whose picture appeared on the cover of *Business Week*. Not entirely forgotten, just radically downsized.

The latest story posted to the site was about his relationship with Ed Gaverson—once one of the wealthiest Americans, whose fortunes had tumbled considerably in recent years. The company Gaverson ran, Ditsoft, had miscalculated demand for its software and watched its stock fall 90 percent in recent years. A puff piece in *U.S. News & World Report* discussed how Kindle and Gaverson had started a consortium of big technology and telecom companies—including search engines and cable and telephone providers—aimed at spurring 100 percent consumer adoption of the Internet. They were promoting what they were modestly calling the Next Next Big Idea.

Glenn Kindle and Ed Gaverson made hundreds of millions of dollars building computers and the programs that run them. So why do they want to start giving away technology for free?

Kindle, a venture capitalist whose fortunes rose and fell with the dot-com boom, and Gaverson, the mercurial founder of Ditsoft, are fast friends—and sometimes business rivals—with a novel idea. They believe that in the not too distant future, computers, mobile phones, handheld devices, and other gadgets will be free—and so will the Internet access that connects them together.

The pair have argued that government- or advertising-subsidized growth of Internet infrastructure will fuel advances in American productivity—spurred by the reliance in every facet of life on automation and inexpensive devices. They and their powerful corporate allies have rallied some interest in Washington by arguing that America's per-capita penetration of high-speed Internet adoption is 8th in the world, risking the country's competitiveness.

Kindle and his pals have profit on their minds too. They believe future returns will come when people use those devices to buy goods and services over the Internet, download video games and music, or watch advertisements while they surf the Net.

A tagline of their concept might fairly be: First connect, then collect.

Kindle prefers a loftier explanation. "Teach people to fish and they will eat. Connect them and they will create more efficient, as of yet unimagined ways to harvest the oceans—and the heavens," he told a gathering at Stanford Business School earlier this year.

Among the companies helping to advance the concept are major Internet search engines. One search company, AmericaSearch, has floated the idea of offering free wireless access in major downtown areas in exchange for sending users advertisements targeted to them based on their location. The mobile phone companies too have been flirting with delivering not just text-based but voice-mail commercial messages.

But a prevailing question is how much of their idea is science and how much is fiction—and New Age marketing-speak— born of an effort to help them reclaim their mantle atop the technology economy.

I closed the link.

I had to—to keep my eyeballs from exploding. It wasn't Glenn Kindle I hated. It was that tiny part of him that was manifest in Annie. My fists balled and an old fantasy surfaced—me holding Annie's father by the feet over the edge of the Golden Gate Bridge. I hit my fist rhythmically on the desk.

I jumped out of my skin. Not from anger. From the hand on my shoulder.

"It's 3 a.m."

It was Erin.

"I'm just . . ."

"You're obsessing." She looked at the computer. "Is this site important?"

I looked at the screen. It was a story about a recent award given to Kindle Investment Partners by the American Society of Software Engineers. It wasn't important in the slightest. It was . . . distraction. It was crap. Erin closed the computer, took my hand, and pulled me toward the bedroom.

"I never visited."

She looked at me quizzically.

"The place where Annie died. I never went back—after it happened."

She got into bed next to me. She took my hand. "You can visit . . ."

I finished her thought. "But you can never go back."

Perhaps. But what if the past came back to me?

She said, "Tomorrow is going to be a big day."

25

It was raining. I felt myself slip in and out of consciousness. Was it another watery dream?

If so, my dreams had gone from surreal—to very real. My face was wet. I opened my eyes and bolted upright. Erin stood beside the bed, dressed and armed with a glass of ice cubes. One was aimed at my face.

It should have been funny, but I felt a surge. I tried to get a grip. Was I really upset? More likely still tired. I shook my head—like a dog after a visit to the ocean—to reorient.

I'd had five hours of sleep during which Erin said I tossed and turned and chattered. I woke up as I'd gone to bed, fully clothed.

We drove in silence to San Francisco. I dropped her off at her car so she could run errands while I went to breakfast with Danny. I glanced at the headlines through the plastic of the newspaper magazine racks while I waited for him at Mel's Diner. "Police Stumped by Café Explosion" (*Chronicle*); "Cops: Terrorists Didn't Rock Tea Time" (*Examiner*); "Feds Lend Weight to Café Investigation" (*Oakland Tribune*); "Did We Bring It Upon Ourselves?" (*Weekly*).

I was about to put my token into the box to pull out a *Chronicle* when I saw Sergeant Danny Weller pull up in front of Mel's. I didn't need a paper—my information about the explosion was coming from the inside. Danny stepped out of a brown sedan with a red cherry on top. He had parked in a loading zone.

"I'm having ham and eggs," he said by way of greeting. "Side of flapjacks."

"You are a man of great vision."

"Tell me about your conversation with Aravelo."

Talking to the police is like talking to parents. And schoolteachers. And elected officials. Except none of those people carry .40-caliber Berettas. Police represent the ultimate authority figure. You like them, want to please them, and you hate them. Just for their mere existence.

I've had friends who are cops. I had one for a neighbor once. He liked to smoke dope and he was more than happy to share. I got pretty comfortable with him, but I always knew the pecking order. Same with Danny. He'd let me get pretty comfortable, but with a turn in his tone, I could see who was pecking at whom. What did he want to hear from me? What was I prepared to say? The road was forking. I went down the middle.

"It was more like a monologue."

"Monologue?"

My head pulsed again, accompanied by a leg twitch. This was new—a rapid-fire jitter of my foot. I excused myself to the bathroom and splashed cold water on my face. When I got back, I told Danny that Aravelo had shown me a picture of a woman and asked if I'd seen her.

"Had you?"

A newfound intensity. I shook my head.

"Then Aravelo told you to stay out of his investigation?"

His investigation. Not *our* investigation. Not *the* investigation.

"He accused me of causing the explosion," I said. "Danny, I'm not really sure where this is . . ."

"Unbelievable. Un. Fucking. Believable. How could he . . ."

Danny understood.

"You mentioned a laptop. Tell me about it."

I reiterated to Danny that it had belonged to someone at the café. Danny asked me if I thought it was connected to the explosion. It struck me as an odd question, coming from a cop. I thought: Danny is a cop, isn't he?

I looked at my empty coffee cup. Two cups and still not thinking straight.

"I would very much like to see it—the laptop," he said. "Actually, that's not true. I don't want to see it. I want a brilliant technician I know to see it."

"What the hell is going on, Sergeant?"

It was about as much tough guy as I could muster.

Danny laughed.

"Story time," he said.

He took a sip of water.

"I want to know what your angle is," I said.

Danny put his hands forward.

"Hear me out. Do you remember Valerie Westin?"

Valerie Westin.

"The Lingerie Larcenist," I said.

"I busted her. Aravelo took the credit."

The Lingerie Larcenist had gone into banks, opened her raincoat, and displayed a bodacious body—clad in black stockings and a lacy bra. She showed them a holster and a sexy little Glock .45 as well. She was more modest about her face. That remained covered with a ski mask. But the poor distracted bank tellers looked at her guns, and her gun, and forked over the dough.

"I put the case together. I found the tie to her earlier crimes in Omaha. I found her address through an ex. I've got zero to show for it."

"That's a great story," I said. "But you still haven't answered my question."

"You want to see my cards. Here:

"Aravelo is a power broker inside the department. Maybe *the* power broker. That's why he got this assignment. That's why he controls who does what. And who gets what credit. And what promotion. And, by extension, what power and salary—and real money."

Money, what money?

"I can't prove anything. But Aravelo lives in a $750,000 pad on Fillmore, and I hear it's mostly paid for. He's just a savvier version of his punk brother."

Implying what, exactly? Aravelo was dirty? That Danny would be willing to take graft too? He switched tones.

"If you want to swing in the wind," he said, digging his fork into a pile of grease and cheese, "be my fucking guest."

Interrogation. Peace offerings. Threats. Was Danny the good cop—just trying to set things right?

"Your father," I said.

He put down his fork.

"What about my father? Leave him out of this."

It was worth a gamble.

"You said he needed a transplant. You need the money."

He took a long pause.

"Dad's finances were vaporized by the dot-com bust. Netscape, the browser guys. The stock dove and dad chased after it. His whole life's philosophy is that being right is less important than being decisive. Commit. FDR, JFK, McCarthy, Reagan, didn't matter, if they had conviction, he respected it. He made up his mind about Internet stocks and away he went."

He stopped himself by clearing his throat.

"I could have used my rightful promotions a long time ago. It won't be near enough money to help my father. Not near enough. But every little bit helps. And there is a principle here. A man ought to have the right to take care of his family. I can solve this café explosion, and you can help me set things right."

"What exactly are you asking from me? Why *me*?"

He had grown particularly calm. "Clues. Stuff Aravelo

might be overlooking. Stuff I can put together with information I'm getting from inside," he said. "Why you? Because you may have them—even if you don't know it. Plus, this is personal for you."

I flinched.

"What's that supposed to mean?" I said. Did he know something about Annie? The note. I'd told him about the note. Is that what he meant?

"Jesus, Nat. You almost got blown up. And you're a journalist. A good investigative journalist. I saw what you did to Aravelo's punk-ass brother.

"And after the café exploded, you went out there and found that waitress. Didn't you?"

That waitress.

"I need eyes and ears, Nat. My whole job is amassing eyes and ears, and putting together what they see and hear into a coherent picture," he said. "I'm guessing you wouldn't mind having an insight into what is really going on. We can work as partners on this." The words were trite, but the tone sounded sincere.

"Horse trade," I said.

"How's that?" He leaned back.

"I'm not blindly feeding you information. You've got to give me something. At least to establish . . ."

We both waited for me to finish my sentence.

"Trust," I said.

Danny pulled out a wallet. He took out twenty and put it on top of the check. "The café is owned by Idelwild Corporation. It's an investment arm of some of the major big-time corporations."

Hardly a revelation. I'd already read it in the newspaper.

"C'mon, Sergeant. Is that a test to see if I'm paying attention?"

Danny put his hands to his face and rubbed his eyes. He craned his neck back.

"Okay," he said.

Okay. Okay what?

"The waitress," he said.

The waitress.

What about her?

"Did she tell you about Michigan?"

"Yeah. She told me—she grew up there."

"It's also where she almost spent the rest of her life—in jail."

"Erin? For what?"

"Blowing something up."

26

Romp Studios."

"This is a joke."

"The offices of an adult film production company went to the ground. She beat the rap. But then she got sued."

He handed me a printout from the East Lansing Superior Court. It had the name Erin Iris Coultran, a date six years earlier, and a long number that I guessed to be a docket number. I listened to Danny's explanation in a daze. He said that, as near as he could piece it together, a pornography company had started shooting films in East Lansing, trying to recruit women from Michigan State University. Not long after a profile of the company appeared in the local weekly alternative newspaper, its offices were destroyed. Erin was part of a small group charged with what looked to be a political or religiously motivated attack. She was not convicted, Danny said, but she still faced a mountain of debt from the civil suit.

"So are you saying that Erin blew up the café?" I asked.

"I have no evidence that the waitress caused anything."

He said he had a friend at the FBI run down the names of people at the café and Erin Coultran's was in the database.

"I don't know if the charges were dropped, or if she was acquitted—or precisely the dispensation."

Erin. Blew. Up. The. Café. I let the words rain down. They didn't go together. Did they? Something tugged at me—something unresolved about Erin. Too many coincidences. At the least, she had been way less than frank.

"Lieutenant Aravelo asked me about her."

For a second, it looked like Danny's eyes widened. "Anyway, I'm expecting details soon about the Michigan case. I will forward those that don't violate her right to privacy."

I looked at the paper and shook my head.

"I take it you don't think Erin is capable of such an act of violence." Sounding more like the sergeant with every passing moment.

"Nope. Can't be."

He pulled out a stick of gum. He offered the package to me.

"I do my puzzles with a pencil."

I asked him why, what he meant.

"I put a lot of words in the crossword puzzle that ultimately don't fit. But you can't be afraid to put down some words that ultimately don't work. Do the same with Erin. Take your time, see what fits."

"Why not just ask her to fill in the blanks?"

"I'd advise against. You'll scare her off. She won't tell you anything and she might run."

He suggested I continue spending time with Erin, if that's what I chose to do. "Use your listening skills. Try on different ways of looking at her. See which one is the best fit. She'll get clearer. They always do."

After Danny drove off, I considered the essential question: Could Erin have blown up the café?

She'd given me no indication of violent tendencies, yet she'd been violent enough to attract the attention of the FBI. On its face, anything underhanded by Erin seemed implausible.

Unless.

There had been a fire at Simon Anderson's house. Possibly started by a female electrician. *Arson. Explosion. Fire.*

Then again, if she was as straight as my initial gut instincts told me, what did that say about Weller? Why would he impugn her?

Maybe there was a third possibility: Erin and Weller were on the up-and-up. Weller was exploring options and alerting me to pertinent evidence; Erin was on my side, but simply hadn't told me something about her story. It could be a coincidence. That seemed plausible enough, given what I had learned so far about each person. Just then, Erin called. I sent it to voice mail.

I beelined to the nearest Internet café—the modern public library. I did a search on Erin Coultran, cross-referencing her with Michigan, East Lansing, Arson, Lawsuit. Each search turned up empty. Most newspapers don't keep their archives online, and hadn't even started building them until recently. I found a brief reference to the demise of Romp Studios. An item at the site of an adult film magazine mentioned a fire at the studio as one of the examples of backlash against pornographers in the late nineties.

Then I researched Danny Weller. There were a handful of stories about his crimefighting, including one about the Lingerie Larcenist. He was a bit player, and a stand-up guy. A brief mention in a column in the *Examiner* mentioned that Weller and his junior partner, Officer Velarde, were among those assigned to rotation on the homicide shadow investigative squad. He checked out.

I checked my e-mail. My editor, Kevin, had sent three messages. The last one was just a subject line: "What's up?"

When I was a sophomore in high school, the dog ate my homework—a six-page paper on *The Red Badge of Courage*. I'd set the paper down under a well-lit window, and put my uneaten peanut butter and honey sandwich on top of it. The sun did its job of melting everything, and then the dog came in and cleaned up the mess. The teacher did not believe me. It should have taught me to come up with better excuses.

My phone brain story was due that afternoon. I needed

something better than: The café explosion ate my homework. My subject line read: "I'm just polishing off the final draft."

I was going to have to come up with something better soon, but I had bigger things to worry about. Like the intensifying pain shooting down my back, which felt like linebackers were performing *Swan Lake* on my spine. I looked at the clock on my phone and realized it had been an hour and a half since I got to the café. If I wanted to make it to Stanford Technology Research Center on time, I was going to have to speed again.

During the ride down to Palo Alto, Erin called twice, but I sent the calls to voice mail. I had a meeting with a geek about a laptop. What was hiding in that laptop that she wanted so desperately to see?

27

Mike's office was a study in obsessive-compulsive disorder. Everything was stacked, ordered, and dusted. Five pencils sat in a row on the desk, their tips of identical length. It seemed almost dainty compared to Mike, who had played linebacker at Stanford. He had a slight but chronic bend at his elbow from arthritis, caused by blows of helmet to joint, that was noticeable to anyone with anatomy training. When he typed on the computer keyboard, the pain in his left arm caused him to peck letters one at a time with his index finger.

On his wall were two posters. One was of Douglas Engelbart, the man credited with inventing the computer mouse, and, in turn, with making computers more user-friendly. Engelbart was an icon for people who wanted to make bits and bytes a little more human. The other was of Eldridge Cleaver, a man who wanted to make humans a little more human. Whether its presence had anything to do with Mike's own heritage—African American—never seemed relevant to anything. One of Silicon Valley's attributes was that it never seemed to give a damn about race. If you could make the green, you were on the team.

Mike's only trouble was that he suffered the social condition of being overly friendly. He would try anything, go on any outing, hang out with any group, say yes to any invitation, and become ever present if you let him. He was reliable, smart, and nearly funny, but he was just slightly tone-deaf and so he couldn't understand that not everyone was that happy all the time, eager to have fun, or altogether sincere in their social planning. He had to be kept at arm's length or his friendship could be overwhelming.

"Dude, was your friend a hacker?" he said. He was fond of the title "dude."

He was relatively social for an engineer, but he was still a geek. We weren't going to distract ourselves with niceties. He didn't ask why I was interested in the laptop. We went right for the technology.

"This encryption program is a doozy."

Hackers get a bad name. The term can refer to the jerks who break into computers and destroy Web sites. But not all hackers are malicious. Some hackers take apart systems in order to improve them, work outside corporate channels, find new ways to attack problems. When the title is said in a certain tone, it is a tribute to someone who, tech-wise, has got it going on.

"I might have overlooked it. But the disk seemed way too full given the applications. There had to be something else on there."

I mustered enough of the two required ingredients—concentration and patience—to follow his thinking. He was saying that when he first looked at the computer, he noticed its memory was very full. But on its face, there weren't enough big programs to be taking up so much space.

"I did some digging," he said. "And found this."

He was in the computer's directory—about fifteen submenus down from anywhere a person without a PhD would look. All that popped up was an icon for a computer application with the title "GNet." Just like Mike had told me on the phone.

"The program is half a gigabyte. Huge—especially considering that it wasn't showing up in any of the main directories."

A big program. Possibly hidden.

"So what does it do?"

"Can't tell you, dude."

He had his index finger on the computer's nipple, controlling the onscreen prompt. He put the prompt on the GNet icon. He clicked. Nothing happened.

"Cut to the chase," I said.

It was uncharacteristic for me. Mike looked up at me dispassionately, like he was examining a computer with a virus, and jumped ahead. He said he thought, at first, that the program was corrupt, but it had been activated recently.

"Activated?"

"The logs show when a program is working. Just like you can tell in your word processing program when you most recently worked on a given document."

He showed me the computer's log. It had a date. Three weeks earlier.

"I tried about five hundred ways to open the app. I even loaded some all-purpose software I thought might pry it open enough for me to glimpse its raison d'être."

He paused.

"It should have hit me a hell of a lot earlier. Most times when a program is encrypted, it asks for a password. Or it tells you that entrance is forbidden. That's how you know it's encrypted."

"But you weren't asked for a password?"

"Nope."

He leaned back. He was in the Geek Teaching Zone. He explained that he was able to see in the computer logs that each time GNet was activated, so was a different program, AXcs*82.

"That's the name of the encryption program," I said.

"Yep. Very tidy. Very sophisticated. It is in stealth mode—blocking attempts to access GNet. But whenever the program is activated, the encryption is opened too—and therefore activated."

I leaned forward.

"Meaning you didn't get into the program either?"

"Dude, give an old dog a little credit." Then he added, with a smile, "But just a *little* credit."

I waited for the punch line.

"I didn't break the encryption code. But I did manage to find the signature of its author."

"The author's identity?"

"Sort of a tagline you typically find associated with a program. It can tell you something about the author. Or the company."

I nodded.

"I printed it out," he said. "This stuff is typically jargon, or an oblique identifier, so it typically doesn't tell you much. Seems to be the case here."

He opened the piece of paper. I looked at it. I felt that little bit of me still tethered to reality had just become unglued.

28

Forty-eight hours earlier, just before the world exploded, a woman handed me a note that saved my life. Written, seemingly, in the handwriting of my true love. There had been no way to make sense of it.

Maybe I'd imagined the whole thing, maybe it hadn't been her handwriting at all. Or maybe it had been a ghost—a specter in a red Saab.

Until that moment, I didn't have any reason to favor any of these explanations.

"I've been in the Valley a long time," Mike said, stabbing his index finger at the words on the piece of paper. "I've never heard of this."

But I had. I knew it well. I knew exactly what it meant. The name on the paper, the name of the company, or person, or memory that had written the encryption scheme on Andy's computer.

Strawberry Labs.

Annie's childhood dog. Strawberry. The Labrador retriever.

The past had returned.

29

After Annie died, I took brief custody of Strawberry Too, the Lab Annie had named after her first dog. But my apartment was too small and the dog liked to throw up. I reluctantly put S2 up for adoption. I tried to make it symbolic of my getting over Annie's death, but it wasn't that neat.

One thing Annie's death brought me was the idea for a magazine story that turned into my next foray into medical journalism. I wrote about the neurology of grief. Researchers had begun to use magnetic resonance imaging to identify the parts of the brain used when we experience all different sorts of emotions, including grief. They mapped reactions as people thought, felt, and remembered in real time. The research tried to hone in on to what extent grief emanates from the limbic cortex, where we think emotions originate, or the hippocampus, where we form memories. It was the nascent study of the neurobiology of attachment. If we identified its origin, could we mitigate the pain of loss?

The signs of Annie's passing were everywhere, and not all of them I could have predicted. One day two men in suits knocked on my door. They introduced themselves as IRS investigators and said they'd come on a routine matter. They asked about my employment status. Specifically, if I'd ever worked for Kindle Investment Partners.

"No, I'm an ex."

"Ex-employee?"

"Ex-boyfriend."

I told them that I had dated Annie for just over a year. I was about to launch into the story of her death—the abridged version.

"We're sorry for your loss," the taller one said. "And you never worked for her—in a professional capacity?"

I explained to them that I'd graduated from medical school and was trying to make it as a freelance journalist. The tall one cut me off.

"Just one final question. Did you ever travel to New York with Ms. Kindle?"

A stab of pain. The Empire State Building. The Kiss. I nodded.

"And you weren't working for Kindle, or Vestige. Did you deal with their accounting?"

Vestige. That was the company we'd visited in New York. It had been one of the start-ups owned by Kindle Investment Partners. I assured them I never worked for either company.

"When you were in New York, did you attend a meeting regarding Vestige—pertaining to the company's pending public offering?" the tall one asked.

I remembered the meeting. I'd attended long enough to give Annie some documents she'd left in the room. I told them I'd stopped in to the meeting for a few minutes to say hello. They seemed satisfied.

"Like I said," the tall one said. "We're sorry for your loss."

"Can I ask . . ."

"As you know, the Kindles have a substantial amount of wealth," he explained. "The government just wants to make sure everything is in order."

"It's routine," his partner added.

In the morning, I called Kindle Investment Partners. Glenn Kindle and I both loved his daughter. I didn't like the man and he didn't like me, but for the sake of her memory, I wanted to make things right between us, and find closure. It was the least I could do for my nearly future father-in-law.

That didn't happen. I couldn't even get him to come to the phone, not for at least six more weeks. That's what the receptionist at Kindle Partners told me, in her usual hyperprofessional tone. When I told her who it was, she softened considerably.

"Oh, Nat. I'm so, so sorry. Annie was such an amazing person."

Diane, Kindle's receptionist, had been at the funeral, but we hadn't had a chance to talk. She explained that Mr. Kindle was taking time off to grieve and had sequestered himself in Europe. I thanked her.

"Diane. One quick question. What if I have a question about Annie's affairs? Could he be reached then?"

No, Diane said, not even then, but there was one option.

"You could try Dave Elliott."

Dave's office was in a high-rise building that looked out over the Bay Bridge. It separates San Francisco from Oakland, the "haves" from the "have to commutes." The bookshelves behind Dave's desk were sparsely appointed with a few law books with the spines intact, like they'd never been cracked open. A putter leaned against his desk.

"I've got a 2:15," he said.

I looked at the clock to the right of his desk. It was two o'clock.

"I've got a 2:05."

"What can I do you for?"

I told him about the IRS. He took it in.

"Thanks for the tip, buddy. I'll check into it. Have Tim validate your parking at the desk."

The words and tone were friendly enough, but I felt simmering anger. I asked him what the IRS wanted. Had something happened with Vestige? He told me it was almost certainly routine, but neither of us was fooled by my question. I was pissed about Annie's death.

"I charge two hundred dollars an hour for law," he said, smiling. "Twice that for psychotherapy."

Dave looked as his clock. He launched into a fairly simplistic description of Kindle Investment Partners, the venture capital game, Annie. Her reputation as a rising star in the community caught me by surprise.

"In the venture circles, they said she'd bring glory to Kindle Investment Partners. Her technology instincts were amazing—marketing, engineering, everything. Start-up companies wanted to work with her. Competitors feared her."

"Annie?"

"The Smiling Assassin."

It rang false.

"People like that attract attention. Even after they're gone."

"Were you in love with her too?"

He chuckled.

"C'mon, buddy. This is the big leagues."

"Meaning what?"

He let the bad taste swirl around in my mouth.

"You and Annie had a great thing. I'm not blind. You were something special to her. You provided her with a real texture, romance. I think it's something you should be proud of."

I considered shoving the putter two feet into his colon, but he kept pulling me back from the edge.

"Listen. You're going to find something terrific again. It's in your blood—finding real connections. If you want to chat more, don't hesitate to call. In fact, why don't you give me a call if you ever want to hit the Olympic Club for a round."

It was a part of Annie's world I'd just as soon have left behind, but when it haunted me again just a few weeks later, it was my own damn fault.

30

A month later, I called Annie's close friend, Sarah Tenner.
"Nat," she said when I called, like she'd never heard the
name before.

We met at a bar. The one thing that I hadn't been able to
do was give myself permission to let go. I just couldn't get over
the hump. Annie seemed to haunt me all the time. I told Sarah
I loved her eulogy to Annie. She softened, and we toasted to
our lost love.

"Annie was far from perfect," Sarah said. "You damn well
know it."

"She did occasionally have a hangnail," I said.

"Let yourself focus on her failings. It'll help you move on.
She could be competitive, manipulative, even a bitch sometimes, a little nuts."

I shook my head.

"You're being pathologically naïve."

We got drunk on martinis and reminisced. Sarah urged me
to move on. She said that's what Annie would have wanted.
She pointed out that we'd only dated for a year.

"I knew Annie my whole life. I loved her as much as any
friend. But I am trying like hell not to lionize her. She didn't
deserve that."

It was the difference between friendship and true love.
Sarah and Annie's other friends couldn't see what I saw, or feel
what I did. The intensity of two people in love can only be ad-
mired from the outside, not shared or even fully appreciated. I

felt like a dope, but I unloaded on Sarah all the things I missed about Annie. It was a laundry list of small moments and big emotions, a dripping whiny poem.

Sarah looked me in the eye. "I know this is hard. That's the way these things are. But Annie was not as much of a romantic as you think. She would have wanted you to move on. I know that's what she wanted. Because she told me so. You made her feel something she'd never experienced before. She was fascinated by you. She said that whatever happened to you two, she wanted you to be happy."

"Meaning she expected something bad to happen?"

"That's not how I took it. She meant, like, if you guys should break up, or whatever. She meant that she considered you so special. Some kinds of affection transcend whatever tragedies befall a relationship."

Sarah added, "There's someone I think you should meet."

A month passed before I took Sarah up on her offer.

Her name was Julie. She was one of those lucky few creatures whose double helix was tailor-made for this particular period on the planet earth.

She was five feet ten inches tall, thin, with breasts that preceded her by just enough to demand attention, but not enough to cost her credibility. She had shoulder-length blonde hair—of a shade that suggests playful and easily underestimated. She looked like something that Hugh Hefner would put on the cover of an issue about Girls Who Make Everyone Want to Emigrate to America.

Julie had, in no particular order, been in the Peace Corps, a singing quartet that toured Eastern Europe before the fall of the Wall, a trivia game show in which her family had won $5,200—and the most overhyped trip *ever* in the history of game show prizes.

"Let me guess," I said. "They put you up in the Motel 5?"

"Motel 5?"

"It's like a Motel 6. But you have to bring your own cock-roaches."

She was the kind of woman who made you want to make her smile, who smiled even if you didn't deserve it. She smiled.

It was easy conversation. She didn't mind me one bit. When I told her I liked to play midnight golf (sneaking onto the course at night and hitting glow-in-the-dark balls), she said, "I'd like to try that. We should go sometime."

"So how well did you know Annie?"

"Didn't have the privilege," Julie said. "A real tragedy what happened to that girl. How well did you know her?"

I hoped the ache in my chest didn't show.

Two months after that, I went to an oyster bar with Rochelle, a piano teacher when she wasn't doing public relations for the local cable company. She was thirty-two, but the important number was her blood alcohol content, and mine. She plied us both with booze, we made small talk. One segue led to another that led to her apartment.

I'd never bothered to consider bringing a condom. I took the one offered from her bedside drawer with a feeling of inevitability. Afterward, she went into the bathroom to freshen up, and I wiped away a tear. Three months after Annie died, I thought, and I'm in purgatory, fighting back tears while some woman's tabby cat sniffs at the bottom of my still-socked feet.

And so it went. I was sappier than I should have been, than I'd ever expected to be. Angrier.

I eventually found some solace in a woman—not one wielding a bouquet, but a needle. The weapons of the good witch Samantha.

I first experienced her powers about six months after Annie died. Shiatsu massage. Sam laid hands on the leverage points of my tired corpus—the insides of my knees, my ankles, my beltline, and the bony outline of my jaw. Then shot me through with bolts of energy. I graduated to acupuncture, the needle.

Sam knew I was skeptical of the New Age arts. She knew I thought massage was something you got on a hard plastic table at an athletic club. Then she made me a believer. Her treatments were as real as anything I'd learned in Western medical school. They put my world in slow motion. She helped me find something I'd never looked for, or considered. Silence.

When she was done with me on those Sunday nights, and sent me out in the world, it was okay that things were quiet. It was okay that Annie wasn't there, that she was not coming back. And I could see her more clearly; I could see the imperfections that her abrupt, tragic end often distracted me from.

I escalated to meditation, slack-jawed breathing, and acupuncture. I didn't quite become some nut and berry picker and eater. I remained a sometimes judgmental red-blooded American male who believed that the greatest salve to any problem was two shots of tequila and a compact disk compilation of U2's greatest hits.

Sam and Bullseye weren't my only friends. They weren't even the people I spent the most time with. That would have been the fellows from the YMCA. The misfits of Monday, Wednesday, and Friday basketball between 4:30 and 6 p.m. Gym rats. Guys with delusions of great athleticism. And delusions of great social skills. They played imaginary games of one-on-one with visions of supermodels inside their heads. But they had a perverse sense of loyalty to others of their species.

And there was a neighbor. Sanjiv Bubar, a manager of Ant Hill Records. Not that a tiny store hawking used rhythm and blues albums (actual vinyl) needed a manager, but that was his title. Music, by the way, wasn't his deepest passion. His real love was making model airplanes.

He would knock on my apartment door long after the infomercials had taken over the airwaves. I'd find him standing there, stinking like glue and holding a facsimile of a Navy experiment that had flown only two missions over Prague in World War II.

Sanjiv had something in common with the others—with Samantha and Bullseye, and the gym rats. They had hit a plateau in life. They weren't striving or fighting. They had settled in, and they were more or less contented with it, living a life without judgment—of me. If they were judging themselves, they were doing it outside of earshot.

Not like my medical school friends. I still kept in touch with them, but I'd fallen out of their pace. I couldn't muster the energy to care the way they did, or maybe to feign caring the way they did.

One night, I came home late from the Past Time bar and found Sanjiv standing in the doorway of my apartment looking grave. Someone had jimmied into my apartment and robbed the place. The cops said it was going on in the neighborhood, a sign of a new collective dependence on crystal meth.

Gone were several of my big-ticket items: a PlayStation 2, a microwave, stereo, computer, monitor, and printer. All replaceable, except for the work I'd failed to back up. The place was a wreck. Whoever had broken in, the cops said, was probably looking for pot and prescription drugs.

As I looked around the place, I noticed Sanjiv standing beside the refrigerator. I watched as he picked up the picture of Annie and me on the Santa Cruz boardwalk that lay amid the ruins on the floor. He looked at it. He thought I wasn't looking at him, but still he seemed self-conscious when he decided not to put it back on the refrigerator. He slipped it into a drawer in the kitchen. The drawer that keeps the tape, and glue. The thumbtacks. The Tic Tacs. The pictures of dead girlfriends.

I think he was thinking it was time I stopped building replicas of Annie in my mind. Something must have resonated. Maybe it was the tenderness in Sanjiv's decision. I left the picture in the drawer.

Time started to pass normally, no longer at the pace of grief, maybe even faster than it had before. The fog of Annie finally started to clear, after two years.

I got a toehold with my writing, and I amassed a small body of work, including something that actually made me proud.

At San Francisco General Hospital, an elderly (but not decrepit) man had come into the emergency room wearing a black baseball cap with a red Safeway logo on it. He complained of headaches. The doctor, who happened to be a friend from medical school, took off the cap. And found maggots crawling around an exposed part of the man's brain. The insects were actually saving the man's life.

Evidently, the man had gotten into a car wreck months earlier and had cracked open his skull. But whether through age or early dementia or ignorance, he'd not gone to the hospital, despite having exposed a tiny portion of his frontal lobe, the part of the brain responsible for emotion and judgment, among other things. It is possible to live without the lobe intact, as lobotomies attest. It was very likely the missing lobe clouded his judgment so much that he never bothered to go to the hospital.

Meantime, his lobe had gotten infected, which should have killed him, but maggots got there first and began feasting off the bacteria. They kept it from spreading. It was a fascinating conundrum for the doctors of San Francisco General. They had to clean his wound, without allowing bacteria to take hold. They succeeded, and had a great cocktail party story.

Until the doctor told me something else of interest: The man's wife was in the early stages of dementia. After his car

accident, she had called the insurance company, which was obligated to send a care worker out for an in-home visit. It failed
to do so, even after she called several more times (then forgot
about it, thanks to her own dementia).

The couple was not alone in their experience. Thousands of
elderly Californians were not getting the follow-up home care
they were entitled to under their insurance policies. According
to lawsuits, at least four people had died in the previous two
years as a result.

After two months of investigating, I wrote a story in the
California Medical Journal. The story, I was told, prompted
the state legislature to put the heat on insurers.

My stories fed on one another. Work and life took on a
rhythm, and an honesty. There were fewer downs and ups.
There weren't the great joys or pits I'd once known. Maybe I
was growing up.

Or, just maybe, I was being lulled to sleep.

31

Where is Strawberry Labs?"

"Would you believe I might actually know that?" Mike said. "Nat, this isn't for a story you're working on, is it?"

"I need to know where it is."

"I was curious myself. I couldn't find any mention of it on the Net." He typed a few sentences or commands into his keyboard. "But I did do some IP mapping."

Mike said that the author of the encryption software hadn't left any further information in his signature. The signature didn't say the who, what, or where of its author. But the encryption program did provide some indirect evidence of the author's whereabouts.

"Indirect evidence? C'mon, Mike."

"Whenever someone signed on to GNet, they had to get through the encryption program. To do so, they signed on through a remote server."

"A computer located at Strawberry Labs," I said.

"I can't tell you the physical location of Strawberry Labs. But I can tell you the Internet address—I can tell you in rough terms the Internet protocol address used by the company."

He paused.

"You want some ibuprofen?"

I realized I was gripping my neck and rubbing.

"I'm good," I said.

He shrugged.

"When people sign on to the Internet, they do so from a location that has a unique set of numbers. That set of numbers corresponds typically to an Internet service provider."

"Like America Online."

"Like Felton Community Net."

"Felton," I said. "South of San Jose."

He nodded.

Felton.

I wouldn't even have to stop for another tank of gas.

I asked Mike not to say anything about his findings, mumbling something about it being part of an investigative story. I grabbed the laptop and exited Stanford Technology Research Center. On the hood sat Erin. Before I was barely within earshot, she said, "I thought we were in this together."

I muttered, "I thought we were too."

What should I say? What could I say?

At the least, she had neglected to tell me she was accused of felony arson. It didn't seem like a small detail to leave out, given the prominent role fire suddenly was playing in our lives. At the most, Erin had actually committed felony arson, several times.

"My phone went dead," I said.

I sent an e-mail and it bounced back; my phone battery went dead; I didn't get your voice mail, how weird!

If we owe nothing else to the great advances in telecommunications of the twenty-first century, we at least should give it credit for availing us of a myriad of new excuses.

I might as well have told Erin the dog ate my peanut butter and honey homework.

"It rang five or six times every time I called," she said, paused, then added, "Spare me," in a resilient tone I hadn't heard from her before.

"I didn't want to miss the appointment with Mike."

"I was worried about you. Jesus."

I studied Erin's face. Worry, fear. What else?

"I figured you must have come down here," she said. "I wasn't sure where else to look."

"You just figured I'd come down here?"

"What's your problem?"

"What's my problem? My problem is I want to know what the hell is going on."

She balled her fists together. Her eyes flickered.

"We're on the same side here, right?"

She looked at my arm, which I had folded over Andy's laptop. "I want to know what's on the computer too. Did he open the diary? Let me see it."

The diary. Of course. I should have looked in Mike's office—so I might know if there was anything of interest before Erin made her appearance. I put the laptop in the trunk.

"Let's check it out when we get there."

There are silences and then there are silences. The forty-minute drive to Felton started innocently enough, then grew into a silence of the professional variety. Cold, seeping Arctic air. My side wasn't born quite of animosity, but of safety and strategy. I was waiting for an opening to explore, to get a feel, without pressing. Per Danny's admonition, I should have been aiming to keep my conversation with Erin relatively normal, but the best I could muster was a thinly veiled pout.

"Tell me what's wrong," she finally said.

"My head feels like a steel drum at a Bob Marley concert."

The phone rang/vibrated. Battat and Bard. The offices of Murray Bard. Neurologist. Andy's doctor.

"Hello, Dr. Bard."

Dr. Bard made a brief attempt at pleasantries, asking if I'd been a classmate of Dr. Fernandez and whether I was still located in the city. I answered in the affirmative to both questions, technically not a lie even though when Dr. Bard asked about my location he was almost certainly referring to where I practiced medicine.

"I'm between consults," Dr. Bard said. "What can I do for you?"

"I'm calling about Andy . . ."

I looked at Erin. She mouthed, "Goldstein."

". . . Andy Goldstein." Then I switched languages—into doctor.

"Headaches. Insomnia. Rapid cycling of moods. Came in for an EEG."

Dr. Bard took a memory break. He saw hundreds of patients. Without a chart in front of him, they didn't entirely exist.

"He jumped off the Golden Gate Bridge about three weeks ago."

He responded after a pause. "I remember him now. Thin gentleman. Hyper. Not surprising for a meth addict."

Erin hadn't told me anything about Andy using drugs.

"He told you about that," I said, with open-ended intonation.

"Dr. Idle?" said Dr. Bard. "I can't remember—what were you treating Mr. Goldstein for?"

"I wasn't his doctor. Just a friend."

"If you want to come by, I can pull his chart. Call my receptionist to set up a good time."

"Wait, Dr. Bard. I could really use your insights here."

"Please say hello to Dr. Fernandez for me." He hung up.

Erin had been watching me anxiously.

"What was wrong with Andy? What did they do to him?"

They.

"You didn't tell me Andy was taking drugs."

"What?"

"Was Andy a drug addict, Erin? What aren't you telling me?"

"Andy? Drugs? No way. What kind of drugs?"

"Meth. Uppers. The kind of thing that keeps you up all night and makes you walk off a bridge."

Silence.

"What's going on, Erin?"

"Nat, Andy was . . . my best friend. I knew everything about him. He was totally straitlaced," she responded, her voice rising. "Drugs were not his . . ."

"His what?"

"His vice. His vice. He didn't have a single vice in the world, okay? Andy was a good, loving, kind, generous man."

She leaned back and turned her head toward the window.

Half an hour of silence later, we arrived in Felton, which looked more like a movie than a town. I felt like I was on Lot B of Disney, where they shoot scenes of a quaint downtown, shopkeepers spending their coffee break raking leaves.

I went to the one gas station and asked the one middle-aged full-service attendant for directions to the, hopefully, one Internet service provider. Felton Community Net. It was just a few blocks away, the portly man said.

When I pulled up to it, I said to Erin, "I'm sorry in advance for what I'm about to ask."

32

I told Erin that I wanted her to go into the Internet service provider and con them into giving her the address for Strawberry Labs.

She put her hand on my knee and cooed, "I really want to look at Andy's diary."

"We're in a hurry. One thing at a time."

She grabbed a bottled water from the backseat and a manila envelope from my stack of papers. On the envelope, she wrote "Strawberry Labs." She got out of the car and walked into the Internet service provider. There was a kid who looked to be about seventeen years old behind the counter. Just after she walked in the door, Erin tripped, spilling water from the bottle onto the front of her T-shirt. She was good.

As I waited, I thought about Heather Asternak, whom I'd met six months earlier. I'd just wrapped up the story about Timothy Aravelo, and was looking to write about something that had zero chance of yielding a subpoena. Enter Heather, a dermatologist.

I was writing a story about a trend among medical students: In growing numbers, they were abandoning bread-and-butter specialties, like family medicine, in favor of subspecialties like dermatology, where the hours were more manageable and the money much better.

What struck me first about Heather was her heavy makeup—unnecessary given her youth and natural attractiveness. And when, over french fries and lemonade, she gave her reasons for choosing dermatology, she sounded like something she was reading out of a manual.

I asked enough questions to keep the conversation going, then shut up and listened. She told me where she grew up, what drew her to medicine, when she fell into her first love—cooking. We ordered a second round of lemonades. She said how frustrating it was to have a soufflé fall. I nodded, as if to say: There is no perfection.

"You love cooking, don't you?" I said.

She took a big gulp of lemonade. She looked toward the corner of the restaurant. More specifically, she looked away from my eyes.

"I cheated on my boards," she said.

Just like that. I tried not to suck too hard on my straw.

"I've never told a soul."

Heather was technically not a doctor at all, at least as far as the state licensing boards were concerned. She told me that she'd pursued dermatology because she didn't trust her abilities. She thought she could do the least amount of damage.

I never figured out what happened with her. I never told anyone about it. But I stored it away as a valuable insight—a lesson on how to wait out a revelation: (1) Care, and (2) let the source fill in the silences.

That was my plan for Erin, who had performed masterfully with the seventeen-year-old. She told the young man she'd driven down from San Jose to courier some documents to Strawberry Labs, only to realize the office that sent her had left the stupid street address off the envelope. She couldn't get anyone on the phone at the San Jose office, couldn't find Strawberry Labs in the phone book, and wondered if he knew anything about the area. Nope, he couldn't help her. She looked distraught. Anything he could do to help? she asked. She was having a really rough day. Wait, he said. What a coincidence, Strawberry Labs was a customer.

"Three miles into the canyon," Erin said to me coldly.

*   *   *

I stopped at the one coffee shop in town and ordered the tallest, most powerful drink on the chalkboard. Then I asked the
young lady behind the counter to add two shots of espresso.
She was probably wondering: Where is the elephant he's planning to revive?

We wound up the canyon, through an increasingly dense
green forest. Dirt side roads emerged, and our address came
up on the right. We drove a quarter of a mile in through dense
overhang and came to a gate. Behind it were three houses.
The one in the middle was the most modern. It had the look
of a log cabin, but a perfectly manicured one you'd find in the
pages of *Architectural Digest*.

The buildings to its left and right seemed similarly empty.
Or, at least, there were no sounds or movement to indicate that
we were sharing the wilderness. The building on the left was
a rectangular pine shed that stretched fifty feet into the forest.
Probably storage. The building on the right was a single-story
residence, stained dark with red curtains drawn. It looked
sterile. If this had been a campsite, it would have been the in-
firmary. Attached to it was a single-story garage.

"The most sinister bed-and-breakfast I've ever seen," I
said.

Said Erin, "We want the one in the middle."

As I approached the front door, I had a surge of reassurance
and courage. Not from any sudden sense of perspective, or its
loss, but from the sign.

"Strawberry Labs," it read. In small black handwritten letters on a piece of wood hanging by the door from a wire.

It's just a Silicon Valley software company, I thought. Perhaps the arm of something sinister, perhaps not. These were
just engineers. Engineers didn't merit this kind of suspicion.
That's what I told myself as I rapped my knuckles on the door
of the business named after my dead girlfriend's dead dog.

No answer. I rapped again. No answer. Erin pushed open the door. We entered a messy room dominated by a round oak dining table covered with mountains of paper in total disarray, as if someone had come in, found an unkempt pile of papers, and then given it all a good going-over with a leaf blower.

The openings in the middle belonged to two stairwells, just to the right of the front door, one set of stairs going up, one headed down—presumably to the garage.

"Hello," I yelled, then took a step toward the stairs leading upward. "Anyone home?"

No answer. I looked back at Erin. She was looking down the other set of stairs. I turned back toward the stairs heading up, and climbed. At the top, I saw three doors. All closed. The door closest was the one to the left. Instinct drove me to it, or maybe it was the pungent smell.

The door opened easily. My eyes flashed first on a bank of computers. The image gave way quickly. To Plexiglas cages, at least a dozen, more like twenty, stacked four on top of each other. Each with at least one rat, some with five or more.

It took me a moment to realize they were dead. It looked like they were in suspended animation. Their lives had stopped mid-breath, as if the taxidermist had already visited, pulled their stuffing out, and sewed them up.

Only one thing could do this: highly potent poison. A theory verified when I looked to a table to the right and saw a handful of small medicine-sized bottles of strychnine, opened, one tipped on its side. I crept closer to one cage. Near the bottom, in the middle of the stack, five gray rats inside. On the cage, there was a handwritten nameplate: "A6-A10."

I fought a wave of nausea. I pulled my shirt over my mouth—if there was disease here, I'd be well served not to inhale too deeply, though it was probably too late.

Something else told me disease wasn't at play—it was the two bald spots at the top of each rat's head, toward the back of the skull. They'd been shaved, as had their erstwhile compatriots. Cage upon cage, each dead rodent shaved, each with two bald spots exposing rough skull. Except one. The gleam caught my eye. On the top right. B4. Black hair, in a cage by itself. The rat wore a thin metal band around its head, held tightly with screws. Two thin black electrical lines were attached to the back, leading out of the cage. Before I could discern where it led, I heard the scraping noise.

I spun around. How had I not bothered to look in the corner of the room?

One more cage, with one more rat. I moved toward its Plexiglas home. "A11" was still breathing.

"You're going to be okay, little fella," I said.

Had it been poisoned too, and survived, or merely overlooked by the assailant? My emergency training didn't extend to rats. And saving A11 wasn't really the point. What had happened here? Torture? An experiment? Both?

I returned to B4, the black-furred critter with the metal headband.

I'd seen testing labs in medical school. This looked consistent—lots of cages and rats, yielding lots of data. What kind of data? Why?

"Oh God."

It was Erin. I turned around. She had her hands at her mouth. We locked eyes, hers registering terror, then a sudden resolution.

"Nathaniel," she said. "We have to get out of here!"

I looked at her, not grasping her urgency. I turned back and pulled on the cage door.

"Nat. Now," she screamed. "The house is on fire!"

33

"We're going to die in here."

I didn't see or smell anything burning, so I wasn't sharing Erin's urgency. That's when I heard a throaty boom, followed by an aftershock. Something in the bowels of the log structure had exploded. The house turned momentarily into a waterbed. We swayed. I fell to my left, losing my grip on the cage, touching a knee to the floor.

I was bathed in heat. A swirl of dangerous and cruel air surged up the stairwell.

"The basement," Erin said. "There was a pool of gasoline by the furnace."

She pulled at my shoulder again.

The basement. It sounded so distant when she said it. Two floors and three galaxies away.

"I need a second to figure out what happened."

"No, we have to get out of here."

I followed each of the wires connected to B4's head to where they led. Nowhere. They lay on the ground in back of the cages, unattached to anything. But each had a little tag. One wire had the word "stim," the other read "wave."

I started pulling at the door to B4's cage, to lift it. It was locked to the cage beneath. All the cages were attached. I needed a tool.

"Dammit."

"Leave it," Erin shouted.

I didn't respond.

"Give me the car keys."

"Help me look, Erin."

"I'm leaving. Now."

Erin stood by a window overlooking the front of the house, staring resolute and contemptuous. She caught my eye, then turned to look out the window.

"Look!"

"What?"

She was pointing.

"Nat!"

Another burst of hot air surged from the stairwell. And I looked where she pointed, out the window. A spit of flame jumped up in staccato leaps like a spring of orange water.

"I know. It's a tinderbox. I need your help, Erin."

"No!"

No, it's not a tinderbox? Or, no, she wouldn't help?

"Look! A car—driving out of the gate," she said. "Please. We have to go. Now! Move, or give me the car keys and stay here and play detective yourself."

I couldn't respond. I couldn't be drawn away from the room. I wanted to have control over one goddamn thing. All the helplessness of the preceding few days felt like it had come down to this moment. What had happened here?

Erin was pointing out the window. I saw a single flame whisk at the top of the edge of the window. And I felt a brush of heat graze the bottom of my feet. I moved closer to the window to look for what Erin had seen. There was nothing. Maybe it was hidden from view. Maybe it had already made its escape.

Arson.

Erin.

"Erin, did you . . ." I said. "Did you? . . ."

"What?" she said. Not hearing, or understanding, or pretending not to.

I shook my head. No way. My brain felt muddled and fuzzy. No time to think. No clarity. I looked at Erin. She caught my eye, then started moving. Sprinting. But it looked like slow motion.

She bounded down the stairs.

I took a step to follow her.

Then turned around. I wanted a second look at the operation center called Strawberry Labs. Was there anything I could imprint? Any clue? Anything I could testify to later?

I swiveled my head across the lab. Everything blurred together. Rats, medical equipment, a bank of computers, nothing discernible. No smoking gun.

I gave a final glance to the still living rat, the hearty soul known as A11. I yanked open its cage door. The critter scampered out and I pushed it off the table. It ran three steps, stopped, sniffed, fled to the stairs, slid down a step, stopped again, and pulled itself back up, then began frantically circling the room. Under the edge of its cage, something caught my eye. Pinned beneath was a tattered piece of paper. I reached two fingers through the bars. The paper looked to have names and numbers. It was technical, with decimal points, and something familiar. At the bottom, the scrawled words: "Password—Vestige."

I clenched my teeth in thought, and I felt piercing warmth. On my feet.

The floor was on fire.

The baseboard was pulsing red—the foreplay just before the real heat started.

I stuffed the piece of paper in my front pocket.

"Time to go."

I looked back at the stairwell and saw a lick of flame. I took a step to the stairs. A surge of black smoke billowed out of the opening. Danger.

The window.

I looked to my left, above a table holding a computer monitor. Another window. Overlooking the side of the cabin. I jogged to it. I peered outside. Flames surged more persistently up the side of the house, though still not regularly enough to form a wall. They seeped from the garage. Or maybe even the first floor.

I yanked the monitor off the table and tossed it through the window. Cool air. I toppled the table.

I moved to the window. Suddenly, an explosion and a surge of flames. I looked down. Fire bathed the house's side. If I jumped, I was leaping into a cauldron. I looked back at the stairs. Smoke churned from the stairwell. I sprinted toward it, and got rebuffed by a surge of flame, jutting up toward me.

That's when I realized the full extent of my mess. I could see that eight stairs down, the stairwell took a ninety-degree turn. It meant I had visibility about halfway; if I made it the first eight steps, I would turn the corner into an uncertain fate.

I looked back at my surroundings. I'd remembered something—about the room, and about medical training 101. There it was. Under the table I'd overturned—a small green-and-blue area rug.

I yanked at the rug, dragged it back to the stairs, and wrapped it around my shoulders.

"Now or not at all."

I took a step toward the top of the stairs. I pulled the rug over my shoulders. I realized that the moment I turned the corner on the stairs, I'd have to make a decision: If the fire wasn't too bad, I'd walk out the front door; if it was bad, wrap myself and roll. And pray.

I took a step toward the stair and felt a dying man's last wishes. Let me live long enough to find out what happened to Annie.

I took the next step, the wool rug wrapped around my

shoulders, dragging down from my back and behind me like a cape. Smoke streamed around me. I took the final step before the turn of the stairs in silence, then heard an explosion. A burp from the guts of the house. Something highly flammable had caught fire. The explosion had a domino effect. The noise was followed by a burst of heat and a stream of fire—coming around the corner, right at me. Instinctively, I fell back onto the stairs. I began sliding on the rug. Back down the stairs. I braced my foot against the wall.

I flailed frantically, grabbing for a wooden rail. I snagged it, succeeding in slowing my descent, then I halted the slide altogether. I used the leverage to pull myself to my feet.

I stepped back toward the turn in the stairs, then turned the corner. Flames were covering the first floor and the staircase just a foot below me.

Eight steps separated me from the floor.

I pulled at the corner of the rug and yanked it toward me, turning into a human enchilada wrapped in woven wool. I let myself fall backward. I pulled the rug on top of me, rolled, and saw a life flash before my eyes. Not mine, Sonny Ellison's. For just a nanosecond, I thought of a young man who had come into the emergency room when I was a medical student. His Civic had dived fifty feet over the edge of Sea Cliff onto the rocks. The gas tank exploded. Ellison lived, and I never forgot him, or what the human body could sustain in pursuit of its own survival, like the bumps slamming into me as I rolled down the stairs. And suddenly stopped.

I was at the bottom of the stairs, consumed with heat.

I flung open the rug from around my shoulders. I'd hoped it would stamp out the flames in my immediate vicinity, plaster them to the ground.

I got lucky. The rug opened toward the door. The ultimate red carpet.

The porch was hot, but not engulfed in flames. I tumbled down two concrete stairs and fell onto the gravel in front of what would soon be the ashes of Strawberry Labs.

There was Erin. Ashen-faced, covered in char, standing beside the car.

"What the hell is going on, Erin?"

"Thank goodness. I thought you were going to die."

I ambled toward her, trying to gauge her expression. Sincerity? Fear? Outright manipulation?

Suddenly, I grabbed her by the shoulders.

"What are you doing, Nat?"

"You left me in there to die."

"You're crazy. You're freaking out."

She spun away from me, insisting she'd seen a red sports car leave the property. "We have to go!" she said. Dazed, I climbed into the car. The house was gurgling and bursting. A surge of heat bathed us. Then another wave, this one internal. A fierce pulsing, the headache again. Erin pulled the keys from my hand and put them in the ignition. I kept her from starting the car. I looked back at the compound, the house in the middle now ablaze.

"What happened to Annie?" I said.

"What the hell are you talking about?"

"What's Vestige?"

She turned the keys in the ignition.

I said, "Time for the police."

I sped down the mountain, looking for a phantom sports car and a cell phone signal. I couldn't find either. Just before Felton's town center, there was a four way stop. A road sign said it was ten miles to Santa Cruz. It might be impossible to go back in time, but you can at least visit. Time for a trip down memory lane.

"You like fire," I said coldly. "You like to see things burn?"

The rat lab, the café, a pornography studio, Simon Anderson's house.

"What are you talking about?" Erin said.

"Let's start simple."

"Simple?"

"I want to know the real reason you didn't like Simon Anderson," I said.

It had been kicking around in my head, a relative coldness in the way she described him, the fact that she didn't get out of the car at his funeral, or when the Anderson house burned down, looking at the ruins of someone she had known well. It didn't seem like her style, even if, as she said, Simon Anderson had been a player.

"I really don't know what you're talking about."

"Now, Erin."

I turned the car toward Santa Cruz.

Silence.

Finally, she said, "How did you know?"

34

Erin pulled her knees up to her chest. She was looking out the window with a distant, defeated stare.

I hadn't *known* Erin had lied to me, but I'd suspected, even before Danny's warning.

"He didn't get that far under your skin just because he flirted with the waitstaff," I said.

Erin turned to me.

"The Napa mud gave him away."

Napa. The epicenter of Northern California's wine country, three hours due north of our current location. Maybe Erin liked to start her confessions in the middle.

"At the Four Seasons, they keep the mud baths ninety degrees, so the minerals get good and baked into your skin. Simon called it the 'dirt shirt,'" she said. "I told you Simon was a word person. And a lying son of a bitch.

"He didn't tell me he was married for three months."

Erin said they met almost immediately after she started working at the café. He came in almost every day, ordered a caramel latte and wrote on his laptop, and checked his stock prices on one of the café's three Internet computers. He made friends with everyone. They were drawn to his charm and wealth, which he commented on just enough to establish its existence. He was witty and sure of himself and Erin didn't have anything else going on.

They kept the whole thing private. He never invited her to his house. They spent weekends away from San Francisco together—in Napa, drinking and bathing in mud. It turned out that those were the weekends his wife took their autistic son to a special clinic at UCLA. Eventually, he got caught by his wife, or so he claimed, and came clean with Erin. Over time, she came to see this was serial behavior.

"He was a sinner to his core," she said.

Andy came along shortly after. He and she experienced a much different attraction, the strongest one Erin had felt. "He was the first person who made me feel that the lifestyle I was living was okay. When I moved from Michigan, I knew someone like him was out there."

They had a fling too, but it didn't stick and gave way to something more than that—mostly platonic and deep.

"Six months ago, he started getting distant," Erin said.

It correlated with a time that Simon and Andy became good friends. Both men liked to talk about books and writing. Andy started babysitting for Simon's kids. He wanted a family of his own.

"What does that have to do with you, Erin? C'mon," I said, filling in the silence that followed. "You were jealous? Is that it?"

"No."

"He was your best friend, and your relationship got strained, and then he died. It was easy to blame Simon."

"You're reaching."

"Enlighten me."

"You couldn't possibly understand," she protested quietly. "What Simon did was so terribly cruel."

"Did he kill Andy?"

"I'm not sure."

"What makes you think it was even a possibility?"

"Simon was a seducer and a manipulator. He got inside

Andy's head. Andy got depressed. He felt so conflicted. Alone."

"Enough to kill himself."

"I need to see the diary," she said.

The phone rang. It was Danny. The reception was choppy. "Turn . . . news. Radio . . . news." I was hearing every third word. I told him to call me back. I told Erin to find a news station.

I saw an unpaved entrance to a cove beside the Santa Cruz pier, the cove where I'd watched a flotilla and an amphibious team try to find Annie's remains. A sign read, "Emergency Vehicles Only." I drove in.

Maybe I just wanted to pretend the last four years hadn't happened. Maybe I wanted to go back *before* Annie. At least before I got the excruciating headache. Maybe it was the thick sea air, but it felt like the insides of my brain were pushing against my skull. The linebackers that had been dancing *Swan Lake* on my spinal column had taken steroids. My eye twitched, my legs were cramping.

Erin found a news station.

"A major development in the investigation of this week's café explosion in San Francisco."

I slammed on the brakes and put my hands on top of Erin's, for the purpose of stopping her from changing the dial. I had reached a clearing where road met beach. I looked out over a gorgeous blue sea.

"Sources at the San Francisco Police Department said they are looking for two people in connection with the explosion, which took at least five lives. Police sources said they want to question a San Francisco resident and a café employee who survived the blast. Police declined to say whether the people are official suspects or what their motive might have been. We will provide details of this remarkable breaking story as they emerge."

Two possible suspects, sitting in my car—an employee, and a San Francisco resident. Could there be any doubt who they meant?

And I knew goddamn well I hadn't blown up the cafe.

Were the cops on the same page?

I felt a surge of excruciating pain. A migraine, I thought. It felt like my skull was peeling back, letting a harsh wind scream through the opening. I opened my door just in time. I threw up.

I picked my chin off the ground and looked at Erin. She was stone-faced.

"Did you?"

"Did I what?" she said. "Did I *what*?!"

The light hurt. I closed my eyes and squinted.

"What about Michigan, Erin? The fire?! Goddammit! What aren't you telling me?"

She responded by opening her door. She stepped outside and started walking.

"Erin!"

But I couldn't continue, or follow her. Whatever it was that was tormenting me, it had won. I leaned out the door. I purged again. Bile and stale air pouring out in heaves.

Seconds later—or maybe minutes—I heard a noise. I lifted my eyes. I caught a reflection in the rearview mirror. Of flashing lights. I turned my head to look at the newest visitor. A police car had parked behind me, blocking my escape.

35

As the cop exited his car and walked toward me, I wiped my chin and considered my options. According to the radio, I was wanted in connection with the explosion of a quaint San Francisco neighborhood café. If the officer knew this, I probably was going to be arrested. That seemed like a rotten way to spend such a cloudless day, or the next forty years.

That left my alternatives as lying or leaving in a hurry. I didn't like my chances either way.

"You okay, sir?"

Sir.

"This beach is restricted," he said, walking to the driver's side door. "Eighty-five-dollar fine. But you look like you could use a break."

I looked up to find a giant mustache and ears. The cop didn't exceed five and a half feet. But he had the facial hair of a man twice that size. A handlebar mustache, and round ears protruding from the sides of his cap. I wondered if it might be from acromegaly, a condition that causes facial features to get coarse and pronounced over time.

"Tempting to come down this way," he said. "But I tell ya—when the tide gets high, it's a son of a gun out here."

I told him I'd get out of the way. But he started right in chatting about what a beautiful day it was, and what a terrific view. In San Francisco, you get used to everyone being in such a rush, but Officer Ears just wanted to take a few minutes to reflect and sip a cool lemonade on the porch.

I fought off the nausea and took a chance on his goodwill. I told him that I'd lost a friend in a boating accident about four years earlier and was wondering how I might find out more about the accident—could I get incident reports or the like?

He said I could do a Freedom of Information Act request, if I wanted to wait for a couple of months, or I could try to talk to the officer in charge of the investigation. He said I could ask the clerk at the Santa Cruz Police Department. He said I could use his name.

First, I had another stop. By the side of the road. I turned on Andy's laptop and called up his diary. I combed through pages of seemingly innocuous entries typed in shorthand. The short entries appeared to span a couple of years, though they were denoted by day and time, not by date and year.

> **Thursday, 10:10; saw art flick with e. (playful). I ask you: is the definition of an art movie anything that has moral ambiguity . . . another run-in with d-wad. Only reason he runs the dept is no one else wants it. Position does not equal wisdom.**

> **Sunday, midnight or thereabouts. head cold. Hate taking meds. Can't let it keep a fellow down tho. Got research done at Sunshine, napped in car for an hour, bowling with S. (2nd gm = 210).**

I mostly skimmed, until I got toward the end. I was drawn by a couple of entries with a word in all caps. It read:

> **Dinner with the wiz over bridge. parked in the headlands. YOWZA.**

Then a week later.

> Friday night in san anselmo on wiz's dime. Ate lobster
> and a fat choc souffle and one thing led to another. Are
> you kidding, asks I? An unequivocal no. woke up at 8 and
> didn't get out of bed untl 2.

Then:

> bought the new j. mayer at Amoeba. Copied for wiz
> and got smiles and admonitions (cool!). Worked out with
> free pass at gym du gorilla. Told e id meet for dinner then
> bagged out. deadlines, deadlines

I did a search back through the document. I found the first
entry that mentioned the wizard.

> Wednesday: 6—book shopping in am. Afternoon at
> the 'shine. met book writer of kids' fantasy. proofread my
> summary; too many adjectives says he. Helpful grammat-
> ical wizard. (face man)

I turned it over in my head. "e" could be Erin; who was
the Wizard? Simon Anderson? He was a book writer. Had
something happened between the Andy and the Wizard? Was
it obvious?

The computer beeped. The battery life was waning.

I looked toward the end of the diary. The entries seemed to
reinforce Erin's reports. Toward the end, more capital letters
caught my eye.

> Wiz sick too. Headaches. He's pissed. Or something
> to do with a new flame? Who is Tara? Whatever, whatever
> WHATEVER.

The computer beeped again. I looked at the clock. There

was still time to get to the Santa Cruz PD. I'd have to finish probing Andy's personal life later.

My head was spinning. I couldn't shake the tremors and nausea. Other than exhaustion, no ready diagnosis came to mind. They say a lawyer who represents himself in trial has a fool for a client. They also say: Physician, heal thyself. Why are doctors expected to be more adept self-service professionals than attorneys?

The clerk at the Santa Cruz Police Department must have been thirsty—there were five empty diet Coke cans on her desk. Maybe the caffeine was why she gave me her full attention. Or I looked just as brutalized as I felt and she took pity. Maybe it helped my cause that, moments after I arrived, Officer Ears walked by and said hello to me. "Give this fella our top-notch service," Ears told the clerk, with a smile. The clerk listened to my plea but said that unless I knew the case number, she probably couldn't give me the name of the cop who investigated Annie's death. I did have the exact date. She clicked and clacked around her database. She told me the search would take more time. After five minutes more of poking around, she said she could she call me when and if she found something. I gave her my cell phone number.

I pointed the car back to San Francisco, and phoned Danny. He sounded particularly professional as he informed me the police wanted to interview me. He asked me if I wanted to meet him so he could escort me into the station. I said I would think it over. Then he hit me with the bombshell. He said the police knew I'd been hanging out with Erin and that was problematic.

"They found explosive residue at her apartment," Danny said.

"Someone was attempting to blow her place up?"

"Someone was using her place to make explosives."

A few minutes later, a couple of miles out of town, my phone rang.

"Where are you?" Erin said. "You're really not planning to leave me here, are you?"

"You need to turn yourself in."

"I didn't blow up the café. I swear to you. Nathaniel. Please. I am begging you. You have to believe me."

"They found explosives at your apartment."

"No." She was crying.

"Who are you working for? Who are you working with?"

"Please come get me," she said, now sobbing. "I can explain."

36

I called Samantha and asked her and Bullseye to meet me at the acupuncture studio in Daly City in ninety minutes, explaining I needed their help.

Then I drove to the Santa Cruz bus station, where Erin had said she'd be waiting, and indeed, she was standing outside, looking like she had nothing left to give, or lose. I asked her to remove her jacket and I did my best imitation of someone at airport security. I let her get in the car.

"Start talking."

"What do you want from me?"

"Is Annie alive?"

"I swear to you, I have no idea. I've never met Annie. I've never seen Annie. I think you're losing it, Nathaniel."

"Romp Studios."

For a moment, silence.

"How do you know about that?" Suddenly sharp.

I reached into my wallet and pulled out the arson report Danny had found.

Erin was crying again, but she finally started talking. "The third year of my marriage got really brutal" was how she started her story.

It wasn't so much that her husband hit her, which he didn't do all that often; it was what the future held: a lifetime in purgatory. He wanted kids and she secretly took the pill.

"The bloodline stops here," she said.

She stopped talking to her mother and any friends who might hold a mirror up to her. She devoted herself to church, where she was befriended by two women, one of them a mother of five kids who was sickly sweet but fire and brimstone. The woman blamed everything on forces destroying families.

"I don't know why, but I confided in her. About everything—about taking birth control, and having trouble in the marriage. I wanted absolution, or maybe to get caught," Erin said.

The woman invited Erin to join her on a crusade—to sneak late at night into a small office park on the outskirts of town. A back office belonged to Romp Studios. The woman first asked Erin to go, then threatened to tell her husband about the birth control if she didn't.

"So you were forced?"

"I swear I wish I could say that. I took a gasoline can and poured it over everything. I went crazy. I told myself that the men who hired women to do sex movies were just like my husband."

When she was caught, Erin said, she copped a plea and turned state's evidence.

"It made me hate myself even more," she said quietly. "I was a pawn in everybody's everything. I ceased to exist as a person."

My gut told me that Erin was telling the truth. It didn't exonerate her; she was capable of great violence. Maybe something at the café had set her off again.

"Tell me about Simon and Andy."

"Will you help save me?"

"You made your bed, Erin."

"I didn't do anything. The cops want me. Aravelo's been calling me every day. But *I swear to you* I'm innocent."

So Aravelo had been on to Erin. Of course. I was interested in the why.

"Did Simon and Andy have an affair?"

Erin nodded. By then it came as little revelation.

At first Andy was babysitting for the Andersons. She thought the two men had writing in common. She denied to herself that Andy seemed drawn to Simon—because she saw Simon as such a jerk and Andy as such a good friend. It dawned on her slowly that Andy was probably gay. That might explain why their own physical relationship was so short-lived. He finally confided in her—about Simon, and how it wasn't his first encounter with a man. Simon seemed relatively safe; married and interested only in conquest. Still, Andy was hurt when Simon blew him off completely. Erin said she felt betrayed too.

"And then he started getting angry, and tired, and mean," Erin said.

"Was Simon having headaches too? Or acting strange?"

She shrugged. "Yeah, I think. Maybe. Andy said something was bothering Simon. I don't know."

"Was there someone named Tara at the café?"

"No. What are you talking about?"

"I need to know."

"He slept with a lot of people. I've never heard of Tara."

She seemed genuine in her uncertainty about the woman Andy had mentioned in his diary.

"You're not telling me everything."

"What do you want from me?" Erin said. "Andy had been my best friend. And then suddenly he wasn't. He was a stranger."

"And you blamed Simon."

"How else can you explain it? How else can someone who is your best friend in the world turn against you? He was the first and only person to really understand what I was trying to become. He let me be weak. He didn't press. He didn't take advantage. Then he got sick, and frantic, and . . . he died."

"That's why you did it."

"No."

"You lit those fires, didn't you?"

"No, Nathaniel."

"Just admit it, Erin."

"Stop! Stop it!" she said. "You're acting just like Andy."

I already was on the edge when my cell phone rang. It was the clerk from the Santa Cruz Police Department. She had come up with the name of the officer who investigated Annie's death. Suddenly, upon hearing the name, I realized there was no one in the world I could trust.

37

The first time I almost died from delirium, I was seven years old. I was sleeping on sheets with bright red fire trucks soaked through with sweat. My temperature had hit 105 degrees. I was so sick and delirious that I didn't have the strength to cry. Luckily, my mother came to check on me. She called the doctor, who told her to pack me into a bathtub of ice. I remember looking up at my mother from the bathtub and thinking: She really loves me.

The symptoms I felt acutely in Santa Cruz were not letting up, so I put Erin behind the wheel and scribbled directions to the Daly City studio. I lay down in the backseat and used a pair of gym shorts for a pillow. I was a six-foot nerve ending. I felt each bump in the road, each piece of gravel embedded in my skin. The sounds of passing cars became feverish images.

Annie sat on the dock. Her feet dangled over the water. She held a mouse by its tail. A dark figure took shape below the water. It leapt. It broke the surface of the water in a splash. It snagged the mouse in its mouth. It was me.

"No!" I screamed.

I felt a hand on my face. "It's the liver," said a voice.

I opened my eyes. Samantha was touching my cheek. Her other hand was probing my body. Like a doctor checking a child for an appendix.

"C'mon, sweetie. We'll get you fixed right up."

I tried to protest. We had to go. There was no time for acupuncture or whatever the Witch had in mind. In my delirium, my subconscious had been at work. Some things had begun to fall into place—as unbelievable as they seemed. On wobbly knees, I walked to the trunk, pulled out the computer.

"I'm fine," I said.

Erin took a step toward me. So did Samantha. I surveyed my compatriots. Samantha, granola and tofu incarnate. Bullseye, a human protractor with jagged edges. Erin . . . a striking balance—between dignity and vulnerability. Wasn't she?

I stumbled. Erin moved forward quickly. She held out her hands. I took them. What was wrong with me?

"I'm sorry I doubted you," I said.

She squeezed my hands.

I felt a spasm of pain in my head. I collapsed.

38

Samantha's alchemy defied all the conventions I'd learned growing up. It mocked my medical training. True, medical students learn respect for the unexpected. The divine. The weird. That's one reason the most oft-heard phrase among doctors is: "I can't rule anything out."

Doctor, is it possible this surgery could lead to complications?

I seriously doubt it, but I can't rule anything out.

Doctor, can some self-taught spiritual guru reeking of herb-based deodorant poke needles into my back and pull me from the brink of collapse?

I seriously doubt it, but I can't rule anything out.

I lay on an acupuncture table in Samantha's studio.

The walls had a maroon hue. Soft light shone from a lamp with a white Japanese shade. A foot table near the door held incense and a CD player.

She pressed the play button on the CD player. The room came alive with the ethereal sounds of flutes and a distant wind. I had a hazy memory of Bullseye carrying me onto the table.

I pushed up on my palms.

"I have to go, Sam," I said. "There's no time."

My instinct told me I had to move, to act. But my brain was too foggy to remember or piece together why. The laptop, it had to do with that, and the café, and Erin and me wanted for murders that someone else committed. Rotten police, and a gnawing feeling that, given all the violence, Annie really was dead, and not from an accident but as part of some conspiracy I couldn't see and that now was visiting me. But it hurt too much to try to put it together.

She put a hand on the back of my neck. She held it there. For more than a minute. I relaxed my arms, my resolve melted.

"Let go now," she said.

My bare chest felt cool against crisp white sheets. The music began to make its way into my consciousness. I flashed back. To the dozens of other times Samantha had worked her witchery. I always was conscious of the first pinpricks. They reinforced my skepticism. But slowly, I would focus instead on the music. The notes carried me away. I would float along with them, imagining them as animate objects, mostly animals, like brightly colored elephants and chimpanzees and flying fish.

Eventually, I laughed. No matter the stress in my life. Samantha said it was the proof that I'd let go of the stress. Spit out the poison from my viscera and cleared my eyes, nose, throat, gullet, and windpipe.

Can the Witch save me?

I can't rule anything out.

Samantha put the first pins into me. I blanched. It was more painful than I remembered—white heat puncturing my taut outer casing.

I flashed on the cages. Rats locked up, ignited into a funeral pyre. Samantha put a pin inside my elbow. I nearly jumped off the table.

She again put her hand on the back of my neck. Her fingers rough, but pointed. They found their button. Slowly, I felt calmer. She kept her hand there. She put a needle into the fold behind my knee.

I began to feel the music flow like syrup. My lips turn slightly upward into a smile. The Witch was in control. "Time to let you cook."

I barely heard Samantha's words. It meant she had filled me full of needles, and set them to conduct vibrations and heat. The pins were connected through thin wires to an electrical system. It made some pins warm and others vibrate. Crazy, but I didn't question the Witch.

I heard her leave the room.

As she left the room, I entered a tunnel filled with soaring harmonies. I saw floating notes and strange animated creatures on the horizon. Time passed. Seconds. Minutes. A millennium.

Eventually, I felt the door open. I must, I thought, be fully cooked. I smiled limply and didn't bother to open my eyes. Samantha would tell me when it was time to come back to life. I felt a hand graze the back of my neck. Then grip it. Rougher than usual.

"Where is the laptop?" said a man's voice.

Samantha?

I began to lift my head. First slowly, in a haze. Then with a jerk. I didn't get very far. The hand around my neck pinned me to the table.

That's when I experienced a stab of excruciating pain.

Whoever was pinning me down had pushed an acupuncture needle into the square of my back.

"There isn't much time," the man said, sounding almost gentle. "Where is the laptop?"

Andy's laptop, I thought. Hadn't I given it to Bullseye?

He pushed the needle deeper. I screamed.

39

Suddenly, blessed relief. The man steering the needle extracted it from the middle of my back. Mercy. Pain's most wicked incarnation.

Someone was holding down my neck, while someone else restrained my feet.

"Andy's laptop. Where is it?" said the man holding on to my neck.

He took a needle and reinserted the tip into the base of my neck. I could feel it break the skin, and for an instant I imagined the cells dividing. But he didn't push very hard, just enough for me to feel my muscle's desperate resistance.

"What happened to Annie?" I breathed out.

He responded by applying pressure, slow but persistent. I saw a flash of white. I realized it was only the start. He could hit a major vessel and, at some point, my spinal column.

I looked to my right. I could see a pant leg, blue fabric. I reached for it and pulled, weakly attacking. He twisted the needle, and I pulled back, the leg moving easily outside my grasp.

"We'll tell you what you want to know when you tell us where the computer is," said the person holding my feet.

I recognized the voice, just at the same moment that I realized something about the person holding down my head. On his arm, near his elbow, was a red rash, scaly. Psoriasis. It all jibed with what the clerk from the Santa Cruz Police Department had told me.

They were partners. Velarde had been the behemoth cop who had investigated Annie's drowning. He was doing the intravenous work on my neck while Danny Weller tightened the grip on my feet.

Amazingly, Samantha's treatment had actually had an impact. I was feeling the most clearheaded I'd been in days.

"This is making me sick," Velarde suddenly said, easing off. He pulled out a pair of cuffs and locked my right arm to the table.

"What are you doing?" Danny asked him.

"This New Age shit is making my brain hurt."

Velarde turned off the CD player and put on the radio. He tuned in to a light rock radio station. I was going to be tortured to the soaring sounds of Celine Dion.

"This one is for Timmy Aravelo," Officer Velarde said. The cop I'd helped put in jail for battery. He began twisting a needle on top of my right shoulder—preparing it for deep insertion and a direct shot into muscle.

"Ease off, Ed," Danny said. "Aravelo was a blight. Like his brother."

"Brothers in arms," Velarde responded. "Besides, don't forget who's paying your medical bills."

Whitney Houston came on the radio singing "The Greatest Love of All," and Velarde started to hum along. He steadied a needle against my neck. I could feel him about to press it in again. I winced in anticipation and realized the extent of my fear; Samantha had placed at least a dozen needles all over my backside. He could pierce my lower back, the inside of my elbow, the tender flesh behind my knee. I felt woozy, like I might pass out.

"Tell me what I need to know," he said. "Or you can take the eternal swim in the Pacific with your girlfriend."

I couldn't muster a response.

"We'll get there, Edward," Danny said, calming his partner.

He loosened the grip on my feet, but held them tight enough to prevent me from getting up.

"Listen, Nathaniel," he said. "I tried to get you to cooperate. But these guys—they don't have a lot of patience."

He was the good cop again.

"We just ran out of time. And they were getting pretty angry with all the poking around you were doing."

"Danny, tell me—what do they want? What does Glenn Kindle want? Give a dying man a little parting gift."

He brushed past me.

"So if you'll just help us out and get us that fairy's laptop back, we can all go about our business."

"Okay," I said. "Hold on. Let me catch my breath."

I felt his grip loosen. Was there any possibility of escape?

"Aravelo—they didn't reopen the investigation into him," I said. "You made that up, Danny."

I felt him cuff my leg to the table.

"That's right. I needed to create some trust between us."

"Yeah, okay, you needed information. I get it. A little misdirection is one thing," I said. "But *this* isn't you."

Danny let go of my right leg. I yanked at it and got two inches off the table before the metal bit into me.

"This is useless. Have at him," Danny said.

"What could she possibly be thinking?" Velarde said, as Whitney Houston was hitting the big key change in the final chorus. "How could she marry a jackass like Bobby Brown?"

I tried one more appeal to Danny.

"You're a compassionate man, Sergeant. All that stuff about your father. Was this the son he raised?"

He'd talked at length about his relationship to his ailing dad. A torturer didn't do that, did he?

"It'll make him feel better to get the money for his new liver," he said, then added quietly, "I've made up my mind."

"Enough," Velarde said. "I'm giving you one more chance. We'll put you to sleep, just like the waitress."

"Erin?"

"I did you a favor with her," Velarde said offhandedly. "They found some nasty shit at her apartment."

"What are you talking about? It was planted, right?"

"You're still way behind the eight ball, buddy boy."

"What the hell are you talking about!?"

I started struggling again, now maniacally. Velarde let out a rodeo whoop. I realized he must still be screwing with my head about Erin, just before the pain began to set in. He put his thumb onto the needle. I took a flyer.

"Wait. Is this more fun than killing lab rats?"

"Quiet down, Sherlock."

"*You* burned down the lab. You destroyed the evidence of that . . . freaky neurology experiment," I said, fishing. "You killed those poor animals and torched the place. You are a crazy . . . fuck."

If any part of me still doubted how dire my straits were, the denial was quickly disappearing.

"Interesting theory," he said.

I felt the needle start to sink into my skin.

"You're right about one thing. I'm a crazy fuck. Now, where is the laptop?"

I gripped the sides of the legs of the table, bracing for pain. I found my mind wandering—to the hero algorithm. I calculated. Was there any way to save myself, or should I go down in a hail of false bravado?

I could tell them I'd given the laptop to Bullseye. They'd probably then hunt him down, and bounce anvils off his head until he confessed to the computer's whereabouts. As a bonus, I figured once they got what they needed out of him and me, they'd bleed us both.

Alternatively, I could play tough, or mute. I could spare Bullseye and probably Samantha. Besides, how many chances do you get to be a hero?

From the radio, the sultry voice of Norah Jones filled the

room. Just as Danny joined the act. I felt him press gently on a needle stuck into the fleshy part of my calf.

"Danny, there are half a dozen people who know I've been talking to you," I said. "You'll be the first place they look."

Velarde tightened his grip on my neck. I fought for air.

"Idle threats." Danny sounded tired and resigned.

"Please."

"Last chance, Vance."

It was hopeless.

I said, "I can't." As much bravery as I could muster.

I felt the pressure lessen on my neck. Velarde leaned in close. "I warned you."

I gripped the sides of the table in preparation. I was not disappointed. Velarde found his leverage on the needle poked into my neck. Then, finally, it came. Full force. He shoved down like he was digging for China. I wondered if he'd found my spinal column, in an odd moment of intellectual curiosity. And a surreal, unspoken plea: Why couldn't I be killed to Springsteen?

Then white-hot agony. Just before I passed out, Velarde removed the needle. The relief was instant. Consuming.

"I'm just getting a better grip," Velarde said. "Here comes the fat lady."

I let my mind flow free. I indeed imagined a lady. A beautiful, dark-skinned angel. Annie. I reached to her, looked into her eyes, and searched them for an answer.

When I felt the needle enter my body, I opened my throat and let out a wild cry. Nothing came out. Nothing was left.

In the far distance, I heard a click, clack, click of an ethereal Peace Train. Underneath its wail, a voice, "I'll finish him," and the sound of a metallic click. The last thing I heard was a series of pops. Commotion. Then blackness.

40

Death is a blonde with a gun. She looks familiar.

Soft light surrounds her. It attaches to her skin like bread crust. It bends and warps when she rubs salve on your wounds. When she puts the pill on your tongue. When she rights your limp body.

She says, "This will help you sleep."

Maybe everyone sees the same vision.

Then she leaves. But not before she puts something in your lap.

A cell phone. Even in death, a phone.

41

The pharmaceutical industry has figured out sleep. It's dreams they can't do a damn thing about.

Sleeping pills do a great job of shutting down the brain; unfortunately, that's not the essence of good rest. When dolphins sleep, they shut down half their brain while the other half stays alert. It's partly because in the ocean the predators work taxicab hours; it's also so the dolphins can play. So too, our brains get refreshed by the surreal romps of our deepest journeys into sleep.

I had descended into a dreamless, timeless place as bleak as death. But you don't wake up from death, or, if you do, it probably doesn't hurt as much as the pain I felt when I found myself in the fetal position on the bloodstained floor of Samantha's studio.

I peeled open an eye. The heavy grog of hangover encircled my brain. Suddenly pierced by a shooting pain when I shifted the weight from arm to back. "Holy Mother Shit," I groaned.

I fell back on my stomach, turned my head to the right, and said, "Still ticking."

Images suddenly returned in chunks.

Gunshots. Velarde falling. A sandal, beneath a jeans-clad leg. A cool hand—turning my face to the side. Hazel eyes, exploring. Then blackness.

Did the blonde angel subdue Velarde and Danny? Did she kill them? I put my elbows on Samantha's table. I breathed deeply, sucking in the sweet, stale air of combat. More images came this time, held together with synaptic rope. The woman cleaned and sterilized my wounds, removed my manacles, gave me pills. I told her I'd seen her before. In response, she'd handed me a cell phone.

"We'll call you," she said. "Rest."

We. Who was we? Who was she?

I looked on the floor at a mobile phone. A perfectly innocuous Motorola phone, flipped open. Was I expecting a super-secret spy cell phone? "Damn," I said in the direction of the phone. "I'm going to have to bend over to pick you up."

I reached left hand over right shoulder to diagnose the damage administered by Weller and Velarde. The muscle movement brought a kaleidoscope of pain, but I could move without collapsing.

I felt the spot near the base of my neck, where Velarde had gone to town. It was covered with a piece of gauze, taped inexpertly to my back and neck. I took stock. I wasn't suffering blood loss and hadn't taken a hit to any major organ. Someone had sterilized my wounds. Besides, I thought, Samantha probably had sterilized the needles to begin with. The wounds wouldn't kill me, I thought. I had probably passed out not from imminent threat of death or even shock, merely from pain.

I slowly bent over, picked up the cell phone and studied it. Looking for . . . I wasn't sure what, nothing in particular, which is precisely what I found.

The phone was turned on. On the display, the clock read 6:15 p.m. Could it be that I'd been knocked out for only two hours? Or was it two hours plus one full day? I closed the phone and reached to put it in my pocket. Until I realized I was wearing boxer shorts—no pants. Where were they?

In the corner, in a pile, along with my wallet and phone. Right where I'd left them all when I undressed to get acupuncture.

What had happened to Samantha? And to Erin? Didn't Velarde say that she was knocked out. Or worse?

With adrenaline trumping pain, I donned pants and shirt. I opened the door to Samantha's small studio. Outside of it was an anteroom—a small waiting area where Samantha's clients would read yoga magazines on an overstuffed orange chair, and where she would sit, meditate, and wait for them to cook.

As I peeked past the door, I braced for the worst. I felt another burst of adrenaline. There sat Samantha on the big orange chair, her head hung to the side, eyes shut.

"Samantha!"

She didn't stir.

I stepped toward her. I grabbed her wrist, felt for a pulse, and found a strong one.

"Give me five more minutes, Bullseye," Samantha slurred quietly.

She seemed to be in a heavy drug sleep, the likes of which I'd probably been in minutes before. I desperately wanted to shake her awake and ask her what she'd seen, but I didn't think I'd get much useful information. I also thought it better to let her sleep. I put my hand on her cheek.

That's when I noticed the key. It was dangling from a string around Samantha's neck. I didn't remember Sam ever carrying a key that way. I reached forward and supported the key in my fingers. From its logo, I could see that it belonged to a Ford.

I walked to the front door of the studio—a mere three steps given the office's diminutive size. I looked out onto the dirt parking lot of the industrial complex. It was, as it had been when I'd arrived, empty, with one exception: a Ford Explorer, evidently belonging to the key dangling from my ring finger.

It was a curiosity, then a sudden source of anger. Who the fuck was playing with me, and why?

"What the hell?"

The answer, once again, came from my pants. The mystery phone was ringing.

As I opened the flip phone, I remembered the strangest feeling. Déjà vu. I felt like I'd been in that exact moment a thousand times before. I tried to shake off the sensation, and put the phone to my ear.

"Hello," I said tentatively. "This is Nat."

"Turtle," said my formerly dead true love. "I've missed you so much."

42

I'd had reunions with Annie before. Often on a bench in Golden Gate Park. I would sit with a bag of sunflower seeds. One seed for me. One for the squirrels. Two for me. Two for the squirrels.

I was the picture of contemplation, pity, and piety. I exuded a kind of contrition—like if Annie were watching from the afterlife she would know I was living with the proper cool reflection of one who has lost a true love.

But she wasn't in the afterlife. She was fifty yards away and walking toward me, her smile broadening with each closing centimeter. Even when we locked eyes, she wouldn't run. I would finally stand. But wait too. Savoring. Then, at last, she wouldn't contain her legs. She'd sprint into my arms.

"This isn't possible," I'd whisper into her hair.

"I'm here, Turtle," she'd say. "It's really me."

I'd bury my head in her hair. Then she'd laugh. We'd kiss while the squirrels stood on hind legs and applauded with their paws.

I had the fantasy a thousand times in the months after Annie disappeared. It was usually a variation on the same theme—though one component of the story always seemed to change. The explanation for how Annie had returned to me. How she had survived her slip and fall into the Pacific.

I could never conjure any suitable explanation. So I left it to nebulous and fantastical: She had hit her head and been carried to safety by dolphins; or she had been kidnapped by sailors on a foreign cargo ship and made a harrowing escape in the shark-infested waters off New Zealand.

The explanation for her presence was hazy and unimportant. But the moment we reconnected—*that* I had always imagined in exquisite detail. It was ripe with joy and, above all, laughter. Nothing at all like the way it actually happened.

43

"Annie," I said, then paused. "Is it really you?"

"Are you alone?" she said.

That voice. I'd know that voice in a wind tunnel, with my ears stuffed with both cotton and the drummer from Nirvana.

I looked around the parking lot. Was she asking if there was anyone around me? Not that I could see.

Before I answered, I paused. I took one more look at my surroundings. Was any of this real? Maybe I'd actually entered the afterlife, and it looked a lot like an industrial park.

"Annie," I said.

"It's me, Turtle."

"Am I dead?"

Annie swallowed hard.

"No. We're not dead."

I looked up at the sky.

"This isn't possible."

"It's really happening. But we don't have much time."

"Annie, I don't know what's going on. I don't know whether we'll talk again. So I've got to say this: I've missed everything—your hands, and the way you smell when you get out of the shower, and . . ." I paused, then continued. "I take that back. I like the way you smell and look all the time and under all circumstances; even if you never bathed again, you will still be the greatest-smelling person ever."

A laugh. She laughed, but only lightly, thinly. Still, I felt the heart tremors.

"Nat, there's no time. Are you alone?"

"You've got to tell me what's going on. Where are you? How long have you been . . . out there? Annie, did you save me at the café?"

"I need to know if you're alone, Nat. Can we speak freely?"

I felt a blush of admonition drench my skin. I felt woozy. This was cornered Annie.

"Yes," I said.

"I'm in danger, Nat. We're both, obviously, in danger."

I felt my knees weaken.

"Did you find the Explorer?"

I looked at the black sport utility vehicle, then at the key in my hand. I told her I'd found it.

"Annie—I need something. Explain . . . how did you not contact me? All these years?"

Before she could answer, I added, "Were you in a coma?"

"When I see you. I'll explain everything. Why I couldn't see you. And we'll have chocolate shakes, and I'll fall asleep with my head in your lap, and we can dream."

My heart grew three sizes. But still I wanted to demand answers. I wanted to scream for an explanation. My mouth was almost too dry to speak.

"You need to be in Nevada—tomorrow afternoon," she said. "There's a map—in the glove compartment. With precise details."

"Nevada," I said, with not nearly the shock I was feeling.

"Boulder City. Not far outside of Las Vegas. It'll take nine hours. Nat, no airports or police. It's too dangerous."

That one part I pretty much had figured out. Especially as it related to the police. Just hours ago, they were using a scythe to play pin the tail on my donkey. The phone nearly slipped from my hand. It was slick with perspiration. I wiped it off, and switched hands and ears.

Annie said, "We're taking care of your friend. We're protecting her from them."

"Friend."

"Erin," Annie said. "She's very pretty."

I recognized Annie's tone of voice. Jealousy. I'd heard it dozens of times during our relationship. Never merited, and always preceding an argument. Its presence here was preposterous, but there wasn't time to be defensive. That could wait, at least, until I brought up the other woman in my life.

"Samantha," I said. "What happened to Sam?"

A pause. Like Annie put her hand over the phone. I heard muffled voices, then Annie returned.

"She'll be fine. She'll have a headache for a few hours," Annie said, then added without a segue, "I love how much you care about people around you."

The overture was lost on me. I was stuck on an earlier sentence. We're taking care of her, Annie kept saying. *We?*

Then a shooting pain.

I felt myself lose footing, my legs buckled, the earth slithered underneath me, the onset of another shrieking headache.

"Something's wrong with me, Annie. I don't know if it was the acupuncture, or . . . it's something that's been going on for a couple of days. Since the explosion."

"What are you talking about?" she said, sounding earnest and intense.

"My head. It's—it feels like it's exploding."

"Nat, focus. I need you to tell me when it started. Are you disoriented? Nauseated?"

"Yes. A couple of days ago. I'm thinking it's post-traumatic stress disorder, but bad. Or . . . what?"

After a brief pause, she spoke. "Dammit. Goddammit. Let me think for a second." She paused again. "Can you get hold of some amphetamines—like Ritalin, or even crack? Low, low doses of crack would be fine."

Ritalin. The stuff people take for attention deficit disorder? Crack? Me?

"You're just tired, Nat. If you can't get something stronger, fuel up on sugar and caffeine. It'll keep you going."

Sugar and caffeine.

I wanted to go back in a time machine.

"Are you qualified to prescribe sugar?"

I was hoping for a connection. I got the opposite—a disconnection.

"I have to go now," she said, her tone intensified. "Nathaniel, I need you to bring that man's laptop."

I gulped for air.

"We can trade it for our freedom."

Our freedom.

"I can't wait to see you, Turtle. Don't forget the laptop. It's everything."

The line went dead.

I stood up. Blood, what was left of it, took the A train from brain to extremities. I paused to let dizziness pass. I looked at Samantha, still slumbering, then I staggered toward the Explorer.

Annie was alive. How could that be? But I heard her, the warmth, coupled with that toughness I'd had so much trouble grasping in our year together. More of that than I remembered. Still, it was Annie, and her whereabouts were locked inside the mystery Ford.

As I put the key into the door lock, I was struck by an impulse. Fighting the pain in my neck, I leaned under the car. I looked at the underside. Did there appear to be anything out of the ordinary, or dangerous? Like a bomb?

Nothing looked suspicious.

I pressed my hands against the ground in the form of a push-up. I rose to my feet. A phoenix—with blue canvas high-tops. Annie was waiting. So was Erin. I opened the car door. "I'm rebounding," I said.

I climbed into the car, and was struck by the antiseptic smell of leather scrubbed clean. Without hesitation, I reached for the glove compartment. I opened it and found a cream-colored envelope. Inside that, a map—of Nevada. It was in black and white, except for the circle in blood-red pen around

Boulder City. A town apparently so small that it was denoted by the littlest typeface on the map. It wasn't far from Hoover Dam and Lake Mead.

There was a typewritten note on the edge of the paper. It instructed me to be in Boulder City the following afternoon. I had almost twenty hours to get to my destination. I glanced back at the paper—at the few additional words typed there. "Will call with an address," it read. The note wasn't signed, it was stamped with the image of a turtle.

On autopilot, I carried Samantha to the car and set her in the back seat, where she continued to metabolize sleeping medicine. I started the car.

Sometimes my moments of creative clarity happened in the middle of the night. Other times in the shower. Once during a particularly depressing series of one-night stands eighteen months after Annie's disappearance, while I was mid-coitus with a woman who made bracelets by enclosing colorful plastic around strands of human hair. This time, it happened when I was in reverse.

I was thinking about the sound of Annie's voice, just the mere, extraordinary sound of it, and her instructions: to bring the laptop, to stay awake eating sugar and caffeine. I was navigating the behemoth SUV out of the lot. I hit the brakes.

The car stopped. My mind careened forward. I was struck by a series of seemingly unrelated images. Andy's laptop, which everybody seemed to be craving, his headaches, and apparent addiction to uppers. The caged rats, with the holes in their skulls. Someone was experimenting on rat brains, measuring their brain activity.

Eat sugar, said Annie. *Drink caffeine. Better yet, take uppers.*

I had my first guess at what might be happening.

I reached into my jeans. I felt what I was looking for—the tattered and bloodied piece of notebook paper I'd taken from inside a cage at Strawberry Labs. Along the left side of the paper were written numbers, which I knew to be names: A1, A2, up to A15. Then B1 to B5. Some with C and numbers.

At least three dozen. More than I had seen. Missing, and presumed dead.

Beside each name were four columns. One read "food," the next, "stim"; the next two had the headers "NOR" and "DA." I couldn't be sure what that meant, but I had a strong guess. Norepinephrine and dopamine. Neurotransmitters, measurable through urine sample. They helped control attention span and impulsivity.

Also, the rats had shaved heads, consistent with the placement of electrodes. Like someone also had been measuring their brain waves. Attached to B4's wires had been two words, "stim" and "wave."

Stimulation? Brain waves?

Food? Stim? The concept rang familiar. Wasn't it a classic experiment? What would rats choose, food or stimulation? But why? What did that have to do with this?

"No way," I said, almost in the form of a question, then answered myself. "Not possible."

I flashed on the image of Andy's laptop, its space bar cracked and indented. He typed the word "ping" over and over. Like a rat clawing at a lever to obtain more stimulation. Was Andy doing something similar? Could the computer have been acting as a stimulant? Could it elevate anxiety and adrenaline—to dangerous levels? Could it be elevating mine?

"Not possible."

I reached for the super-secret spy phone. I fumbled it in my slippery hands, looking for the feature that told me what numbers I'd received calls from. Annie's number was listed as blocked.

I scrolled the menu looking for anything else that could tell me her whereabouts. Was there a way to find her—immediately? Not in twenty hours, when it might be too late. I looked in the mirror. A chalk outline of a face looked back, eyes peering through whiskers and disease.

I dialed directory assistance and asked for the number for Glenn Kindle. Unlisted. I tried Kindle Investment Partners. I found myself at the voice mail of Glenn's administrative assistant, Diane McNulty. Good old Diane. She wasn't around either. I called the operator again and asked for any Diane McNultys in the surrounding area. There was a listing in Redwood City, a few miles north and a few tax brackets south of Palo Alto.

Before I knew it, I'd been connected to Diane's number. And shortly thereafter, I heard another voice from the past.

"Hello."

"Diane?"

"This is she."

"Howdy, Diane McNulty," I said, employing the politician's trick of repeating a name. "It's Nathaniel Idle—Annie's old boyfriend."

There was a pause.

"Hi, Nat. My goodness. How are you?"

Warm. Like a grandmother who just wanted to invite you in off the porch and give you a cold glass of lemonade.

"Diane. I need to find Glenn," I said abruptly. "It's essential that I reach him."

Again, a pause. "I'd be happy to get a message to him tomorrow. Can you give me a call at the office?"

I sunk my head into my shoulders. She was a smiling Cerberus, a dog at the gate happily wagging her tail, but whose protective powers were not to be underestimated in the slightest.

"Can I reach him tonight?" I said. "I can't impress upon you how important this is."

"Oh, I don't think so, Nat. He's in transit to Las Vegas. He's speaking at TelCom, the annual trade show with telecommunications companies," she said. "I bet you're calling about Ed Gaverson. Aren't you still a reporter of some kind?"

Ed Gaverson. The founder of Ditsoft, Glenn Kindle's friend and sometime business rival.

"Isn't it a tragedy? On top of the world—and he does . . . that. . . ?" she said, lowering her voice. "This is all off the record, of course."

I was a juggler, a spinner of plates, a sword swallower, with someone sharpening knives already ingested. Something happened to Gaverson?

"I need to talk to him about . . . Annie," I said.

"Oh, Nat," she said quickly, innocently. "I know how hard that was for you. I promise to let him know right away you'd like to chat. Is it the anniversary?"

Diane had no idea what I was talking about. I wasn't sure if, and how much, I should tell her. What if I told her about Annie, and she told Glenn or whoever had Annie fighting for her life?

Who else would have Annie scared to death?

"How can I reach Dave Elliott?" I asked.

"Oh yes, that's a good idea. He's in downtown San Francisco."

A hop, skip, and a jump. I turned the car around and pulled out of the parking lot. In the rearview mirror, I again caught a glimpse of my face—illuminated by fading sun. The light accentuated the red lines burned into my eyes. If I didn't get answers soon, would I even survive long enough to see Annie?

44

The operator gave me the phone number for Dave Elliott's law firm and, when I asked sweetly, the address too. Elliott was in the Kindle inner circle. Maybe he could bring me inside the circle too.

I felt pulsing of my cranial veins. I recognized it now as the precursor to another set of dancing linebackers. My mysterious flulike symptoms, or a wave of exhaustion. When I'd sensed something wasn't right with me, Annie had very nearly validated my intuition. Perhaps Dave Elliott could make it clearer still.

Sugar. Caffeine.

Somebody tell the FDA: The most powerful drugs in the world remain unregulated, and available cheap at 7-Eleven.

Moments later, I stood at the counter of just such a convenience store with a basket filled with the stuff of an eleven-year-old's erotic fantasy. A box of Cocoa Puffs, a 44-ounce coffee, a half dozen Snickers, four Milky Ways, a six-pack of Jolt, twelve sugar doughnuts, and, for protein, Slim Jims and prepackaged peanut butter crackers. And various other assorted snack items that I'd always wanted but lacked the medical counsel to buy or ingest in good conscience.

I exited the convenience store, ignoring the curious gaze of an overqualified employee. I climbed into my car and looked around—for police, or other antagonists. I'd become a fugitive from the law—and my dentist. I devoured two candy bars and slugged a mouthful of muddy coffee. It pasted me with a surge of sugar and caffeine.

I headed downtown. With any luck Dave Elliott would be doing what lawyers did best. Working late.

As I drove, I flashed on my editor, Kevin. I still owed him the story about the impact of cell phone radiation on the brain. Was I so conditioned by school that I could think even at a time like this of my financial and work obligations? I almost laughed.

Finally I'd found a worthy excuse. *Kevin, I was planning to get my story in on time, but I was murdered.* If that didn't buy me a few extra weeks, I didn't know what would.

I called my attorney. "Dude," he answered after the first ring. "What's up?"

I had to hand it to Eric Rugger, attorney-at-law. He might not know how to connect with the common man on juries. But he did a great job speaking the language of the common teenager.

"Great news," he said. "They have not reopened the Aravelo investigation. I talked to my sources; you've got nothing to worry about."

"Yeah, I figured that much out. Hey, here's some more great news: I'm wanted for blowing up the Sunshine Café."

"If you're serious, we need to get off our mobile phones. They can tap these calls."

"I'm innocent. I don't give a shit who's listening."

"Nat, are you talking about the reports on the radio that the police are looking for two survivors of the café explosion?"

"Yep."

He paused before he spoke again.

"That might just be a tactic. It might mean you're wanted

for questioning. It's a way of making sure you cooperate. You need to turn yourself in immediately. And you need to get off this phone. Tell me where to meet you and we'll go together."

That seemed like a good idea on the order of pouring lemon juice down my back.

"You spent a year at Justice, right?" I said.

Eric had spent a grad-school summer at the Justice Department.

"Nat, I don't see . . ."

"I need a favor," I said. "I need you to call any friends you might have at the SEC. Ask about a company called Vestige Technologies. V-E-S-T-I-G-E." I told him it was in New York and had some problems several years ago.

I had barely hung up with Eric when I looked up to see the cross streets of Front and Mission and a gorgeous dusk view of the Bay Bridge. I didn't pause for long. I needed to get into the building quickly if I had any chance of catching David Elliott.

I parked the car. One more call. I picked up my phone to dial, but stopped, remembering Eric's admonition—*they can tap your calls.*

I put my phone down and picked up the blonde angel's cell phone. I gathered that my use of the phone was a secret. Except to Annie, or whoever she was working with. I got out of the car and went to a pay phone to call Bullseye. No answer.

I called the Past Time bar. The phone was answered by Ally, who tended bar twice a week. She put Bullseye on the line.

"Is Sam with you?" he said. "I haven't heard from her since I left her studio a couple of hours ago."

"Bullseye. I need you to sit down."

"As opposed to what?"

He was in his usual terse mood and probably wasn't all that concerned about Samantha's absence.

"Sam's okay," I said. "She's gotten a little mixed up with the nonsense involving me and the waitress."

"I'm standing, Nathaniel."

I looked up the side of the building that was home to Dave Elliott's office. Same joint I'd visited several years earlier, when I'd quizzed him about Vestige Technologies. Bullseye arrived within ten minutes. He looked at me: "Holy shit."

Then he turned to Samantha. He leaned over, kissed her forehead, and stood looking at her in silence for a full two minutes.

"She's been drugged, but she's okay," I said. "She needs rest, but I think she can do without a doctor for now."

He brushed a wisp of her hair off her forehead and behind her ear.

"I'm going to kill somebody." He took Samantha's hand. "And I'm not nearly as ticked off as she'll be. She hates ingesting any synthetic chemicals."

"Did you call the cops?"

He lifted her gently into his car. "Dennis," she said, stirring, using his given name. "You smell good."

"No police. Please," I said. "Do you still have the laptop?"

He climbed behind the wheel of his car.

"I hid it. On a table in my living room. Do you want me to do something with it?"

I nodded. I gave him Mike's cell phone number. I told him to ask Mike to make a copy of the laptop's hard drive, fit the computer with a tracking device. I wasn't sure it would work, but I figured if anyone would know, it would be Mike. I begged Bullseye for discretion, a melodramatic and unnecessary request.

Moments later, I walked into Starbucks and bought two lattes and one individually wrapped, three-dollar butter cookie.

I entered Dave Elliott's building and walked to the guard station.

"Badge," demanded the guard, a portly fellow with a ham-sized fist dug into a bag of tortilla chips.

"Coming up." I put down my snacks and dug into my pocket. "By the way, you want this extra latte and cookie? Johnson asks me to get it, then he calls to say he had to scamper home to his wife."

"Serious?"

"Where the hell did I leave my badge?" I said, as if talking to myself.

"Don't sweat it," he said, snagging the latte.

I took the elevator to the eighteenth floor, where Elliott kept his office. The glass reception doors to the law firm were open too, and there didn't appear to be a soul around. Inviting. What luck.

I made my way down a hallway, passing the photos hung on the wall of serious-looking law partners dressed in pinstripes. There was a light on inside when I arrived at Elliott's office door. I had hardly begun to debate whether to knock when I heard a voice from inside.

"Nathaniel, what took you so long?"

45

Dry cleaning," Dave said. "That's the key."

He stuck out his hand.

"What the heck happened to you?" he said. "And to what do I owe this visit?"

"You tell me."

He'd known I was coming. Was he tracking me?

I put out my hand and gave him an aggressive shake. His palm was slick. He turned away to face the room.

"Diane said you might be heading this direction."

He leaned over his desk and squirted his hand with an industrial-strength bottle of Purell. I might have been offended if there wasn't so much more on my mind, and if it didn't happen so often these days. Especially interviewing medical professionals, or business executives; they immediately went into their pockets to disinfect. They did it not just with me, but with each other, with whomever. Sometimes they didn't grip hands at all but just touched fists. Germophobia. The handshake had given way to the hosedown.

What I had was much worse than a cold.

I recognized the room. The big oak desk, beneath a built-in shelf—still virtually devoid of books. To the left of the desk, a window with a terrific view of the Bay Bridge, lit by car headlights and brake lights, and a nearly full moon. At the other side of the room, across from the window, a couch. In front of the couch, a reddish-colored coffee table, with an

ice-filled bucket chilling bottled waters. Dave gestured toward the couch. I sat. I picked up a water, opened it, and
took a slug.

Dave pulled up a chair. It belonged to a second desk, this
one small, to the left of the window. On the desk sat a laptop.
Dave wore a crisply pressed royal blue shirt tucked into gray
slacks. He was just about as I'd left him after our last conversation, but with a bigger forehead. He'd lost a lot of hair.

He picked up a putter leaning against the small desk and
started twirling it.

I'd have to navigate Dave carefully. I couldn't guess what
he knew, but I certainly couldn't reveal anything about Annie,
under the presumption that he and I weren't allies.

"What can you tell me about Strawberry Labs?"

"Synthetic berry manufacturing plant?" he said, then
paused. "Sorry, bad line. You look like you've got something
pretty serious on your mind."

"Are you still working for Glenn Kindle?"

He nodded. Sure, he was working for Kindle Investment
Partners. He couldn't really disclose whom he was working
for, or specific cases. But he'd be happy to talk about some
general legal matters if I wanted to come back during business
hours. All boilerplate. It would have been mind-numbing even
without the creeping headache and nausea. I reached into my
pocket and popped an Oreo into my mouth.

"What about Vestige?"

"Vestige? Is that still on your mind? Listen, I'll tell you
there was a small settlement to the IRS. It's public anyway. But
I really can't discuss any individual cases."

I pulled out my cell phone.

"I'm going to call the police. I'm going to tell them to pay a
visit to you and Glenn Kindle."

It was a ridiculous bluff, given that I was wanted for questioning. But I needed to know what Dave knew, and he caught
on just a second too late.

He said, "Do you really think that's the wisest thing to do—given your predicament?"

He paused, gears grinding.

"You're going to look pretty silly just calling the cops for no apparent reason. You seem tired, Nat. My professional advice—and please don't take this the wrong way—is you're acting a little strange."

If I was reading him right, he had just admitted that he knew much more than he was letting on, and now he was trying to cover. "Predicament": Did he mean the café? Or my illness? Or Annie? And why wasn't Dave calling the cops himself? I couldn't focus.

"Let me tell you my theory," I said.

"I really do need to be getting home."

"Someone associated with Glenn Kindle—maybe Glenn Kindle—is loading computers with . . . a program. Some dangerous program. It causes people to . . . to get sick."

He started laughing.

"The program acts like speed somehow. It affects the attention span, like . . . focus . . . It involves serotonin. The dopamine receptors. It makes computer use more compelling. You get a buzz. You get"—and then I found the word I was looking for—"addicted."

Me, Andy, maybe Simon Anderson. We'd been buzzing. Something was frying our brains. I'd had trouble pulling myself away from my laptop; the endless late-night surfing, the excitability, then withdrawal—nightmares, exhaustion, tremors, aggression, irritability. Hadn't that been Andy's problem? And Annie said I could be calmed with Ritalin, a kind of stimulant, the medication used to treat attention deficit disorder. Maybe that's how the rat test fit in—an experiment to see whether the rodents would choose a certain kind of electrical brain stimulation over food.

"I see what you're talking about."

Was it revelation time?

Dave said he didn't know anything about a dangerous program, and launched into a monologue about the addictive power of computers. When people get an e-mail or a phone call, they get a little jolt of adrenaline—a burst of excitement from the sound and image and also the prospect of receiving something new. The absence of that activity creates a vacuum, and boredom. That's why people feel compelled to place a phone call whenever they're driving along in a car; because they've gotten so accustomed to the burst of brain activity that they feel bored when not stimulated.

It hit me. "And you're trying to perfect this?"

"Jesus, Nat." He laughed. "I have no fucking idea what you are talking about."

"But you just . . ."

"I thought we were talking about modern life. We get conditioned to use our gadgets, right? What do they call it—a Crackberry?"

He was playing me, giving me a nugget, something to think about, then acting like it was an innocuous observation. I extracted a powdered sugar doughnut from my jacket.

"Nathaniel, I'll be honest. You've always been a little dramatic. I thought so when you were with Annie. You romanticized that thing. She wasn't near what you cracked her up to be. Now you're talking this computer nonsense. Next you'll be saying people installed some mythical dangerous program on *your* computer, or that they've been tracking your whereabouts on your cell phone, and listening to your calls. C'mon; do you really think a computer can do what you're describing?"

He sat down in front of the laptop on his desk and started clacking the keys. He couldn't imagine how such a thing as I was describing could work, he said. Could I show him what I was talking about?

Indeed, how could such a thing work? I watched him tap away on the keys. The screen couldn't communicate directly with the brain, could it? He stood. "Show me," he said.

I approached warily. He had put the putter down, and it didn't look like he would attack me.

I looked at the computer and saw the Web page he'd called up. It was a story in the *Chronicle* about the café. A big text box denoted "breaking news." It reported: Local pair sought *in café explosion.*

"What the fuck? Why this story?"

"Why not, buddy?"

I sat at the computer. I clicked on the link and started reading. And suddenly, a buzz. A painful pulsing in my fingertips, like I'd been shocked. A humming in my ears. That headache. My gut—I shook my head. I fought for air. I turned to the side and threw up. More like projectile vomited.

"Spare me." Dave, looking at his shoes. "These are Allen-Edmonds."

I'd never had a migraine. I'd treated them, though. It's like a vise around the brain. The slightest movement, or light, radiates pain.

My gut seized. I fought to inhale—to satisfy primordial urges. This can't be happening. A computer can't do this. I slammed the laptop shut. I gripped its sides, tried to lift my head. I raised it an inch. I threw up again.

"It's on this thing," I coughed.

"You've got the flu, buddy."

"What's on this fucking computer?"

I felt a wave of fury. I pulled myself up and steadied myself on the table's edge. I stepped toward Dave. The corner of my eye saw him pick up a rock paperweight. Was it to defend, or attack?

He cocked the paperweight and swung.

46

The jagged edge of a rock arced toward my head. I leaned forward and turned. The object slammed just below my armpit, into the lat and the ribs. It was excruciating. His momentum propelled him forward and he was nearly on top of me. He cocked his arm again.

I realized I was holding the laptop, which I'd instinctively grabbed for protection. Just as Dave brought the rock down, I held up the computer like a shield, and it took the brunt of the second blow. Dave stumbled to a knee. I turned and swung the laptop. It was blind, but furious, and it hit its mark—the side of Dave's cheek, just as he was turning to look up at me. He wailed and put his hands to the side of his face.

If there wasn't so much fury, and so much at stake, it all might have been comical. Men don't know how to fight. They just know how to threaten to fight. Shoving matches on basketball courts and soccer fields don't count.

Dave rose. He had his hand on a large gash on his cheek. I held my side. Warm and sticky. We both stood there gasping. What to do next?

"You tried to kill me," I said. "You're trying to kill me."

"I'm defending myself against a psycho. Look at yourself."

Dave picked up a phone on his main desk and pressed a button. "Building security," came a voice over the speakerphone. "This is Bob."

"I need help. I've got a hostile visitor," Dave said.

Intervention was something I couldn't afford. When security showed up, Dave had a lot to lose too, but not as much as I did. Annie was out there somewhere. Panting, I took a last look at Dave and ran through the door.

I took the stairwell. I'd watched too much television and had some vague instinct that, if you escaped in an elevator, you risked being met at the bottom by men toting guns. When I got to the bottom, I peeked through the stairwell door at the guard's desk, and found it empty. He must have been attending to Dave. What story was Dave making up?

Moments later, I climbed in my car. I drove away from the building and into a dark, empty street. I heard a siren and dropped my head below the window. When the sound passed, I accelerated again. I drove a half mile to the Bay Bridge. I merged onto it and let the gorgeous span carry me away from the sirens, the muck, the frenetic madness of a twenty-first-century city wired to the hilt.

I steered with my right hand. With my left, I gently prodded the sticky shirt fabric at my right side—at the edge of my rib cage. I'd taken a good gouging. Just how much more than a flesh wound I couldn't conclude, not without jamming my foul paws into my wound and causing so much pain that I would swerve and make it much worse by driving my car off the bridge. It hurt to breathe in too deeply, suggesting a possible cracked rib.

The good news was I wasn't pouring blood or passing out. The muscle is well supplied by vessels and so a more direct hit would have caused a lot more blood loss, at least. It could be a mixed blessing. Less bleeding but slower healing. In either case, faster driving. That's what the following cars' repeated honks were telling me.

I focused on the road. I'd come to the end of the Bay Bridge and found the beachhead to America. Road signs pointed in a million directions—Oakland, Sacramento, San Jose. I took Highway 580, an artery that would lead through the flatlands to Highway 5, the eventual path to Las Vegas. Boulder City. Annie.

I reached for the phone and dialed Leslie Fernandez, my former classmate and lover turned neurologist.

Presuming the computer had somehow attacked my brain, it didn't take an almost-doctor to understand what Annie had been getting at. My brain needed artificial stimulation. Something to take the place of the laptop that had . . . somehow ravaged my own onboard computer. Just how their dirty trick worked would have to wait. My immediate goal was triage.

"It's Dr. Fernandez," she said when she answered.

"Leslie."

"Lover boy." Her voice rose.

"Lover boy needs another favor."

"Sigh. What's up?"

"Leslie, I need a Ritalin prescription. A hundred pills, at least 20 milligrams."

"Nat?"

"I also need Augmentin. Or whatever is the strongest all-purpose antibiotic going these days."

Silence.

"There's a Walgreens in Pleasanton," I said.

"Are you okay? Are you . . . using?"

I laughed, but I shouldn't have. What I was asking wasn't illegal—doctors prescribe for each other all the time—but this *was* serious.

"No. Leslie. Please, no lectures right now. You're not compromising anything. You've got to trust me."

"Okay, lover boy." Not convinced. "I'm here if you need me."

"Actually, one more thing."

"Footsie?"

"Norepinephrine and dopamine," I said. "Remind me."

"Neurotransmitters. Catecholamines."

"Check."

"What's going on?"

"They're stress hormones, right? Corresponding with intense situations. Indicated by a rush."

"Norepinephrine is that and more. In terms of stress, it contributes to controlling primitive functions—activating fight-or-flight: dilating pupils, constricting blood vessels, increasing heart rate. Dopamine is more involved in the pleasure centers of the brain, and also with compulsion and desire."

"Like it controls cravings?"

"Or is indicative of them. Why are you asking me all this?"

"Science experiment. Listen, I gotta run."

"Don't hang up," she said at elevated decibels.

She asked me if this had to do with Dr. Bard and my earlier call. I told her I didn't have time to talk about it, but now she was concerned. She made me swear that I wasn't sick or doctor-shopping, an indirect way of asking me again if I was an addict looking for prescriptions from friends. It was not uncommon for medical students to get hooked and dose their way through life. She was still skeptical when we hung up.

I pulled into a Denny's north of Lake Merritt, an area of Oakland just bad enough that it wouldn't raise an eyebrow if some guy walked in and took a bath in the sink. Cleaning out a gash might be tougher to explain. Fortunately, the bathroom was empty when I walked in, except for a pair of piss-stained jeans lying on the floor beside the urinal. I held my breath, pulled back my shirt, and tried to pretend it wasn't me, but rather some emergency-room stranger whom I'd have treated as a medical student. I put my finger inside the fleshy wound and saw that the stranger was in for good news. The paperweight had grazed his side, missing any major arteries and not breaking scapula or rib. He needed a good cleaning, a bandage, and, it went without saying, hydration and bed rest. A good cleaning would have to do.

Thirty minutes later I arrived at Walgreens. Behind the counter stood a diminutive pharmacist with Coke-bottle glasses.

"Have you taken this before?" she said, handing me the Ritalin.

I nodded.

She reached for a second bag. She looked at me, then looked back at the writing on the bag.

"You have to eat when you take this," she said. "It's a very powerful antibiotic. It can cause nausea and a number of adverse reactions."

On the counter, I laid down cash from the $300 I'd pulled from an ATM at the front of the store.

Moments later in the parking lot, I twisted open the Ritalin and poured two tiny white pills into my hand—double even a high dose. I washed them down with a gulp of warm Pepsi from a bottle sitting in my passenger seat.

What to expect? Would the headache suddenly subside? Or I'd gain newfound clarity? Or be able to sleep? It seemed like a long shot, given that Ritalin is an upper, sort of. It is used widely to treat attention deficit disorder. The concept is that people with ADD have trouble focusing. They appear to be excitable. The theory, though, is that their brains are low on dopamine, and they look for stimulation. They crave excitement—or drama. The Ritalin supplements their brain chemicals. Again, in theory, it allows the brain to not have to scour for new forms of excitement and, in turn, new ways to generate adrenaline. It's an upper that actually can have a calming effect.

Without feeling any immediate difference, I started the car and pulled onto the highway. Would Ritalin have saved Andy Goldstein? Was there technology on his laptop that actually caused him to suffer symptoms like attention deficit disorder?

More to the point: Would Ritalin save *me*? Had I contracted some irreversible syndrome?

He had left me with a million questions. Dave was obviously dirty. Did his computer make me sick? Why not him? Had he suggested that my own laptop computer had been tampered with? How and when might that have happened? That night after the café exploded, I'd come home to find the power on on my laptop and the computer unplugged. It struck me as odd, but not out of the question, that I'd left it that way. Was it all a haze of fatigue?

Was Dave just making conversation when he said people get addicted to talking on the phone in a car? The more I thought about it, the more it seemed clear that he was right. The act of responding to the beep of a call, or an incoming e-mail, is at the very least Pavlovian. You hear the sound, you respond, you get a reward—a message, an input of information, the promise of something exciting. But is that physiological? Does our brain chemistry get molded and refined, like muscles responding to a repeated task?

I thought about the jungle, how humans adapted to survive it. Through random mutation and trial and error, we changed to cope with physical challenges and solve problems in the wild. Was the same thing happening in the digital age? Were our brains evolving to cope with the modern jungle—the computer, the environment in which we interact every day? One thing was clear: Stimulation was everywhere, and growing. It wasn't just phones and computers. It was CNN and Fox News; the screen includes a talking head, a news scrawl at the bottom, and a colorful graphic. Soon enough, they'd stamp a farm report on the anchor's forehead.

Our brains were being asked to cope with an onslaught of information pushed at us rapid-fire.

I picked up my cell phone.

The phone.

Dave had asked if I was paranoid that my phone had been

equipped with a tracking device. A message, or another random taunt? Who was tracking me? Danny Weller? Was he dead?

I looked closely at the phone, but wasn't sure how I could tell if it had a device on it. I took the conservative route. I opened my window and did something I'm sure 99 percent of cell phone users have had fantasies of doing. I tossed the phone onto the highway.

I still had the blonde angel's super-secret spy phone. I called Bullseye. When he answered, I chose my words carefully just in case someone was listening in.

"How's Sam?"

"She's been fully awake for twenty-nine minutes." Ever the mathematician.

"Lucid?"

"Ticked off," he said, expelling a rare laugh. "I reminded her about her Zen philosophy of life, and you know what she said? She said, 'They shouldn't have fucked with a witch.'"

I laughed, sending a seizure of pain down my side. It was worth it.

"Bullseye, you remember what to do?" We'd discussed it only briefly when I'd handed off Samantha.

"I'm a walking computer. I remember the slugging percentage of every member of the 1912 Black Sox."

If only our survival depended on us winning a trivia contest.

"Make sure to call Mike. It's a lot to ask of him, but I think he can pull it off."

"Done and done."

I put the phone down. Then picked it up again. A second call was nagging. To Lieutenant Aravelo.

Maybe he wasn't a bad guy after all. I desperately needed the help of someone in power. But if I was wrong, and a call to Aravelo diminished even a fraction of the chance I would see Annie again, it wasn't worth it.

I instead used the spy phone to remotely check my voice-mail messages. There was only one, a return call from Annie's friend Sarah. There was something urgent in her voice. I overrode my instincts and called her back. Perhaps she was in trouble, or I could delicately elicit something useful.

"Nat? Is that you? Hold on." She cupped the phone and yelled, "Turn down the fucking television! Dammit, this is important."

Same old Sarah.

She bypassed pleasantries and explained that my message had worried her. I'd sounded strange.

"You sound a little freaked out yourself. Are you okay, Sarah?" I refused to commit to tone, let alone substance.

"What's going on? You said you had a question about Annie?"

"Yeah, something about Annie. I'm seeing ghosts."

Long pause.

"You never got over her, did you?"

"Are you still tight with Glenn?"

"I see him around. Why?"

The tit-for-tat was fruitless. But she knew something. She was nervous. But she wasn't giving it up.

"Be careful, Sarah. Something bizarre is going on. I don't really know what. But I just want you to stay aware."

"You're scaring me, Nat. Frankly, you sound . . . a little weird."

"That I'll stipulate to in court."

We said good-bye and I looked into the glare of oncoming lights stacked upon lights stacked upon lights. I took my first deep breath. I felt calmer. Maybe it was the Ritalin, or the distance from the fight. I glanced at the lanes around me, filled with discomfited commuters. They were San Francisco's most determined strivers. Unable to afford homes or rent in the city, they had spread into suburbs stretching as far east and south as they could stand to drive home each night. Like me, they probably had a bucket seat full of snack foods and a desperate yearning. To my right, I found myself drawn to the driver's side window of a white Civic. I could make out what looked to be a middle-aged woman with a thick head of dark hair. She must have felt my presence. She turned her head and caught my gaze. She nodded, commiserating. She turned her eyes back to the road.

I was settling in for the long drive into the Central Valley of California and then to Nevada when I was startled by a shrill ring from the super-secret spy phone. It was Bullseye.

"I'm coming," he said. "But I've got company."

47

By midmorning, I could see it rising in the distance. The Las Vegas Strip. It looked peaceful, like any downtown before the commerce got plugged in for the morning. Its denizens were doing what they did every day about this time: sleeping in. Drenched in sweaty slumber and dreaming about what might have happened if they'd just dislodged themselves from the table thirty minutes earlier.

The town was getting more potent still. I'd read that in recent months, the New York–New York casino had installed a new blackjack table that doubled as a video poker machine. There was the opportunity to play the two games simultaneously, for those not jacking up their adrenaline, and losses, at a fast enough clip.

My poison was caffeine. I got an industrial-strength cup and pulled into the airport. Bullseye was waiting.

"You look like shit with a hangover," he said.

He stood by the baggage claim. Holding out a laptop.

"Where's the company?"

He gestured over his shoulder.

I directed us to the bathroom—to chat in private. It was the kind of melodrama that I figured would drive Bullseye nuts. He feared nothing that wasn't highly mathematically likely. So it probably didn't worry him that someone might be tailing two plainclothed idiots who were meeting in the Las Vegas airport to exchange a laptop.

But I wasn't taking any chances.

In the bathroom, he gestured for me to join him in the full-service stall closest to the left wall.

"Bad odds," he said, shutting the door of the cramped stall behind him.

"How's that?"

He wiggled to the side of the toilet opposite me. He had cups under his eyes and the skin on his chin had begun to break out.

"If you're worried about someone discovering and killing us, you should pick a middle stall. Gives us better escape options."

I couldn't tell if he was serious.

"What if we're trying to keep someone from listening in?" I said. "This way we're not surrounded on both sides."

"Better odds."

He thrust out Andy's laptop. "Here."

It was in just the shitty condition I'd last seen it. I turned it over in my hand and put my foot on the toilet.

"Did everything else go smoothly?"

"Ask him."

"Yeah, just ask me yourself, dude," came a voice from outside the stall.

I popped open the stall door.

"What's the good word?" Mike said.

I shook my head. There stood Mike, the biggest computer geek in the world, wearing a flower-print Hawaiian shirt, shorts, and flip-flops.

"This is the worst covert operation I've ever seen," I muttered.

Mike said that when Bullseye called for help, he figured I

might need some in-person assistance. But the real reason for his presence was plain. Mike was a monthly visitor to Vegas anyway, and his gambling yen earned him free nights at Caesars Palace. They didn't know he was trying to count cards, and he didn't care that he wasn't doing well enough to make the trips profitable.

"Do I have time to get to the tables?" he asked.

"Big mistake," Bullseye replied. "The odds are better at craps."

"Not if you show the proper discipline. You've got to factor in the human element. What is the likelihood *I* can walk away with a profit?"

Bullseye flashed a perverse smile. He had found a friend.

"Shall we side bet on who has better success—presuming you set your potential losses to me in escrow. That way you won't be tempted to give them to the blackjack dealer."

I was amazed. I'd never heard Bullseye talk this much in his life—and at this most inopportune time. I interrupted, reiterating that we needed to track the laptop. I'd outlined my idea to Bullseye before, and Mike said he had come through on the technology side.

"If I don't make it back here," I said, "try to pull the trigger anyway."

Ten minutes later, I was headed southeast.

I was ecstatic to see Annie, but also obviously confused, and angry. I'd always known there was a darker part of her, the part that freaked out when I broke the chair or when she got stressed about work. Had I underestimated that? No. Something horrible must have happened to her. Annie needed my help, and she'd have it soon enough.

Erin's image left nagging uncertainty too. She seemed strong, but also vulnerable and uncomplicated. Yet she'd survived the explosion, having been previously implicated in a fire. The big-boned housecleaner at Simon Anderson's said she'd seen a woman working on the family's electrical system. Erin was there when the rat house exploded.

The cell phone rang.

"Are you close, Turtle?"

"Less than an hour."

Annie gave me specific directions to a condo complex on the south edge of town. I tried to concentrate but was blown away by the sound of her voice. It was in this world but still surreal.

"Are you ready?" she asked.

"I bet you're even hotter now that you're dead."

That laugh.

"Hurry. We don't have much time."

When I asked her to tell me what was going on, she said she had some important things to take care of and would explain when I arrived.

"Nathaniel. You can't imagine the story I've got to tell you."

48

It was nearing noon, and I could sense the heat even with the full blast of air-conditioning. The sleepless night had left me jet-lagged and sweaty. I had given up trying to think and turned on the radio, realizing one of the things that had been yanking at my subconscious.

". . . it just goes to show that all the money in the world doesn't make you happy."

"Thank you, caller. That indeed does seem like one lesson—a lesson that Americans seem to need to learn over and over again. Ed Gaverson's suicide proves that wealth *Does. Not. Equal. Happiness.* This guy was at various times the *wealthiest* American. He had houses, cars, boats, more houses, and he still—forgive me for being graphic—put a bullet in his head. People, listen to me, *you* have the power to be happy, or to be unhappy. Depression, chemical imbalances, all that stuff—it can hit anyone. But *you* are just as capable as America's richest man of recognizing the problems and addressing them. Okay, we'll be back to talk more about the issues of the day on the nationally syndicated *Sizzle Talk*. I'm your host, Roger Templeton."

"Do you suffer from arthritis? . . ."

Ed Gaverson, the head of Ditsoft, one of the largest software companies in the world, was dead. One of Glenn Kindle's close friends, and he had killed himself. This must have been what Diane, Glenn's secretary, was alluding to.

I twisted the dial in search of another station—and more

information. All I got was static, and a new question: Did Gaverson shoot himself, or did someone else pull the trigger?

I turned into Boulder City. I drove through a modest commercial strip, then into a mostly empty, no-frills condomin-
ium complex. When I pulled into a parking spot, I was in a
dream state, sweaty and feral and curious and excited. Yet I
was struck by the most modest of considerations. In my stash
of snack foods, had I bothered to buy breath mints? Gum?
Finding neither, I ingested a handful of Red Hots. Maybe that
would kill the smell of coffee and nerves.

I looked in the rearview mirror at the reflection of red eyes
and more whiskers than the last time I checked. I actually, momentarily, thought: Should I go back to town for a haircut?

Moments later, I stood before the door. Her door. Annie's
door. I pulled a flower from beside the front door and, holding
it in a slippery-wet hand, knocked. No answer. I rang the bell.
No answer. I knocked again and, finally, the door opened. I
forgot about everything.

I looked at a woman with sandy blonde hair. She might
have been Annie's sister—clearly lighter hair, puffier cheeks,
and blue rather than brown eyes.

"Sorry it took me so long," she said. "I wanted to look
pretty for you."

I dropped the flower and pulled her close, feeling her arms
close around me—those tender, fragile twigs that once clung
to me for strength.

Up until that moment, I'm not sure I believed it. Even after
hearing her voice, it seemed she could not possibly, actually be
alive. And even if she didn't look precisely like the woman I
remembered, there was no doubt. This was Annie. She was in
my arms again, and getting a wicked bear hug.

"You've become a professional wrestler," she whispered, and laughed.

She put her hands on top of my head. She ran her fingers through my hair. The way she used to.

"Did you bring the laptop?"

I didn't want to break the hug—for fear that I might not get it back. Or, worse yet, that it wasn't really happening. That this all was *Alice in Wonderland* and any movement would lead to an attack of reality. Annie finally pushed away from me.

"Did you bring the laptop?" she repeated.

I looked at her, bewildered. What could she be talking about, at a moment like this? I shrugged, trying to discern her meaning.

"As you asked."

"Sorry." She looked down, clearing her throat.

She took my hand.

"Turtle, do you remember the day at the boardwalk?"

I couldn't stop looking at her face. It had aged, certainly more than four years. Four years plus extra time for what must have been incredible stress. And something else—surgery.

The puffiness I had seen in her cheeks had been an effort to pad her bone structure. Her hairline was deeper. She was wearing contacts that changed the color of her eyes. It was subtle but highly effective, the work of a true professional hired to make someone perceptibly different without radically altering her looks. I tried not to let my face register what I saw.

"We got a crepe filled with chocolate and you got your fortune told by a palm reader."

"It was a cinnamon crepe," Annie said flirtatiously. "That's the day I've thought about the most. It was perfect. You were perfect. We were perfect."

I tried to hold her gaze. She broke eye contact.

"Do you know what the fortune-teller told me?"

"She said you'd come into money."

Annie pulled her hands from mine.

"That's what I told you she whispered to me. But that's not really what she said."

Annie put her head down, like she was the kind of sad that goes beyond tears.

"She said I would face a difficult choice. But she said I'd choose the path of true love."

She took a step back.

"Your sideburns are longer. Oh, you're hurt."

My light blue T-shirt had been stained ruddy red.

"Courtesy of Dave Elliott."

She put her hand to her mouth. I couldn't tell if it was shock, or anger, or caring. I felt a whiff of doubt; I sensed something in Annie that was rehearsed. I pushed it away.

"They . . . they put some program on my computer."

It was a simplistic way to put it, but that, increasingly, is what I'd come to believe. Annie would fill in the blanks.

"Stunning. Turtle, I'm so sorry. How could he?"

"Your father? What the hell is going on?"

Her face changed. It went hard. Resolve. I'd seen the look only once before—in New York, when I'd stumbled onto her leading a meeting of bankers involved with Vestige Technologies. I suddenly felt the anxiety of recognition that I'd become an adult and that time had passed and was passing, so fast.

"You can't trust anyone," she said bemusedly. Then: "I'm going to finish this right now."

Since I'd last seen Annie, a lifetime had passed. Fish had grown legs, crawled onto the land, and invented the combustion engine, and Annie had hardened. I'd always known a tough part of her existed, but I always believed it was the far lesser part of her spirit.

"I didn't play dead for four years to have it end like this. *He* did this to me. To you, Nat. To *us.* We can't let him get away with it. And now I can stop him for good."

"I don't care about this." I put my hand over my wound.

"It heals. It's not like a broken heart. Annie, remember what we used to talk about. You don't have to crawl around in his muck. Let it go. *That's* how we put this behind us."

It came out adamant. As direct as I could remember being with her. Support, but also challenge. She stepped toward me, and her face changed again—this time it softened.

"When you hear what I've been through, you'll see we have no choice."

49

Do you still love me?" she said, almost in a whisper.

I looked her in the eye and swallowed. I didn't think it needed an answer, but she was studying me—almost clinically.

"Of course."

"What I'm going to tell you. It's private. You can't tell anyone. It's the biggest secret."

"Bigger than when I told you about how I added punctuation to all the Faulkner books in the high school library?"

Laughter.

"Annie, where is Erin?"

"She's fine. We're keeping her safe."

"We? Where is she?"

"Are you in love with her?"

"No, Annie. Jesus. Just tell me where she is."

"She's safe. I promise. She's coming here. Please, trust me for just a little while."

She pulled me into the condo, not exactly the sun-drenched park and clapping squirrels I'd imagined marking our reunion. It was prefab to the max. Annie set me down on the couch, and then hit me with a non sequitur.

"France is a lot lonelier than the guidebooks lead you to believe."

She wore black slacks and a blue blouse, meticulously matched. Even under the circumstances, she looked like she could be secretary-general of the Junior League. She locked the door and peered through a curtain—at the front walk—then pulled it tightly shut. She walked to the kitchen, and I heard pots rattle, then water run. She talked over it.

"That's where I spent the first two years after the accident. There was a country house in the north—not far from Luxembourg."

"So why didn't you call me, Annie? How could you let me think you were dead? Were you in a coma?"

She sighed. "Please, Nat. I've practiced this speech a thousand times and rewritten it twice that. Let me work up to it. It's confusing, even to me, even now."

I nodded.

She sighed.

"I would sit in a rocking chair next to a window that looked out on a small grove of apple trees. To try to keep from calling you, I would count up the number of apples. When I lost count, or couldn't remember whether I'd counted a particular apple, I'd start over." She sounded clinical, then suddenly sad. "Being that isolated, being afraid, being alone like that, it's worse than jail. It's worse than death. You are no longer a person. There is no point in existing."

Annie walked from the kitchen with a stainless steel bowl.

"I despise calendars now. You know why? Because you have to wait a month to turn the page. It makes it feel like time never, ever passes. In the kitchen of the house where I was staying, there was a sweets calendar with pictures of these mouth-watering desserts, like something called the chocolate moat. August had vanilla-bean ice cream covered with sticky cherry sauce that looked like blood. It taunted me. I just couldn't stand the idea that I only got to turn the calendar once every thirty days."

She sat on an oak coffee table in front of me.

"I faked my death and I went into hiding."

She dipped a hot towel into the steaming bowl of water. I held back the shirt from my wound, and my breath, and she pressed a towel into it.

"When I dove off the boat, I thought I was going to die for real. The water was freezing and bottomless and so dark. I swam underneath the boat. There was a mask and a tiny bottle of compressed air."

"A scuba tank?"

"Just enough air for ten minutes. They told me to suck from the nozzle and then swim. Suck then swim. I could hear your voice. I was trying to block you out. If you all discovered me, I planned to drop the mask and air and say I fell overboard. But you didn't. So I swam twenty yards away to a fishing buoy. It was the way we'd planned it. We'd programmed the boat's autopilot to direct it near the buoy. Ten feet down, attached to the buoy's cable, was a scuba tank, weighted down with a heavy anchor, and flippers."

I pictured the scene. Her friends standing on the boat, screaming. Me, in the water, scrambling frantically. How had I missed her?

"It's insane, Annie. I'm having a hell of a time seeing you trying something like this, let alone having it actually work."

She breathed deeply. I was testing her patience.

"I had help. I worked for a month with a private instructor and a meditation coach. I took beta-blockers. And I got a real helping hand from a policeman."

She stood, stretched her arms, and sat down on the couch beside me. She put her hand over my wound.

"Edward."

"Velarde? Officer Velarde?"

She looked perplexed herself. "Yeah. How did you . . ,"

"Is he still working for you, Annie?"

She shook her head. God, no. "For them."

"Dave Elliott? Your dad?"

She nodded.

"Nat, please let me get through this. Everything will make sense. I've been waiting forever to tell you this."

She told me that she swam and floated by the buoy, hovering there, then surreptitiously climbed aboard Officer Velarde's boat. Again, had they been discovered, they would have ditched the equipment and claimed he'd found and revived her.

In the years after Annie's death, I'd come to accept that there were parts of Annie that were more competitive and intense than I had internalized during our time together. But this was beyond anything I conceptualized.

"No way," I said flatly. "That's not you."

She looked out toward the fireplace—like it was a million miles away.

"You really don't understand what was at stake."

50

Can you imagine what would have happened to me in jail?" she said.

I stared through her.

Annie had faked her death and sequestered herself in France. I had to give her the benefit of the doubt. Didn't I? There must have been a logical reason why she abandoned me.

Something else. This Annie didn't feel exactly like the old one. I couldn't put my finger on it. This one seemed much more calculating.

"This is the part where you tell me why you left me."

My curiosity and hurt had trumped my physical pain. I barely registered the fire shooting from my back and side.

"Remember my dad put me in charge of Vestige Technologies? It made software used by big companies to organize and control all kinds of functions—like employee management, sales, and product tracking."

"That's what you threw our lives away for."

She met my stare.

"It had huge profit potential. Kindle Investment put eighty-five million into the company. That was just the *initial* investment."

A hefty sum. This was the heart of the dot-com frenzy, and the price of investing in start-up companies had gotten grossly inflated. But $85 million was unusually serious and it signified that the company's founders believed they had a certain strategy. They must have promised themselves, or their limited partners, that they were going to take the company public and get all that dough back five times over. Glenn Kindle wasn't the type of guy to invest money unless he had a really good idea how it would all turn out.

Annie stood at the kitchen table, zipping up a suitcase she'd folded shirts into, then resting her hands on the bag, as if making a presentation to shareholders.

"Several competitors were racing to go public. We had to beat them. This was a big test for me. We had a chance to succeed on a grander scale than my father could ever have dreamed."

She closed her eyes.

"I messed with the books. I didn't just flat out make things up. I made our deals look . . . rosy. I made us look way more successful than we really were."

"I don't believe it. You committed fraud. You cooked your books."

"Not just ours."

Something had clicked in Annie. She'd earlier been confessing, looking for me to understand, but now she was distant, and seemed to want to get this conversation out of the way. I recognized it from the past—a part of her that didn't like to be challenged.

She said Vestige had a competitor that threatened to beat it to the public markets. The company, like all dot-coms, had hired people at a furious pace. One of the new upper-management hires of the competitor had been a Vestige plant. The plant leaked reports to the press and the SEC suggesting his ostensible employer had been inflating revenue by including in its sales figures vague promises for future orders.

"This was the dirty pool of the dot-com era, the thing you don't read about," she said. "Venture capitalists were taking potshots at each other's companies—in the press, to the major underwriters like Goldman Sachs and Morgan Stanley. Not at first, when all the boats were rising. But when things looked like they were slowing down, we were all desperate not to miss the chance to go public. Everyone was playing rough. We played rougher."

Glenn Kindle's twist was hiring a spy.

It was successful—almost too much so, she said. The press was looking for examples of inflated business models to prove this was another Tulip Frenzy. So was the SEC. The competitor's public offering stalled, becoming one of the chunks of evidence that drove the whole market down in June 2001. But the desperate ploy also caused renewed scrutiny of the market overall, and at the companies in Vestige's sector in particular.

"We undid ourselves too." She smirked.

I stood and walked to the window. I parted the curtains. The parking lot was empty, except for my Explorer, a beat-up blue VW bus, and a big American car. I took a chance. I chuckled.

"Someone's screwed."

"Who? What?"

I paused, buying time, staring out the window.

"What is it, Nat?"

"Poor sucker locked himself out of his Oldsmobile. Or he's trying to steal it."

Annie's eyes narrowed and she headed to the window. I intercepted her and gave her a hug, holding her tight. She resisted, then reciprocated. "Oh, Nat." She pushed away and walked to the window. There was nothing to see. I told her he'd taken something from the seat of the car and must have wandered off. She grabbed her keys and wallet. "I'll be right back."

I unzipped her suitcase. Shirts, a cosmetic kit, nothing much of interest. Except in a side pocket. A piece of paper. It was a receipt from a houseboat rental. The *Monkey*. Located in Slip 47, Callville Bay Marina, Lake Mead. I zipped the suitcase just in time.

"What did he look like?" she asked.

I shrugged.

"There has to be something you're not telling me, Annie. What you're describing doesn't conform to anything you are.

My hunch is that you're protecting someone—maybe your dad. I can't see how or why you'd do that at this point. You have to let that go. I'm not even talking about us at this point. I'm talking about you."

"I really need an ally right now, Nathaniel. More than I've ever needed one. I need you to stay strong, to trust me for a little bit longer."

"You're asking me to trust you but everything you're telling me raises more questions."

She inhaled deeply, absorbing the blow.

"Like I said, the stakes got out of control." She sounded like she might shut down.

"Tell me," I pleaded, palms open.

She said that just before the public markets faltered, Vestige had attracted a new round of high-powered investors. They put $100 million more into the company. They did so based on fraudulent projections and the promise the company would soon go public. Then the sector, the company, and the market started to flounder. It wasn't meeting any of its early projections. The investors could see what was happening.

"We told them that the entire technology economy was collapsing," she said. "The same thing happened to a thousand companies, including some huge ones, like Cisco and Intel."

She said it might have just been another failed dot-com, but there was a difference: Glenn Kindle was a lead investor, one of the founders of Silicon Valley, and one of its most respected venture capitalists. He was worth close to $1 billion.

"A man came up to my father in a Starbucks."

"What man?"

"An investment banker. He'd been involved in Vestige and suspected foul play. He threatened to go to the newspapers and the police."

"Blackmail."

She nodded. "I always hated Starbucks."

I'd been so caught up I hadn't noticed her demeanor. Hers

was a face consumed with defeat; the veneer had softened. She wasn't the investment banker anymore, just a woman—a young woman.

"So your father was behind the whole thing. He made you cook the books." I felt the urge to protect Annie from her father. I was the savior. She stood and stepped back from me.

"No. It was *me*," she said. "Don't you see what I'm capable of? Even now you don't see? It really is remarkable."

"What?"

"My father told me not to inflate Vestige's earnings," she said. The conversation wasn't tracking, but I went with it.

She said her father tacitly understood what she'd done. Glenn Kindle knew there could be serious legal fallout. He wasn't worried about getting sued or jailed himself, since the sophisticated way he'd invested in the company protected him from prosecutors and regulators, but apparently it didn't insulate him from a blackmail demand of $50 million. Her father was worried about his reputation, and his daughter.

"My father felt his paternal instincts. In all its forms—the good, bad, and paranoid.

"He wanted to protect me. But he also saw paying the blackmail as a way to have something to hold over my head. I would have been beholden to him forever."

"So he paid it," I said dryly.

"Then matters got far worse."

As I watched her, I realized I was biting the inside of my cheek. I put my hand to my side and ran it over the shirt. The gash there didn't matter anymore. Annie took a wisp of her hair and curled it behind her ear. I used to love when she did that. She sighed.

"Dave threatened the investment banker."

"Dave Elliott."

She nodded.

"Threatened to kill the banker?"

"Worse, in a way. He amassed a dossier on the banker. He had his own secrets, nothing big. But the kinds of things that ruin families. Dave also picked the banker's son up at school, just to let him know the lengths he'd go to."

I closed my eyes.

"When I found out, I freaked out. I begged him to stop."

"Did your father know?"

"I doubt it. Tough as he is, he never would have the stomach for something like that."

"Stomach. You make it sound like . . ."

"Dave was his designated wild man. An assassin in a suit."

She said Dave felt he was just sending the banker a message: We can make your life miserable. It also was a negotiation. The banker settled for $100,000.

"Pocket change," Annie said. She walked toward me, reached out, and took my hand again. Casually—like it was something to play with while she talked.

"But it didn't make the problem go away. The SEC and IRS planned to investigate. If they'd dug deeply enough, they might have discovered the extent of the problem. It would have been a big feather to tear down Kindle Investment Partners. But we made sure they couldn't pursue the case."

After a pause, she added, "A key suspect died in a tragic boating accident."

If the words had come out of her father's mouth, I was sure they would have sounded like gloating. Annie just sounded sad. Resigned.

"I had no choice but to disappear. If the government had caught us cheating investors, undoing a competitor, *and* kidnapping a child to cover it up, I would have become the poster child of dot-com excess. I would have gone away forever—and you . . ."

"What, Annie?"

"You would have seen what a horrible person I am."

I was struck by a thought. It wasn't: Oh, poor Annie. It wasn't sympathy. It was: Finally. Where had those tears been when she was describing the grand deceit? Perhaps I should have comforted Annie, but I could only look at her in silence.

"Who was the banker—the one that threatened you and your father?"

She picked up the duffel bag she'd just packed. Was she going somewhere?

"His name was Simon Anderson."

For the better part of ten hours, I'd been free of the headache that had held sway over me since the café exploded. It returned. I put my hand on the chair to steady myself.

"Annie. Did you . . . were you trying to kill . . ." I found my voice, but not my emotions, or a singular one. The alchemy was devastation and loss, cut with confusion and still hope. "What were you doing at the café? When it exploded?"

She put her hand on my arm.

"You figured out what they were doing," I said. "You tried to stop them. But it was too late. I need you to tell me you didn't know all those people were going to die. And the rats. You love animals, even rodents. You would never have done those experiments."

Annie cleared her throat. "My father. My father. My father. I know I have a lot more to explain. We've been working behind the scenes to make things right."

We.

As if on cue, there came a knock on the door, and a voice, yelling, as if through clenched teeth.

"Tara," the voice said. "It's me."

"Coming, Cindy," Annie said. "I'm coming."

Annie let go of my arm. I didn't bother to follow. Revelation had become paralysis. At the door stood the blonde angel.

"You're out of time, Tara. You've got to go."

51

Angels don't fly. They drive minivans.

When the door opened, I recognized the face. The blonde angel, the woman with a tight bun of hair and a handgun who'd broken into my torture session and taken out two powerful cops. Now she wore jeans and a leather jacket.

"The meeting is in three hours," she told Annie.

She looked up at me.

"Nathaniel, you've met Cynthia. She calls me Tara. For the sake of discretion," Annie said. "Cynthia works for me. She is assistant, friend, advance man, and bodyguard. She helps me live a very, very careful life. When I can't be somewhere, she is my eyes and ears."

"And photographer," I said. "At the café, right?"

Cynthia didn't say anything. But I realized I'd seen her in the aftermath of the café explosion, I'd caught her taking my picture a bit too intently. She said she'd been a freelancer.

"Turtle, where is the laptop?"

Andy's laptop. She'd expressly asked me to bring it.

"It was in his car," the blonde angel said. "I put it in the van."

Cynthia had unlocked the car I'd driven and taken the laptop. Evidently I was not a sovereign nation. I glowered at her.

Annie held a hand out to Cynthia, as if to say: Slow down. "Give us a second."

She moved to close the door, but Cynthia put her hand on it and said, "What about the other one?"

Annie looked at me, then back at Cynthia.

"Bring her here."

When Annie turned around to face me square on I realized where I'd seen her before. The police station. The photo I'd been shown by Lieutenant Aravelo. The grainy, indiscernible shot of the blonde woman.

"They have your picture," I said.

"What?"

"You came to save everyone at the café. You found out what your father and Elliott were doing and you decided to stop them. But it was too late and you could only save me. Is that what happened? That would be very good to know just about now."

I was teetering again. This time from something deeper than exhaustion, or a disease picked up from my laptop computer, or even uncertainty about Annie's motives. This bordered on certainty. This felt like outright betrayal. This was the possibility that Annie had turned into someone dark.

She dropped her duffel bag to the ground. She brought her hands together—as if asking a child not to act up again in school.

"You've got to stay here, Nat. You've got to trust me. Please. I have a plan. I can expose this, and my father, and make everything right."

Like that, my perspective changed. Annie wasn't in charge. She was fighting demons, and her dad, and she needed my help. Whatever she'd done, she loved me, and needed me. Glenn—he was the epicenter of the problem. Fatigue eating away at clarity.

"I'm coming with you. You're going to meet him, aren't you? You're going to confront your father in Las Vegas."

She shook her head. "We can't risk it. You've got to stay here."

I studied her face.

"Look what he did to me. To us. I have a stake in this too."

"I know how you think, Nat. More than you can imagine. I know what I mean to you. What *we* mean to you. I understand you want to protect me. But he is not going to hurt me."

Annie put her arms around my waist.

"Take your hands off of me," I said, surprising myself.

"Wait here for me."

Her lips touched my cheek. The way they had on our very first date. When we'd been at the Mexican restaurant and I'd told Annie my life story, she'd leaned over to me, kissed me, and said, "I've been looking for you." I'd turned gummy bear.

Annie pulled her arm away from me. She opened the door. I took a step forward, like I might follow, until I saw who greeted us both on the door's other side.

Erin.

Blindfolded and bound.

I looked at her mutely. "Thank God," I finally said.

"Nat?"

She turned in my direction. So did Annie. The emotion in my voice probably caught them both off guard. Not Cynthia. She stood behind Erin, looking perfectly calm. I turned to Annie.

"I'm going with you. I'm not letting you go again." In response to my comment, Annie looked at Cynthia and shook her head.

"Too dangerous. It's for your safety," Annie said, then cocked her head at Erin. "It's for *her* safety. It's for my safety. I don't know who I can trust."

Cynthia nodded. She held a gun. It wasn't necessarily pointed at Erin, nor was it necessarily pointed away. Annie stepped past them, toward the van. Cynthia walked forward, prodding Erin inside the condo.

"I'm going with Annie," I said.

The blonde angel squinted at me.

"You're not going to shoot me," I said to her.

Annie said, "Please, Nathaniel. No."

I took another step forward. Nothing was going to stop me. Nothing, that is, until I heard a protest from an unexpected place.

"Nathaniel. Please don't leave me here," Erin said.

52

I couldn't believe I was watching Annie Kindle walk out of my life. But watch I did, or more like listen. I closed my eyes and heard her close the front door, and open a car door. The engine turned over, caught, and roared to life.

The sounds were palpable. Her thin fingers gripping the steering wheel, turning it to toward Las Vegas. Only they weren't her fingers. When I opened my eyes, I saw Erin had taken my hand. She was gently rubbing the skin between my thumb and forefinger.

Blindfolded, she had found me. I lifted the cover from her eyes. She blinked. She looked tired and unkempt, and had a bruise around her eye. She took in the room.

"I'm okay," I said without conviction. "You?"

She stopping rubbing my hand and squeezed.

"I guess that was Annie."

Erin's legs were tied together by a sturdy piece of nylon, the lines cutting into her Levi's, as though she'd tried to wriggle free. She could walk, but it was more in the form of a shuffle.

Her left eye was black and puffy around the edges, but not swollen shut. The other was red, bloodshot from exhaustion or tears. She gently touched the eye where she'd been struck, pushing in spongy flesh. She winced.

Cynthia studied us in silence and then scanned the open area—from the doorway leading to the bathroom and bedrooms, to the dining room, kitchen, then back past Erin and me, to the couches and chairs, coffee table, and then fireplace.

"Sit," she said.

She pushed Erin in the back with the nose of her gun. Erin stiffened and Cynthia pushed harder. Cynthia was capable of terrible violence, but against me—someone she'd killed to protect? If so, there was no way I was going to overpower her and her pistol, certainly not in sufficient enough time to spring both Erin and me. I felt a wellspring of violence inside of me, fight-or-flight, heightened by my twisted new set of neurochemicals. Cynthia probably wouldn't listen to reason. Maybe she could be charmed.

"Hey, who's up for some blackjack? We can be in Vegas in a couple of hours. The prime rib is on me."

"She'll be back soon," Cynthia said. "Until then, we stay put. End of discussion."

Erin shuffled across the living room to take a seat. I scanned for a phone. Even if I didn't have time to say anything, 911 would get the distress signal and show up. But then what? Would I lose my chance to catch Annie—forever? Besides, there was no phone visible. I walked into the kitchen.

For a moment, I saw myself from the outside. Poor by choice, unlucky in love, crappy at picking out matching outfits, an occasional athlete, sappy about the cat, prone to making choices that disappointed, if not baffled, my family. And I'd never once blown up a bridge. Nothing said action hero. I just desperately wanted to be possessed by one.

"Glass of water," I said, opening a cupboard. "Do you go by henchperson?"

Cynthia didn't respond.

"As opposed to henchman. I'm just wondering if your job title is gender specific."

I turned on the water. I glanced around the counter, unsure what I was looking for. A knife?

"Did you kill those two policemen?" I said. "Water, Erin?"

"Please."

"I owe you my life."

She didn't engage. I asked her why she'd taken my picture outside the café. No answer. I opened up the cupboard to get another glass, and saw a glint. Strawberry air freshener in a spray can. I kept the cupboard open, blocking Cynthia's view. I took out and set down the glass and the aerosol can, now blocked from Cynthia by the countertop.

"You want ice?"

"Where did you put the bodies?" I asked, filling up Erin's glass with water and setting it on the counter. I walked to the refrigerator and pushed the ice dispenser. I scanned the counter to its right. Two cookbooks, salt and pepper shakers, and something shiny—reflecting light from the sun. A green lighter.

"I can't see how you carried Velarde. He was huge."

"You must be really annoying as a journalist."

I laughed.

"My leg is cut," Erin said.

I snagged the lighter.

"I'll have a look at it," I said. "Lie down and pull up your pant leg."

"Give me a break." Cynthia stirred.

"I spent four years in medical school," I said, trying to sound casual. "I'm still qualified to give people the once-over and then overcharge them."

Cynthia eyed Erin as she lay down. I opened the top two buttons on my jeans, shoving the freshener inside, and pulled my shirt over the top.

I set the waters down on a tray and carried them into the living room, trying to block the view of the freshener stuffed in my pants.

I set the tray down and sat next to Erin, leaning in close. She looked at me like my brain was still scrambled. I caught her gaze. I squinted and clenched my jaw. Silent Morse code.

I prodded at the raw skin where rope and jeans had rubbed

against skin. The jeans had been worn through. The skin was irritated but fine.

"You've got to get her to a real doctor."

"Soon enough," Cynthia said.

"It's infected and serious. You can't mess around with something like this."

Cynthia walked warily toward us with her gun in her hand. She raised it and got within a foot, leaning over Erin.

"Put it down, angel."

"Who?" She looked up.

She was staring down a barrel of my jerry-rigged weapon. An air freshener one inch behind the flame from a lighter.

"Put down the gun," I said. "Please. Be reasonable. You know I have no choice but to go."

And suddenly, Cynthia laughed. "Give me a break."

I pulled the trigger on the aerosol can. A stream of fire erupted. But Cynthia easily moved her head aside to avoid getting hit and, in virtually the same motion, swung the gun, sending a spray of fire toward the head of the couch, and then causing the whole contraption to fly from my hand.

I said, "So much for action hero."

It took us all a second to realize my contraption hadn't been totally ineffective. A pillow on the couch had ignited. Erin scrambled away from it. Cynthia sighed and we stood staring at the surreal outcome. Until I saw a flash of metal from the side. Erin hoisted the pot that Annie had used to clean my wounds and slammed it into the side of Cynthia's head.

Stunned, our captor wobbled and turned to Erin and raised her gun, and I dove. I tackled Cynthia to the ground as she pressed the trigger, spitting off three wild shots. With one hand, she covered her head to avoid another blow from Erin, with the other, she tried to hold on to the gun I was wresting from her grasp. Moments later, the angel was subdued.

With the rope from Erin's legs, we tied Cynthia's hands behind her back. We gave her an ice pack. I finally located the phone, dialed 911, and left the phone off the hook.

53

She's going to be okay," I rationalized. "Maybe a concussion, maybe not. A decent amount of pain."

We were on the main drag—heading to the highway and Las Vegas.

"Bullshit. We don't need any excuse. Everyone has limits and boundaries. We're allowed to protect ourselves, and the people we care about. She could have . . . We could have died there."

In the past two days, I'd had fisticuffs in a corporate law firm and set a woman on fire. I hoped Erin was right: Survival instinct had driven my attacks. But another part of me suspected something else was at work. Had my brain chemicals gotten so fried that I'd been inspired to bloodlust? And the adrenaline-drenched belief I could successfully mount an attack?

Then I smiled, thinking about our fight with Cynthia, and Erin delivering the critical blow.

"What's so funny?"

"When you hit Cynthia just then—was that something you learned in your dance troupe? That's what I call a socially responsible karate chop."

On the way out of town, I pulled into a 7-Eleven. I paid cash for a mobile-phone-in-a-box and a prepaid calling plan. I called Bullseye, who answered after four rings. I could hear the bells and whistles of a casino in the background. He put Mike on the phone.

"The laptop is on the move. I need to know where it's going."

I hung up and asked Erin to fill me in on her previous twenty-four hours.

She said she was waiting for me to get acupuncture when two cops showed up. She wasn't sure whether to panic or if they were there to arrest her. One immediately grabbed her—the tall, stocky one with dark skin. Velarde. She pulled away and tried to run.

"He used the nightstick. I watched it coming. I froze. I couldn't move out of the way," she said. "I woke up on the floor of the entryway."

She said she came to with her hands tied. Cynthia was there. She told Erin she'd help her and gave her a sedative. When Erin woke up again, she was traveling in a van, tied up and hot.

Physically, she would be okay, but she needed a doctor. Though she wasn't lethargic or slurring her speech, I had some concern she'd suffered a concussion, and her leg needed attention. Probably just a good clean, a tetanus booster, and some antibiotics, but it would have to be checked out.

"I'm sorry, Erin."

The speedometer hit 90. Erin put her hand on my side—over my bandage.

"What was it like?"

"Getting smacked by a paperweight?"

"You were hit?"

I nodded.

"I meant: What was it like seeing Annie?"

I didn't say anything at first. I blinked back a tear.

"I'm not sure yet."

"I don't see you two together," she said quietly. "What am I missing here?"

It sounded rhetorical.

"So what happened to you?"

I rubbed my bandage with my palm. "Sort of the same thing that happened to Andy."

I told her about Weller, Velarde, and the acupuncture needles, my saving by Cynthia, and the run-in with Dave Elliott. I told her about Bullseye and Mike's assignment, which included putting a Global Positioning System on Andy's laptop. I told her my theory that the computer was so interesting to everyone because it had been loaded with an experimental program, a program that might be very dangerous.

"No, Nathaniel. No. It's not possible. Please tell me they didn't kill Andy that way. Please tell me there was some reason."

Twenty miles outside Las Vegas, I called Bullseye and Mike.

"Bellagio," Mike said. "You'll be in good company."

"Glenn Kindle's there?"

"Andre Latzke and Helen Douglass are in the lobby."

The respective chief executives of Advanced Chip Devices and Sackerd Printer Corp., two of the world's biggest technology companies.

"Can you watch where they go?"

"Sure," he said. "What brings such royalty to this amusement park?"

Five minutes later, I had a partial answer to Mike's question. We were just outside of town when I saw a billboard. "Telecommunications Industry Association—July 20 to 25. Sands Convention Center. Get Connected!"

But it didn't explain the coincidence of their presence at the Bellagio.

The phone rang. Mike said he and Bullseye were inside the hotel—on the fifteenth floor.

"Your friends are inside room 1544."

Moments later, I was on the Strip. I parked in the Bellagio complex, and found Bullseye and Mike playing sudoku in the lobby.

"What's the plan?" Bullseye asked, without looking up.

"Fifteen forty-four. Guerrilla style. That's how I get answers."

And Annie.

I asked Bullseye to take Erin to see if there was a medical center on the premises. I told Erin not to use her name and to say she'd lost her wallet. I doubted the cops would have been looking for her here, but who knew.

"What if . . ." she said, swallowing her thought. "Anger is dangerous. Be careful."

My anger. Their anger? Hers? Erin put her hand on my arm, almost as if to slow me down. I took a pen from Mike and wrote down the name and location of the houseboat I'd found in Annie's suitcase. The *Monkey*, in Callville Bay Marina. I folded it in half and tucked it into Erin's hand. I leaned in close to her and tried not to sound too dramatic.

"If something bad happens, check out this boat," I said.

She winced.

"Mike, can you continue to track the laptop?"

He nodded. "In the hotel, yes, not in the casino. None of it will work in the casino. Not the other stuff either. Too much interference."

He reached into a duffel bag.

"I replaced the batteries in the laptop with a tiny GPS unit. If they turn it on, they'll realize there's a problem. The computer has got to be plugged in to work. Even then, it's got a broadcast radius of about twenty-five feet. You'll need this."

He handed me an electrical cord and power pack. Nothing fancy. An ordinary power jack for a low-tech kind of guy.

From outside the door, room 1544 didn't look unusual. I knocked. No answer, but the door was cracked open. Then a voice. "It's open, Ira."

"I'm with the Kindles," I said, gently pushing open the door.

I looked up, and tried to mask my surprise. My reality had become virtual.

54

I was staring at a living room. To the left was a circular couch facing a wall-mounted flat-panel TV. In the near-right corner, a bar counter. In the middle-right, a conference table, and around it was what set this room apart: the company. Two of the most influential technology executives in the world: Andre Latzke and Helen Douglass. But it was the head of the table that was of the most interest—to me. At the front, sitting apart from each other by the table's width, were the Kindles—Annie and Glenn. I was in a casino. I took a gamble. I spoke to Annie, interrupting two seconds of uncomfortable silence.

"I brought the rest of the GNet data."

Glenn finally said, "This isn't a good time."

All eyes studied me. I was a mess.

"I'm so sorry I'm late, Mr. Kindle. And sorry for my . . . state of disrepair. I got into a car accident. Rear-ended stopping short at a light. I've got to learn to stop making stock trades while I drive."

Glenn stood and took a step toward me, for an instant looking bewildered.

"He helped with some of the tests," Annie said, composed, but deferential. Was she working with her father? Were they at odds?

Glenn turned to the group.

"Will you excuse us all for a moment? Tara and I need to have a private word." He smiled. He was slick. "I know—

we're supposed to iron these things out before the company arrives."

Helen Douglass chuckled.

In this company, Annie went by Tara.

She offered her father a gentle rejoinder. "Should we leave our guests alone?"

Glenn clenched his teeth. If I hadn't known better, I wouldn't have picked up Annie's implicit threat—best not leave me here with this group to get to chatting. The extent of the father-daughter tension was apparently lost on the executives. Or maybe the extent of their cooperation was lost on me.

"True enough," Glenn stuttered.

Latzke, a man with a full head of wavy hair and strong hands who appeared to be assuming a lead role, looked at his watch. "Now where do you think Ira is?" He forced a smile. The good executives never publicly betrayed real feelings.

Douglass leaned forward. "Well, let's get on with it."

I settled onto the couch. I knew little about the two executives. I remembered that Douglass was considered to be more charismatic than substantive, a reputation she often derided in speeches as sexist. Latzke was the consummate salesman. He believed in his company with religious fervor. I couldn't believe either of them was mixed up with the recent dark events, not knowingly. Something else had to be going on.

"When's your keynote?" Glenn asked Douglass.

"Tomorrow morning," she responded, but seemed bored by the subject. "Bring me up to speed."

Glenn took a deep breath. "Why don't we wait for Ira?"

"Because we could wait until midnight," Latzke responded, again with a smile.

Douglass had a sheet of paper in front of her. It looked to be covered with scribbled notes. She glanced at it as she spoke.

"Start with a recap. I missed the Taos meeting."

I was struck by her tone—its lack of urgency. These executives were ice-cream cool; it was clear now that they didn't realize nearly the extent of the hurricane that had visited the Kindles and their pet project.

Annie's head was down. She was sending a text message from her phone. She felt my eyes, looked up at me, and smiled. Was she texting me? I didn't have the super-secret spy phone.

"Key tap and advertising." Latzke aimed his comment at Douglass.

"Right," Glenn said, overcoming hesitancy, regaining the conversation and his composure. He wore a short-sleeved black button-up polo shirt and seemed to transform into the picture of California calm.

"We've developed two methods for intensifying the human-computer interaction. One is the key-tap method," Glenn continued. "Using this method, we give people an imperceptible sensation when they touch the keys on the keyboard. It sends what amounts to a jolt into the pleasure center of the user's nervous system. It is an electric pulse. They touch the key and get a jolt, touch a key, get a jolt. And so on. It serves to reinforce the ordinary sensation that comes from receiving or sending e-mail, or getting some other input of information. The same principle works in variations with cell phones, and other gadgets."

He paused.

"A juiced-up Crackberry."

"I've got it bad already." Douglass chuckled, then stopped. "Can something like that really work?"

"It's already out there to an extent," Glenn answered. "Video game consoles have controllers that vibrate when a player shoots a gun, or their on-screen character is attacked. As I said, our phones vibrate, bringing us to attention. It's a question of refining the technology. And neurology is evolving too, providing us a map for how to give people a positive feeling when they use the keyboard—like a mild dose of caffeine."

After a polite pause, Glenn continued. "In turn, everything

associated with the computing experience is enhanced—the senses are aroused, engaged. The union of the chip and the brain. The users want more and more—and what they do get is intensely pleasurable.

"What this means is the users will get a level of enjoyment out of computing that is tantamount to a pure physical experience. It is an *actual* physical experience. That's what they get out of it. What we get out of it is a user base that will be loyal without precedent. Remember, the essence of making money on the Internet is not just amassing as many eyeballs as possible. That business model fizzled during the bust. The key is keeping them around by giving people a highly intense and interactive experience."

"But to what end, Glenn?" asked Douglass. "Is the business model any more refined?"

The room had momentum now. Even as much as I hated Glenn and was horrified by the undisclosed implications, a piece of me marveled at his salesmanship. This was his Sky-Mall catalog, and he had turned smooth capitalist preacher in its promotion.

"Great question. There are several very fruitful options," he answered. "For one, this technology will be the holy grail of advertising—we'll create an audience of users who are utterly immersed. Already, computers and televisions are so alluring. The lights, the sounds; they are heavy stimulants. We're turning the intensity way up. People will absolutely love looking at what we deliver. They won't be able to tear themselves away from staring at the messages we deliver. Political, commercial, whatever. We can sell them our software, our high-speed Internet connections, our consumer products."

"Sounds like mind control," said Douglass.

The voice that answered seemed to come from far away.

"Not for it's own sake, Helen. This is 2006, not 1984." It was Annie.

Heads turned her way.

"We want to feel connected. We long for a real experience," Annie said. I felt an instant spasm of conflict; her words resonated, but I could no longer take her seriously.

"As you know, Tara's done testing and helped to develop the technology," Glenn interrupted his daughter, then he turned to face her. "But of course that's not a business model."

"Of course," she responded, seeming again to yield to him. "But the business model, the applications, are awesome. And so are the efficiencies. Look, people have come to expect free information on the Internet. They want news, sports, movies, music for free. So in the future, people won't pay for information with money, they'll pay with their attention."

Annie paused. She picked up a bottle of water standing on the table. As she swallowed, her gaze briefly caught mine. Her eyes sparkled. I flashed on a memory of Annie petting her dog and kissing its nose, the moments when her affection seemed undiluted, at its purest. Who was the cold person in her place? Was she playacting? Could I tell the difference? It seemed like she was in love with this too.

She set down her drink and continued.

"In addition to the key-tap method, we have been perfecting the use of subliminal advertising—by inserting images into a Web site's background—ultra-fast, ultra-intense images. This is just what Hitchcock did in the movies, but with a revolutionary twist. Our messages will be highly personal. That's because of what we know of individual user's particular interests from their Internet surfing habits. If someone is a skier, we'll flash travel ads for Aspen; if they like cooking, we'll show them the George Foreman Grill."

"Sounds messy," Douglass said. "What about the FCC? We don't want to be the next tobacco industry."

"'Subliminal advertising' may be a bad choice of words," Glenn said. "Technically, such advertising doesn't violate federal law. But think of what we're talking about here as background enhancements. Maybe the users will even give us permission to run stealth streams of advertising—instant, unseen flashes of personalized communication—in exchange, of course, for free services we provide. Regardless, we're proving that the technology lets us communicate more effectively than ever through vivid, personalized messages on computers, phones, or handheld devices."

"And location-based services too," Latzke said.

"Exactly," Glenn continued. "The GPS in cell phones lets us interact with people not just based on who they are, but where they are. We communicate with them about nearby restaurants, entertainment options, and so forth. They won't be able to disconnect themselves and they won't want to."

The Kindles weren't just talking about creating technology. They were building a kind of drug.

"Of course, this background communication method could also entail simply making the sounds, colors, and entire computing experience more vivid," the wily venture capitalist continued. "All our hope at this point is to develop and perfect the technology and maintain our communication channels with you so we'll be able to move on this when we're all ready."

"You really think this can work?" Helen said.

Annie stepped in again. "Certain of it. As we've mentioned before, I've been developing the technology for more than five years."

Five years. I coughed, repressing an exclamation. Latzke cleared his throat, and spoke. "It's not that big of a reach."

"Society is halfway there," Glenn added enthusiastically. "Video games, compulsive phone, Internet, and e-mail use. We already embrace a cacophony of stimulation. Nonstop, round-the-clock, mile-a-minute data input. When that action is missing, people feel bored. They want a more powerful dose."

Latzke looked at Douglass. "The search engines already are delivering highly targeted advertising—based on a consumer's location, taste, and so on. It's the endgame of individualized marketing to a totally captive audience."

A voice interrupted. "We're *already* hooked." I was stunned to realize the voice belonged to me.

Glenn commanded the turned heads back to him.

"Regardless of the method, we are going to transform the ubiquitous digital devices into the most powerful delivery system man has ever known. We hear all the time in Silicon Valley about the next big thing. This is it. You know it in your gut. This is the inevitable coming together of computer and human. Think of it as delivering to users the sensations of a casino; we're trying to create an environment that people will absolutely love. That will give them an incredible rush."

Annie leaned forward. "Or we would have," she said, adding quietly: "But now we've got a problem."

55

The words were chilly, the tone frigid. And suddenly hard and confident as ice.

So was Glenn's. "Unnecessary."

But before the conversation could continue, there was a loud rapping at the door.

"Rothsberger!" announced a deep, throaty voice from outside.

"Ira at last," Latzke said flatly.

In ambled the thick corpus and many jowls of Ira Rothsberger, the chief executive of one of the largest Internet search companies in the world.

"Couldn't get off the phone with *USA Today*," he exclaimed, sounding like a man accustomed to making excuses. He surveyed the room. "Did I miss a funeral?"

Then he paused.

"Shit. You were talking about Ed. He killed himself, I heard. Jesus. What a fucking tragedy."

Ed Gaverson. Friend of Glenn Kindle and technology executive, and reported suicide case.

"Shotgun, right?" Rothsberger said. "Tragic end."

"He fought depression," Douglass said.

There was a moment of silence.

"I think we're going to have to adjourn for today."

All eyes turned to Glenn, who was bent next to Annie, like he had been whispering to her.

"Jesus H. on a Popsicle stick." Rothsberger sighed. He was

one of those executives imposing enough to make being impolitic seem refreshing, or like there was nothing you could do about it anyway.

"My sincere apologies. We've had some technical difficulties. We need to get them ironed out before wasting any more of your time," Glenn said. "We can reconvene in December at CES."

Latzke stood. So did Annie. She broke a palpable silence.

"You can't let these people swing in the wind. They could wind up being implicated."

"Please."

"What's she talking about?"

"Implicated in what?"

"It's absolutely nothing to worry about," Glenn said.

"Famous last words," Rothsberger said.

Latzke sat back down.

Glenn sighed, exasperated. He seemed to feel no compulsion to share the tragedy of the preceding days with the executives.

"As you know, we've been testing our advertising enhancement methods. We did some very effective tests in a lab setting with paid volunteers. They reinforced just how big this thing can be," Glenn said. "We decided a field test was next."

"Move on."

"One second, Andre," Rothsberger interjected. "Just so I'm clear here. We're still talking about spicing up the computer, so consumers get a real interactive experience. Physical sensations—a real virtual world."

"Check," Glenn said, then cleared his throat and lowered his voice. "Some of our field tests were at the Sunshine Café."

"Where's that?"

"It's the café that blew up in San Francisco."

A collective shudder went through the room. The executives exchanged glances, processing. What were the implications?

"So, what's that got to do with us?" It was Rothsberger.

Latzke joined in. "It's a terrible coincidence. Terrible."

"Exactly my point," Glenn said. "Nothing to worry about."

* * *

In the moment of silence that followed, I did a Cliff's Notes recap of the conversation. These executives had a passing understanding of what they believed—or had let themselves believe—was an innovative but not sinister way to make computing more stimulating. Glenn seemed to share their perspective. But he had always been impossible to read. Annie was the biggest wild card of all. I couldn't afford to let this moment pass without flushing out more.

"Don't forget about the rats."

All eyes swung toward me.

"Strawberry Labs."

"I have no idea what he's talking about," Glenn said quickly.

He shook his head. He blinked rapidly. He seemed genuinely mystified.

"What *is* he talking about?" Rothsberger asked.

"Don't have the slightest idea, Ira," he said, then looked at me. "I think it's time for you to go."

I looked at Annie. She caught my eye, then looked away.

"Animal testing?" Douglass shook her head, then shrugged.

"I absolutely did not know anything about that," Latzke added. "I'm blindsided here. If it becomes necessary, I can assure my shareholders of that."

Annie put her hands out, palms down. Calming the crowd. Glenn ran his right hand through his hair, pinning it momentarily back over his temples.

"Let me explain," Annie said.

"Sit down, Annie."

"Annie?" someone said.

"Tara."

She looked at him. Then she spread her palms up and out, giving him the floor, and sat.

"As I said, why don't we adjourn for the day," Glenn said. "You have much better and bigger things to worry about."

"True. We just need full disclosure. We need to know what our exposure is. You know how the media is. They'll love even the most distant connection between us and a blown-up café." It was Douglass.

"And we're just damn curious." Latzke. "Were there any other tests we don't know about?"

"No," Glenn said. "Absolutely not. You've all known me for years. You know what I'm about. Please, let's not blow this out of proportion."

"Curious choice of words."

"You're absolutely sure, Glenn?"

"Well," Annie said, her voice barely loud enough to be heard, "we might have some exposure as to the nonconsensual nature of the tests."

"Now hold on," Glenn said. "I didn't know . . ."

"Let her finish."

"We couldn't rely on data from subjects who consented to being tested—even if they weren't sure for exactly what. As Glenn said, we all agreed a field test seemed like the next natural step. And I put his plan into action."

"That just isn't true," her father protested.

"We deployed . . . anonymous testing," Annie continued. She sounded the compliant and contrite second in command, duty-bound to tell the executives they'd been jeopardized. "We selected a handful of heavy Internet users, and we tested the tap method on some users and the subliminal method on others. We were hoping to get a sense of behaviors and surfing patterns as captured by the computers on which we installed the software—"

"I assumed test subjects signed consent forms. We can sue you if we're implicated," Latzke interrupted, already in spin mode. I could hear his corporate lawyers talking to the media.

"There's more," Annie said. "The experiments didn't go exactly as planned. Several subjects got sick—first with head-

aches. Then—and I want to stress we're not sure if this is related—one subject *may* have killed himself."

Rothsberger slammed a meaty palm on the table. "Enough,"
he said.

Douglass nearly pounced at Glenn. "You're a maniac. We're
talking about experimenting on people against their will and
then *killing* them. Do you realize who we are? What's at stake
for us?"

"You're protected, Helen," he said. "You are at more than
arm's length from the day-to-day development of the technology. I swear to you, I didn't know about all of this. Whatever
happened was unexpected, an accident. Something obviously
went wrong with the methodology, the intensity of the experiment." Glenn paused, then turned to Annie. "If it really did go
wrong, I have my suspicions as to the identity of the saboteur."

"You can't be serious," she countered.

"I have no idea how, or why, or if the café fire *is* even connected. It's a coincidence, I'm telling you," he pleaded to his
associates.

He sounded genuine, but the jury had already convicted.
The more he talked the guiltier he sounded. Annie piled on.

"I spoke to Ed Gaverson two days ago. I felt obliged to tell
him. He was very pained."

"I need a word in private," Glenn looked at Annie.

"I'm sorry, but we need to get this out in the open. Why
don't you tell everyone what happened to the evidence that
could tie us all to the café?"

Glenn's eyes widened.

"Enough. Please."

She spoke to him. "Where is the computer, the laptop—the
one that killed that poor young man—the one that could ruin
all of us? The one that could destroy the reputation of these
great executives."

Glenn paused. Silent.

"Where is it?" Latzke said.

Annie bent over and picked up a bag. She pulled the laptop from inside of it.

"You can all be implicated by this," she said, holding up the computer. "I went to great lengths to retrieve it when I realized the position Glenn had put you all in. It implicates the tech industry's greatest titans. It could link you to a possible accidental death, but you know the maniacs out there will call it murder. And you can rest assured, I will make sure this is destroyed and doesn't get into the wrong hands."

A silence in the room went from deafening to atomic.

The executives again looked at one another. Frantic. Glenn's mouth was open, his chin hung to his knees. Annie looked at me, and her lips curled up into a smile; self-satisfaction and evil. It was at that moment that I realized she was in total control, and had been the whole time.

There was a sudden quick rap at the door, the sound of it opening, and a voice entering the room that made everyone jump.

"Sorry to interrupt," it said. "But we need to adjourn."

Inside walked a familiar face, with a familiar facial contusion. Dave Elliott. He looked at Annie and nodded.

The executives, furious and bewildered, stood.

Glenn lunged toward Annie like a panther.

56

The executives cleared out in a hurry. Only psychos remained. Before I could plot my first move, father was mowing down daughter.

"What can you possibly be thinking, Annie?"

He was frozen with anguish. I stepped forward, but gingerly.

"What are you thinking? What are you talking about?"

"We needed to put the truth out there and deal with it," she countered. She started walking to the door, carrying the laptop.

"What have you done?" He walked after her. "You blew up the café to destroy the evidence."

She turned and faced him, defiant.

"Give me a break. You knew those tests weren't consensual."

He was stone-faced for a moment, then he smiled, ever so slightly, and said: "No one will believe that. You're taking the fall here."

"How does it feel, Dad?"

"What?" As if he didn't hear her.

"Getting outmaneuvered."

Glenn lost his composure altogether. "You think you can blackmail these people?!" He caught his breath. "This isn't like Vestige, Annie. That was a setback. This is professional suicide. You just don't burn those relationships. And what about the idea? If this gets out, I'll go to jail, you'll go to jail, the press will go crazy, and then, you know what, someone else is going to beat us to it."

It was me who spoke next, expelling knee-jerk commentary. "Don't forget about the murder-and-torture part."

They glanced my way, then Annie spoke to her father in a tone that mixed plaintiveness and accusation. "Would it crush you to see me in chains? Would you come visit me?"

"I can't tell you how much you've disappointed me, Annie."

"I don't think so," she answered with finality. "To be disappointed with me, you'd actually have to feel something."

Glenn's face reddened. He raised his hand, a cross between a schoolboy trying to get attention in class and a cocked arm, like he might strike her. Then something else passed over his face—defeat. I stumbled forward, consumed with the memory of an urge to protect her.

"Annie, you're the one at the biggest risk. Do you understand that you will become persona non grata again? Have you forgotten what it's like to live on the fringes—with no one? If this gets out, that's what you're facing. The wilderness. Something so lonely that a country house in France will look like a Los Angeles mall."

Annie flinched. Now *he'd* frozen *her*. I remembered what Annie had said earlier—isolation was tantamount to death.

I moved quickly. I intercepted her as she neared the door. I took her hand in my left. With the right, I gripped the laptop. "He's crazy, Turtle. Crazy and empty," she said, with a blank look. "I have to go."

"Please tell me the truth. You did all of this. You tested and tortured, set up your father. Help me put this together. Help me reconcile you with the Annie I fell in love with."

"It wasn't working anyway." She sighed, distant, professional. "Make the hypocrites pay. Scorched earth."

"Annie, what are you talking about? What wasn't going to work?"

She pulled her arm away from me—not violently, but enough to get free. I was still holding the laptop.

She opened the door.

A powerfully built man blocked her path. He moved aside so she could go. But when I stepped up to follow, he shoved me back into the room, causing me to reel backward, and shut the door.

Dave chuckled.

"That Electra complex is pretty powerful stuff."

Glenn turned to him.

"You're part of this too. You and Annie, right? You got us in way deep. You've taken this to a different level. Rats? Dangerous levels of potency . . . Right?"

"Defining the cutting edge," Dave said.

Glenn pointed at me.

"What about him?" he said. "What about *him*?"

"He won't say a word."

"Cross my heart," I said.

"Trust me. He won't say a word," Dave said. "Not when he realizes that he's his own worst enemy."

Before I could make a vainglorious attempt to bypass the bouncer, Dave caught my attention.

"Hear me out. This can be a win-win."

I glanced around the room. I bit the inside of my cheek to focus, fending off the familiar cranial pulsing. I held a lot of cards. But one of them wasn't physical advantage. What lengths would they go to keep me here, or stop me? Would they kill me? But if I didn't escape at that moment, would I find Annie? Find out what she'd done, what was in her heart?

I had a decent guess where she would be heading: to a boat named the *Monkey*. To catch her, I was going to have to act quickly, but not so fast that I undid myself.

"Actually, don't hear me out," Dave said. "Hear Sarah."

Sarah.

He pulled out a small digital audio device and hit the play

button. I heard a recording of my voice. It was playing snippets of the message I'd left on Sarah's answering machine.

"*I think I'm seeing ghosts.*"

There was a pause.

"*Be careful, Sarah. Something bizarre is going on. I don't really know what. But I just want you to stay aware.*"

Sarah said, "*You're scaring me, Nat. Frankly, you sound . . . a little weird.*"

"*That I'll stipulate to in court,*" I said.

Dave turned off the recorder.

"Fun with Real Audio," I said.

"Do you understand why you're not going to tell the police about what you've seen or heard, or *imagined* that you've seen or heard?" Dave said. "It's because you're crazy. No one will believe you. In my business, we say that you've impugned your credibility as a witness."

Glenn had taken a seat. He had his head hung between his shoulders.

Dave started down a laundry list of ways in which I was not reliable, or had tainted myself. I'd survived the café explosion, visited the funeral of Simon Anderson, wound up at his house when it caught flames, and been at a fire in Felton. The police had found my fingerprints, and eventually would discover my hair follicles on two of their dead brethren, Weller and Velarde. Then there was video footage from surveillance cameras showing me furtively leaving Dave's office building after he'd called security. And he reminded me that, for good measure, I didn't have a fan club in law enforcement.

"That's the obvious stuff," Dave said. "Then there's Vestige."

"Vestige?"

He reminded me of the visit I'd gotten from the IRS after Annie died. There was more to that interview than I'd realized. I clenched my teeth and fought back the familiar cranial pain as he recounted his tale. When I'd been in New York, Annie had forgotten a packet of information in our hotel room. I'd been a good dog, he said, and had brought the folder down to the meeting. After I'd left, Annie had told the bankers that I was doing some freelance accounting for the company. My name had even appeared on accounting rolls. The packet I'd delivered to her had included some of the inflated projects that got the company in trouble with regulators.

"You're lying," I yelled. "You're fucking lying!"

"And you're acting crazy. Irrational," Dave said. "Look at yourself."

"Dave, this whole house of cards falls apart with a few simple explanations. The police will put that together. Occam's razor—the simplest explanation is that I'm just a journalist trying to expose the truth."

"Sorry, buddy. The principle works in my favor. And what truth? Like the fact that computers kill people? You have zero proof. None. It's totally far-fetched. Or the fact that Annie is alive? Christ, pal, you're suffering post-traumatic stress disorder. No one else has seen her. She died. It crushed you. And you suffered a brutal event that sent your head spinning in all kinds of directions—imagining she'd come back to life or that computers could zap our brains."

Dave hit the play button on my call to Sarah again. He talked over the recording, explaining that a few days earlier, Sarah e-mailed to tell him that I'd contacted her. Dave had said he was worried I had never gotten over Annie's death and was contacting various old friends of hers. Dave had told Sarah he thought it might be necessary to get a restraining order against me, and it would help if Sarah could tape a conversation between us.

"Nathaniel, are you really sure you even know what happened?" He suddenly turned gentle. "You've been very tired. You were nearly blown up. You've been sick. It's very hard to concentrate, right? We're not close to reasonable doubt here. Unless the question is whether you've had a bit of a psychotic break."

I fell into a moment of silence. I wasn't crazy, but my resources were too low to compete with this onslaught. At least right now. Who else had seen Annie? Not Erin. She'd been blindfolded. Only I'd read Andy's diary. The evidence at the café was gone. But there were coincidences, like the fact that Velarde had investigated Annie's death and was dead in San Francisco. Did that work for me or against me?

"Erin will back me up," I protested, but quietly. "She saw what I saw. She was right there with me."

When Dave spoke again, I felt the lights inside my head go bright neon.

"God, you really don't get it. Who do you think blew up the café?"

57

I clasped my hands together and squeezed them tightly under my chin. The room seemed to take on a new smell. Something sweet, like hibiscus tea. It worked its way up my esophagus. I pushed it back down. Dave approached in slow motion. He took the laptop. He was almost gentle. It started to slip from my hands. Defeat.

"Bullshit," I said.

"You never know who you can't trust."

I tugged at the laptop. He let it go. From his jacket pocket, he pulled out a small gun, with an even smaller dart sticking out the tip.

"I'm not a killer. I'm a lawyer. I put people to sleep."

I let the laptop slide away.

"Good. I'd prefer not to leave any evidence in your system."

Dave patted down my pockets. He said he was making sure I didn't have any recording devices. He took my cell phone, and he and Glenn slinked out of the room.

I needed to get to Annie, but I just couldn't muster the energy to move. I couldn't get my head around a central question: proof. What did I even know for sure? The presentation with the executives was clear, real, indisputable. There was a manipulative technology at work. They would attest to that. It wouldn't be hard to back them into a corner. Or would it? If I was written off as a loon, could they simply dismiss me—my claims? Andy's computer—did that hold the key? Even if I had it, could I demonstrate what was on it? Did Andy's diary ramblings amount to anything real? I'd become the poster child for paranoia. Everything else—the dangerous software, Andy, the Andersons—it was all my theories. And Erin? If she was hired by the Kindles, she would come clean. Would she take a fall, or was she framed?

I slammed my fist against the couch. I stood, and sprinted down the hallway.

They couldn't be far ahead of me. One minute, two, tops. Then what? I'd have to improvise. And get lucky. And I'd have to hope Mike had been playing his part, and not blackjack.

At the bottom of the elevator, I scoured the early-evening crowd. Early birds going out, late swimmers still coming in. I heard a raised voice. "Hey, jackass. You stepped on my foot." I looked past a brood of ruffians in bikinis. Mike stood face-to-face with Dave Elliott at the top of some ornate stairs, yelling at him.

Too much of a coincidence. Mike must have tracked the laptop. He was buying time. I slid behind a two-ton couple who made the economics of the all-you-can-eat buffet work in their favor. By the time I got to where Dave had been standing, they'd descended the stairs. I peered down. Dave and Glenn and their bouncer had dismissed Mike and were walking purposefully away. The bouncer cradled the laptop. I walked behind him and grabbed the computer with everything I had left.

I ran.

Ahead was an exit leading to the pool—outside. Escape? Far from it. I couldn't afford to have Dave and his gang get me alone. I veered right, following the sign into the casino. I was still running when I realized I'd caught the attention of a security guard. "Sir," he said. "Slow down. Now."

No cops. Cops meant no Annie. And no proof.

I reverted to a jog, then a fast walk. I looked over my shoulder. Dave and Glenn were a few steps back. I saw the bouncer break off to the left. I entered enormous doors and looked up. I stood in a cavernous casino. Lights, bells, life, passion, fear. I slinked into the crowd, seeking invisibility.

I merged into a group of twenty-something guys, a howling bachelor party. I slid out the other side, into a gaggle of middle-aged women wearing cowboy hats and skin-tight western gear. I turned around the blackjack tables toward a bank of slot machines and looked over my shoulder. No Dave or Glenn.

I slowed, heaved a deep breath, and leaned against a *CSI: Miami* slot machine blaring with bells and rings. Sounds bounced inside my skull. I fought to take in another breath.

When I looked up again, I'd been found. Glenn and Dave were descending from the left, the bouncer from the right. I caught Dave's eye. He shook his head, exhibiting relief and pity. I looked into the lights and mirrors and I could feel the thousands of cameras peering down on me from the ceiling. My sense of smell became suddenly acute.

I felt my hand curl into a ball, I clutched it over my heart.

I fell to the ground.

58

Bit of medical trivia #237: Excluding a hospital, the very best place to have a heart attack is a Las Vegas casino. Even epidemiologists will tell you. You're constantly on camera, and the proprietors know the worst thing in the world for business is a man down. The paramedics in casinos are the West's fastest draw with a defibrillator.

I didn't need a defibrillator or the paramedics. I was faking.

They were on me in seconds. Two men and a woman in white shirts, surrounding me in a protective cocoon, or, rather, protecting people from seeing the fate of some poor sucker. One grabbed for my pulse, another started to affix an oxygen mask.

I sat up.

"Eel," I said groggily. "Very, very bad sushi."

I looked past them. Dave and Glenn were lurking. I saw the bouncer's face. And behind a slot machine, I thought I made out Mike.

I explained to the paramedics that I'd been in and out of the bathroom all afternoon. I told them I could stand up. They insisted that I go with them to the medical clinic.

That's what I was hoping.

Behind us, Glenn and Dave were following.

Ten minutes later, I was sitting three blocks away in a clinic. The paramedics set me in an exam room and, upon concluding

I wasn't a triage case, told me a nurse would be along shortly.
I plugged in Andy's computer and turned it on. I looked at the
screen saver of Andy sitting on a couch, cradling a black cat
in his lap.

I was temporarily free, but I going to have to get very
lucky.

I felt my gut clench. This time, pure emotion. The more I
thought about the Annie I'd witnessed in the hotel, the less
crazy it seemed. The less out of character. Her composure,
outright manipulation, her calculated assault on her father.
The question was how the hell I'd missed it all before. Underneath it, though, something was still alluring to me. I could
imagine how it looked from the outside, like I was a high
school kid pining for a girl who had cruelly mocked me in the
lunchroom in front of the whole school. Had my friends seen
that all along? And yet, maybe there was salvation to be had.
Her motives were unclear, maybe true in some way I didn't yet
understand. I felt my hope dimming, but still alive, anchored
by a feeling of terrible defeat.

It wasn't long before the door opened. In walked Dave and
Glenn. Dave locked the door behind him. He flipped a switch
on the wall. It was a trigger to let outsiders know an exam was
taking place. He opened his jacket and flashed the tranquilizer
gun.

"Okay. You win," I said. "Let's negotiate."

"Much better," Dave said.

"I need to know about Erin."

"She's violent, and angry," Dave said. "The perfect triggerman."

With an impatient tone, he said that just before the café
exploded, Erin was on her break, working on the computer.
She went into the bathroom, turned on the light switch, and
the place went kaboom. The light switch was the trigger. She
survived, but Simon Anderson, whom she didn't much like,
didn't. The cops found residue from explosives in her apart-

ment. And, of course, Dave said, she had a terrible history of setting fires. I took it in with my eyes closed.

"She didn't knowingly blow up the café. You framed her."

Something else struck me.

"She was sitting at her computer and then went to the bathroom. You programmed her. You flashed some subliminal image to cause her to . . . go into the bathroom."

"To wash her hands, actually. Subliminal images of grimy hands," Dave said. "I mean, if you believe the nonsense that computers can program people."

Glenn let out a murmur.

"Impossible," I said. "You're right, I don't believe it. A computer can't make someone do something, or feel something. It doesn't pass the smell test. All of this. Nonsense."

Dave sighed. He didn't have time for this. "Use your brain for once and not your heart. It isn't that hard to fathom. You send imperceptible electrical currents through a keyboard. Nerve endings are stimulated, consistent with frequencies understood to stoke the brain's pleasure centers. You couple that with subliminal advertising. Personal images—a vivid, instant, unseen bombarding of the senses. When you're sitting at a computer, your eyes and whole person are focused on the computer, locked on to it, and the messages are going right into your brain, reinforced with physical sensation. That's powerful suggestion. But it isn't even close to rocket science."

Glenn sagged against the examining table. His jaw was clenched. He inhaled slowly, the practiced move of someone who knew how not to lose control, then addressed me.

"I'm afraid this simply isn't what you think. Yes, Annie is alive. You've seen her. But the rest of it—it's just not true. I had nothing to do with any of this."

"Glenn, stop," Dave said.

Glenn put his hand up.

"We had a terrific innovation. Attention span as currency. Was it brainwashing? No. Listen. People would still think for themselves, we could just make thinking more fun. We'd high-light it. We'd make commerce a highly stimulating experience. It's just a natural evolution. The way it's going anyway. But we saw it. We could have created it. We would have led the evolution. We had some of the biggest executives in the world on board. And Jesus, Dave, you . . . and Annie had to take it to the extreme. They wanted to ruin me."

Dave put his hand on Glenn's knee. "Enough. Don't forget, you've been ruining Annie for years."

Dave turned to me.

"Meeting adjourned." He walked close to me, pulled out the tranquilizer gun. I closed the laptop and handed it to him.

"You have no evidence. Walk away," Dave said. "Do you need further convincing?"

I looked him in the eye. "I think I can live without saying anything."

He walked to the door.

"One last thing, Nathaniel," he said. "You need to put Annie behind you. I'm sure you realize by now. She's not worth it."

"Right. You can't wait to have her to yourself."

Dave laughed. "C'mon, Nat. You don't care about Annie. You couldn't love her. You never loved her in the first place. You just thought you did. You just *imagined* you did. Think about it. You'll see what I'm saying makes sense. Then you can move on. You need to. Annie Kindle is not long for your world."

I shook my head. He was still trying to get inside my brain. The door shut.

I left the room and glanced around the hallway. There, in a chair, reading a magazine, sat Mike.

"Well," I said.

He gave me a high sign.

"Blackjack," he said. "This is going to be one hell of a podcast."

Mike had fitted Andy's laptop with audio software and a tiny microphone. When the computer was turned on, it simultaneously recorded a conversation, then transmitted it to a nearby receiver, in this case controlled by Mike. That way, even if the laptop was destroyed, we had a copy of the recording.

I didn't have time to get further details.

59

The *Monkey* was a fifty-six-foot houseboat. And it had gone missing. It wasn't in its prescribed slip in Callville Bay Marina. Annie had already made her escape.

I stood with my fists balled in the dusk, looking out over massive Lake Mead.

"It left half an hour ago. You can still see it," a voice said.

From behind a bait stand walked Erin. She pointed on the horizon. You could still make out the *Monkey* in the distance, crawling away. I began scanning the marina, but listened to Erin.

"You're alive," she said. "That's a very good start."

"Did you see Annie?"

"The boat was pulling away when I got here."

I could feel Erin come up to me from behind. A shirtless man was cleaning chum from a skiff with an oversized outboard motor. I walked toward him with Erin.

"What are you going to do?"

I turned to face her.

"They framed you."

"Who did?"

"They planted evidence in your apartment. They—" I said, stopping short. I didn't have it in me to tell her she'd pulled the trigger, that she'd been the physical tool used to detonate a bomb. A right time would come. "They used you. The same people who . . . killed Andy."

The implications washed over her face. She was the victim, and yet had been suspected of killing people she loved. I wanted to tell her how sorry I was, that we'd hit the bottom, and that we were going to go home soon. But I'd arrived at the shirtless man. I pointed to the *Monkey*. I offered him the contents of my wallet—$82—for a water taxi.

"Do the police know?" she asked.

"Not yet. Where's Bullseye?"

"I left him in the hotel, sitting in the lobby, talking on the phone to Samantha, listening to her talk."

I climbed onto the taxi.

"I'm coming with you," Erin said, suddenly searing with strength.

I convinced Erin to wait for me on the dock—that I needed to do this next part alone—and jetted out to the *Monkey*. I climbed onto the houseboat and found Annie sitting in the common area. She didn't look surprised to see me. I'd been obsessing over what to say, and still, when I saw her, I couldn't find words. How had it gone so wrong? She finally broke the silence.

"Turtle. You have to understand. I loved you. I *love* you. You were the only person who ever understood me for what I am . . . for what I could be."

The old Annie.

"Stop it, Annie. It's time for the truth. Please help me understand."

"Who knows you're here?"

"No one."

A lie—not just about Erin. Mike had given me another GPS device for my car in case I went missing. With a couple of hundred bucks and a little technical expertise, you can make the CIA look like a bunch of Luddites.

I'd started putting the facts together on the drive. Maybe

the effects of the computer were finally wearing off, allowing me to process. Somehow, Simon Anderson had learned Annie was alive. That must have been what Andy meant when he said Simon was upset about someone named Tara. He was trying to bribe the family again. They had to act, taking him out, along with others they'd experimented on, and destroying the rest of the evidence of their lab tests. Annie and Dave had been partners, piggybacking on Glenn's connections, but going further than he imagined. They planned to undo him all along, I guessed. From her phone, she'd sent a text message to Dave, urging him to barge in on the meeting with the executives. I recounted it for Annie, just above a whisper. She shook her head, in a quasi-admission. "My father and Dave were behind it," she protested, unconvincingly. This topic bored her.

She walked to me and put her arms around my waist. She looked into my eyes.

"I got him good, didn't I?"

I pushed her away.

"You're disappointed in me," she said, soft, sad.

I couldn't reconcile the Annie I'd known with Annie the Conquerer, Annie the Smiling Assassin. It was too simple to describe her behavior as multiple personality disorder. A changeling was more like it. Different shades and shapes and angles, changing light and darkness. But there was a unifying force: selfishness. Annie wanted what she wanted when she wanted it. She felt utterly sincere about her passions. What did she want now? My help escaping? I didn't say anything and silence descended. Suddenly she looked so old, like my grandmother, undone, mourning the loss of Grandpa.

"No, you can't love this. You couldn't love this," she said, with a touch of self-pity, then an edge. "You thought I was pretty. You liked the sex, right? The sex was great. You thought I was witty and smart. What does all that mean?"

Remarkably, she wanted affirmation. It was like the tone she used to muster when she got jealous.

"Not true, Annie. You made me feel something I'd never felt before. I *still* feel it," I said. "True love. Whatever happens, whatever happened."

"You mean that?"

She was a killer, I had to remind myself. But we had loved each other. It's what people pray for, what they die for. Someone who makes them feel all the highs and depth that emotion has to offer. The divine. The feeling of being needed, and understood. Better than any drug. Because you share it.

"Yep. You *made* me feel it," I said.

I leaned against a railing and realized what my gut had been telling me for hours.

"I wasn't your first true love, Annie, was I? I was your beta test."

The epiphany prompted a ringing in my ears. There was another sound. Police sirens approaching the marina.

"Subliminal advertising. On the computer you gave me. When you gave me the desk, and the quill pen."

I took a step toward her. "You put something on the computer you gave me. You programmed me, like you programmed Erin to blow up the café. Like you programmed the rats. You manipulated my feelings. You made our love neon. You made it bigger than life. You made me into an addict."

She closed her eyes. She responded softly.

"Why do you think you couldn't see my flaws? It was primitive. Simple. Subliminal advertising, pictures of me, positive messages."

"Messages and pictures? Those are the bases of our relationship?"

"I watched when you were most drawn to me, what I was wearing and saying. I took high-definition pictures dressed the same way, and loaded them onto your computer. I posed naked. I took pictures of us in bed. I created images with short phrases like 'I love turtle' and 'Annie = happiness,' random images with me wearing Denver Broncos T-shirts, and eating your favorite foods. I loaded an audio file with my name and played it at very low and high frequencies. A hundred experiments. Every time you were on the computer, you were flashed with the images, when you surfed the Web, checked sports scores, sent e-mail, shopped, played Scrabble with your grandmother."

It seemed, at last, like something real. Yet on some level, it rang false. Intellectually I could grasp what had happened; it was the most profound, inescapable assault. I was fighting myself—head and heart. Blow for blow. My own realization undermined by incredulity.

"Bullshit! It's not that simple. You can't deny what we felt. I loved you even after your vicious computer was gone. You can't take that away from me."

Annie took my hand. I pushed it away.

"I used to watch you when you were on the computer, wondering what you liked more, me or my digital incarnation."

"You were manipulating me? I was nothing to you—an experiment."

Silence.

"Then you put something on my laptop five days ago too?"

"No."

"No?!"

"You didn't have me tortured?! You didn't order those cops to torture me?!"

"Dave." Quietly. "Dave hated you. He was jealous. After the café , . . He . . ."

"It doesn't make sense. Why would you save me from the explosion? You never cared about me. Why save me?!"

Annie plopped onto the couch. I practically sprang toward her. She recoiled.

"Because you loved me too," I said. "You can't *imagine* what we felt, Annie. You can't invent it. You can't digitize it. You can't fake it."

She paused.

"I will grant you that no one ever made me feel the way you did," she said.

"You will *grant* me?"

"When we first met, I couldn't believe you felt that way about me. How I started to feel. How the whole thing made me feel. I couldn't trust it," she said. She'd sewn up the psychology nice and tight.

"It was real. It was the goddamn real thing! You were *it*. I loved you from the moment I laid my eyes on you. I loved your laugh. I loved your smile. I loved your passion."

"That's why you were perfect."

"Because I was inspired by you?"

"Because you're a romantic. Because you're the kind of person who leaves a career in medicine to become a writer. Because you wrote me poetry—the goofy kind that rhymes. Because you believe in intense emotion."

"Stop rationalizing!"

My yell rocked the boat.

I heard a rush of cascading water. Speedboats were getting close. The police.

Annie stood, her eyes widening. She ran out of the far door of the cabin, onto the deck. I followed her into the pitch black. She moved to the front of the boat. Police headlights were coming. I could hear voices. I moved close enough to see Annie's face. She'd turned hard. "If they frame me, I'll go to jail forever."

"Frame you? Jesus."

"They don't get it," she said. "They're missing it."

"Missed what?"

"*You're* still missing it. My father is finished. He was small-time. I didn't need him, or his precious executives. They were convenient. They gave me structure and resources but I hung those flailing hypocrites out when I realized their use had passed. They don't know a damn thing about real connection, especially my father. Anyway, this won't stop anything. People want the connection. They need it. They crave it. It's what matters. It's already out there."

"It's over, Annie."

She walked to the railing. She paused, then softened just a bit. I swear I saw a tear.

"A few months before I went away, I had lunch with Sarah," she said, sounding suddenly rational. "I told her that if something were ever to happen to me, I wanted you to be happy. I wanted you to find someone to be with. I mean that still. I want you to be happy."

I smirked.

"Erin seems quite amazing. See how easy it is to replace me?"

Annie had closed her eyes. She opened them again.

"I have to go. This time, no tricks," she said. "Will you try to save my life?"

"What?"

"You know how to save lives. You told me on our second date. Can you save mine? Will you?"

Annie was not impervious to pain. She could dress it up all she wanted, but the thing we felt, however engineered, meant something to her. I meant something.

"You're right, you know," I said.

I heard a voice on a bullhorn. "Stop your engines." The police were almost near enough to climb on board.

"Right about what?"

"I didn't love you. I could never have loved you."

Annie flinched. That flinch I'd seen when her father told her she'd have to disappear.

"STOP THE ENGINES. NOW."

Annie climbed onto the railing. Her voice was childlike—a whisper.

"Will you save me?"

I heard the police climb into the boat.

I grabbed her arm.

"Don't forget me. Don't forget how we made each other feel."

She caught my gaze, then leapt. Gravity broke my grip and I scrambled to the railing. When she hit the water, she looked up at me, churning her arms, and she smiled.

60

The boat exploded in lights and chaos. I pointed an onrush of police to the spot where moments before I'd seen bubbles. It took less than a minute for the first officer to dive in. A hand restrained me from diving in myself, or maybe I was just paralyzed.

The hand belonged to a familiar arm—that of Lieutenant Aravelo.

"We tracked you to Vegas. You and your friend have a lot to explain."

"Yeah, us meddling kids," a voice said.

It was Erin.

Aravelo scoffed.

"They wanted me to identify Annie," she said.

I stared into the water, and pointed.

Erin put her hand on my shoulder. She let it slide down my arm, onto my forearm. She took my hand and gently rubbed the webbing between my thumb and forefinger.

EPILOGUE

Some people consider the extraordinary beauty of our world to prove the existence of God. How else to explain the aspects of nature so perfectly suited to human comfort and joy?

But another explanation is that humans and our surroundings evolved together for millions of years. Of course we see our world as beautiful; we've been growing in concert with it, fitting together with it, and surviving thanks to it. Nature may not be evidence of the divine, but, rather, the ultimate living room in which our rear ends and the couch have been forming together for our entire existence.

What is distraction? What is true?

Three months after Annie disappeared for the second time, *American Health Journal* published my article on the scientific basis for the physiologically addictive qualities of computers. It either was unintentional or subconscious poetry that inspired me to sit down in a café (not the one that exploded, at least) to read the finished product in print.

THIS IS YOUR BRAIN ON E-MAIL
by Nat Idle

A small but growing body of evidence suggests that human interaction with computers is altering brain functions, and affecting mood and productivity, not necessarily for the better.

While the science is nascent, it indicates measurable impact on neurotransmitters from the continual stimulus-response feedback loop created when people send and receive information from computers, cell phones, and other digital gadgets.

The issue first emerged three months ago, after a prominent Silicon Valley venture capitalist and his cohorts were discovered to have allegedly developed technology aimed at maximizing the stimulatory effects of computers. The financier, Glenn Kindle, is awaiting trial on murder charges in the deaths of experiment subjects, and has pleaded innocent, asserting that his company was trying to understand and develop new ways to enhance the computing experience.

The larger issue, of whether the brain could be impacted by computer interaction, now seems answerable in the affirmative, though the research is largely derivative. One early study at Michigan State University mapped images of people's brains while they were playing video games and was able to demonstrate that players' brains look similar when stimulated to those of individuals with compulsive aggression disorders.

Allegedly, cohorts of Glenn Kindle were involved in rat experimentation to see if the rodents would abandon food in favor of feeding the pleasure centers of their brains with electrical stimulation thought to be similar to that experienced by heavy computer users.

A perhaps more telling initial indication of the possibility and prevalence of computer-based addiction is anecdotal. Around the country, psychologists and counselors are reporting a growth in the number of people professing "addiction" to their computers and Internet use. This phenomenon—entailing people feeling a compulsive interest in surfing the Internet, checking voice mail, and using their phones, often at the same time—had previously been considered to be an act of volition.

In light of the arrest of Mr. Kindle, and his company attorney, David Elliott, there is some concern that a more traditional form of addiction is plausible. Indeed, some counselors have begun treating the activity like a physical compulsion, urging if not complete disconnection for users, then limited interaction—relegated even merely to work hours—to try to mitigate the impact of the stimulus-feedback loop.

The medical theory behind computer-based addiction has some parallels to attention deficit disorder. The constant digital stimulation created raises the level of certain neurochemicals. When the stimulation ceases, the body craves elevated levels of chemicals. Yet it has been difficult to determine precisely how the technology might work, and thus impact the brain. Complicating the pursuit of answers is the bizarre fate of Kindle's daughter, Annie Kindle. Glenn Kindle's attorneys assert the young woman was the mastermind of the computer-stimulation technology. But this allegation has been difficult to substantiate; around the time of her father's arrest, Ms. Kindle disappeared—diving into Lake Mead to evade authorities. She is presumed dead.

Also anecdotal has been an appearance of what some counselors are calling a new round of cases of extreme computer addiction—hundreds of people who seem so entranced by the computing experience that it is cutting into every aspect of their lives. Characteristics of the "illness" entail frequent, compulsive multitasking, and a pressing urge to fill life with stimulation or distraction. Sufferers feel bored in the absence of something to do, and tend to seek out a focus, an activity, even an intense discussion—the kind of emotional spur that Freudian thinkers would refer to as drama.

Curiously, the emergence of this strain has coincided recently with what computer experts are saying is the appearance of a new variant of computer worm; like many worms, it causes pop-up advertisements, but these images are subliminal, flickering only briefly on the screen.

Counselors say that if people feel their computer has contracted the worm, if they increasingly feel unable to understand why they are constantly drawn to their gadgets, they may be under powers greater than their control. The only choice at that point, experts said, is to unhook.

At that point in the story, the text was interrupted by a graphic—a visual conceived by my editor, Kevin—that showed a mystical beam of particles traveling from screen to brain. It prompted me to laugh aloud.

"Medical journals don't have a reputation for being that funny," a woman's voice said. Erin took a seat at the table next to me in the café. She wore the uniform of someone who had just been on a jog, her hair in a ponytail.

"You get your comedy from the *New York Times*," I reminded her.

A few weeks earlier, Erin had introduced me to a game she'd invented called "How'd They Die?" She would read me an obituary and I would have to guess the person's cause of death.

I was hanging out with Erin a lot, and even learning to appreciate her interest in free-form dance.

My physical symptoms induced by the computer had faded, actually, very shortly after I disconnected myself from the loaded laptop. Samantha helped, throwing some wicked spiritual voodoo my way, though I took a decided break from acupuncture, and Bullseye aided my healing with what he referred to as his holistic beer-and-big-screen-TV treatment.

My feelings about Annie took a predictable path from disbelief to anger, and then wound up in a less expected place. While I no longer romanticized Annie herself or wanted her to return—I'm done dating sociopaths—I continued to wrestle with the feelings she stirred. How could I distinguish between the healthy version of passion and the destructive version of the same thing? Once you've felt such connection, real or imagined, how do you not yearn for it again?

Maybe alcoholics feel just that way—forever knowing the most beautiful taste in the world will kill them. How does any of us know if the short-term obsessive pursuit of something we love—working, nutritional eating, following celebrity love lives and daily news developments, gambling, exercising, reading—comes at the expense of long-term happiness?

What is true, and what is distraction? What is love?

Maybe it depends for each of us on how we metabolize emotion and experience, or simply what we choose to believe. With each passing day, I gain a little wisdom that lets me recognize which people and experiences are my own fifth of Jack Daniel's.

The next love will be less great, and greater.

ACKNOWLEDGMENTS

It takes a village to create a work of fiction. In that spirit, I humbly thank:

My parents. Dad, for teaching me about big ideas and awe. Mom, for teaching me to look and listen for the tiny moments and emotions that matter most. I love you both.

My selfless bride, Meredith Jewel (last name to be determined), for patience, stability, persevering affection, creativity, personal and editorial insight, and the ability to ignore bouts of weirdness and see the greater good.

Barney, Bob, Brad, Cheryl, Josh, and Trish (alphabetically ordered), for the early encouragement, crucial feedback, and plot and character ideas otherwise unseen.

Sara-Jane, for grammatical genius (this is wrong somehow, isn't it?).

Alex, Ana and Zach, Annie Richtel, the Concerned Fellows League, Dr. Ratey, Erik, Gary, the Grove, Jake, Jay, Kara, Karen, Kevin, Leah (and your mom), Noel, Rick, Skol, Stacey, Susan, the Syers, Tic, and the cadre of Stanford MDs, for reading, encouraging, providing joy, beer drinking, and liar's dice (I own you).

Hot chocolates and guacamole, for essential snacking.

Laurie Liss of Sterling Lord Literistic, amazing agent, fighter, a book's midwife.

Jonathan Karp, (exacting and brilliant) editor and publisher. You've got the sixth sense. And to the Twelve's Nate Gray, Cary Goldstein, and Mari Okuda.

In memory of Alyse Neundorf, who graced the world with a fierce and compassionate love.

Thanks to you all and those unintentionally forgotten but deeply appreciated, for what has been an unequivocally collaborative effort, and to all the writers who have inspired me. And, again, to guacamole.

Matt Richtel

ABOUT THE AUTHOR

MATT RICHTEL is a reporter for the *New York Times*. Since 2000, he has worked in the paper's San Francisco bureau, covering technology and telecommunications.

Under the pen name Theron Heir, he writes the syndicated daily comic strip *Rudy Park*, which is published in newspapers around the country and was dubbed by *Newsweek* as one of the contenders for new signature strip of the decade.

Matt grew up in Boulder, Colorado, and lives in San Francisco. He can be reached at mattrichtel@gmail.com or through his Web site, www.mattrichtel.com.

About TWELVE

TWELVE was established in August 2005 with the objective of publishing no more than one book per month. We strive to publish the singular book, by authors who have a unique perspective and compelling authority. Works that explain our culture; that illuminate, inspire, provoke, and entertain. We seek to establish communities of conversation surrounding our books. Talented authors deserve attention not only from publishers, but from readers as well. To sell the book is only the beginning of our mission. To build avid audiences of readers who are enriched by these works—that is our ultimate purpose.

For more information about forthcoming TWELVE books, please go to www.twelvebooks.com.